D1617609

The Zen of International Relations

The Zen of International Relations

IR Theory from East to West

Edited by

Stephen Chan
Professor of International Ethics
Dean of Humanities
Nottingham Trent University, UK

Peter Mandaville
Assistant Professor of Government and Politics
George Mason University
Virginia, USA

and

Roland Bleiker
Senior Lecturer and Co-Director
Rotary Centre for International Studies in Peace and Conflict Resolution
University of Queensland, Australia

First published 2001 by
PALGRAVE
Houndmills, Basingstoke, Hampshire RG21 6XS and
175 Fifth Avenue, New York, N. Y. 10010
Companies and representatives throughout the world

PALGRAVE is the new global academic imprint of
St. Martin's Press LLC Scholarly and Reference Division and
Palgrave Publishers Ltd (formerly Macmillan Press Ltd).

ISBN 0–333–68822–8

This book is printed on paper suitable for recycling and made from fully managed and sustained forest sources.

A catalogue record for this book is available from the British Library.

Library of Congress Cataloging-in-Publication Data
The Zen of international relations : IR theory from East to West / [edited by] Stephen Chan, Peter Mandaville, and Roland Bleiker.
    p. cm.
    Includes bibliographical references and index.
    ISBN 0–333–68822–8 (cloth)
    1. International relations—Philosophy. 2. China—Foreign relations—1976– I. Chan, Stephen, 1949– II. Mandaville, Peter, 1971– III. Bleiker, Roland.
    JZ1305 .Z46 2001
    327.1'01—dc21
                                                            00–66902

10   9   8   7   6   5   4   3   2   1
10   09   08   07   06   05   04   03   02   01

Printed and bound in Great Britain by
Antony Rowe Ltd, Chippenham, Wiltshire

Contents

Part IV   The Zen of International Relations

Acknowledgements

Indeed, let more stories be told. If this volume accomplishes that, or makes some space for that, the editors will feel very pleased. As ever, they look to resume another stage of their own story-telling at the next Pan-European conference.

Debts are owed to John Groom, for reasons mentioned in the introduction; and also to Osmo Apunen, who was the co-editor of an original volume of conference proceedings from Paris that, sadly, fell by the wayside. Stephen Chan's contributions were variously rehearsed at the Universities of Kent, Tampere, Aberystwyth, Nottingham Trent, Southampton, and the London School of Economics. He thanks all the students and staff at those institutions for their patience, and hopes the scepticism, in particular of Southampton, may be a little redressed by this volume. He thanks Vivienne Jabri for her loyal support, and Ranka Primorac for her loyally raised eyebrows; and Janet Elkington for womanfully word-processing so much of this, retaining every successive version on her overcrowded disk.

Notes on the Contributors

Roland Bleiker is Senior Lecturer and Co-Director of the Rotary Centre for International Studies in Peace and Conflict Resolution, University of Queensland. He has also taught at the Australian National University, Pusan National University and the University of Tampere. He is the author of *Popular Dissent, Human Agency and Global Politics* (Cambridge University Press, 2000) and a number of articles in scholarly journals.

Qing Cao has been Associate Professor at Hangzhou University, teaching Comparative Cultures. A graduate of the International Academy of Chinese Culture, Northeast Normal University, and the University of London, he is completing his PhD at The Nottingham Trent University. He has contributed to both Chinese and English language journals, and has also co-authored and co-edited books in both languages.

Stephen Chan is Dean of Humanities and Professor in International Relations and Ethics at Nottingham Trent University. He has served on the faculties of Kent and Zambia, and has advised several governments, international institutions, liberation movements and third world opposition groups. Formerly an international civil servant with the Commonwealth Secretariat, he participated in the transition to independence of Zimbabwe. He has recently established the Kwok Meil Wah Foundation, to assist third world causes.

Xiaoming Huang is Lecturer in East Asian Politics, the School of Political Science and International Relations, Victoria University of Wellington, New Zealand. Trained in international relations, Dr Huang received his LL B and LL M from Peking University, Beijing, and PhD from the USC, Los Angeles, with a strong interest in comparative IR theory. Before joining Victoria University he had held various teaching and research positions at the East–West Center, Honolulu; the United Nations University, Tokyo; the Wilson International Center for Scholars, Washington, DC; the Center for International Studies/Pacific Council on International Policy, Los Angeles; the University of Tampere, Finland; the University of Trondheim, Norway; and the University of Pittsburgh. Dr Huang's primary interest in teaching and research focuses on institution and culture in modern politics. His current research projects include a book-length manuscript on the institutional conditions and consequences of the Asian model of development. Dr Huang's recent publications include an article in *International Studies Quarterly* (1997) and an edited volume, *Strong Market, Weakening State and the Political Economic Transition in East Asia* (2000).

Peter Mandaville is Assistant Professor of Government and Poltics at George Mason University in Virginia. His research interests include transnational Muslim politics, non-Western political theory and the philosophy of community. He has published in journals such as *Millennium* and the *Review of International Studies*, and is the author of *Transnational Muslim Poltics: Reimagining the Umma*: (Routledge, 2001).

Mehdi Mozaffari is a Professor of Political Science at the University of Aarhus (Denmark). He was formerly a Professor at Tehran University, a lecturer at Université Paris 1 (Sorbonne-Panthéon) and a Senior Fellow at Harvard University. His recent publications are: *Security Policy of the Commonwealth of Independent States* (ed.) (London: Macmillan, 1997); *Fatwa: Violence and Discourtesy* (Oxford: Aarhus University Press, 1998) and *Pouvoir Shi'ite: théorie et évolution* (Paris: L'Harmattan, 1998). His current research project is focused on 'Globalization and Civilization' and 'Emerging of a New International Law and Ethics'.

Houman A. Sadri is an Assistant Professor of International Relations at the University of Central Florida. He joined the Department of Political Science at UCF in 1995 after earning his doctorate from the Woodrow Wilson Department of Government and Foreign Affairs at the University of Virginia. His book, *Revolutionary States: Leaders and Foreign Relations*, was published by the Praeger Press in 1997. Dr Sadri is also the author of several professional articles and book chapters dealing with different aspects of foreign policy and international relations.

Hidemi Suganami is Professor of the Philosophy of International Relations in the New School of Politics, International Relations and the Environment at Keele University, England, where he has taught since 1975, having previously studied at Tokyo, Aberystwyth and London. His publications include: *The Domestic Analogy and World Order Proposals* (Cambridge University Press, 1989) and *On the Causes of War* (Oxford University Press, 1996). He is currently working on a joint book with Andrew Linklater on the English School of International Relations.

Wang Yi is now Programme Manager for SBS Radio in Melbourne and concurrently Visiting Fellow in the Department of International Studies, Nottingham Trent University. He has conducted teaching and research in China, Australia and Britain, currently focusing on Chinese politics and foreign policy, Australian politics and Australia–China relations. Most recently, he was World News and Current Affairs Producer at the BBC World Service in London.

1
Introduction: Within International Relations Itself, a New Culture Rises Up

Stephen Chan and Peter Mandaville

> Already the ingenious beasts are aware that we are not reliably at home in our interpreted world.
>
> (Rilke)

What the West did not realise, according to the Sinologist, Rudolf Wagner, was that both students and political authorities, at the 1989 Tiananmen Square incident, used the same Chinese rhetoric of absolute and exclusive truth. As long as they maintained that rhetoric, meaningful dialogue and compromise were impossible: each side was excluded from the truthfulness of what was said by the other.[1] In short, notwithstanding their construction of a Franco-American Statue of Liberty, and their identification with the democratic revolutions of France and the United States – not to mention the Western sympathy to their cause and their symbolism – the students were not speaking democratically. What the West did understand was that the students had attempted a political protest, and thus analysed it with the instruments of a Western political science. In the years afterwards, seeking the icons and typologies of that political science – ideologies, parties, manifestos; the organisation of grievances and aspirations – the West took a long time to recognise the Falun Gong as a political challenge to Beijing. It did not take Beijing so long. Using legislation that forbids the misuse of religion and Qigong, the authorities have cracked down upon the Falun Gong; which, all the same, refuses to go away.

What is Qigong? It is a series of exercises that promote health. At successive, ascending levels, however, these exercises cultivate the Qi – the internal energy spoken about by esoteric martial artists, but

1

unknown and unknowable to Western science and medicine – and not only confer health upon the practitioner, but extraordinary powers of perception, the projection of strength, and the channelling of the invisible energies of the cosmos itself. In short, with the practice of Qigong at its heart, the Falun Gong is, in a word, irrational. It is not, therefore, susceptible to rational instruments of control and the rational processes of politics. Nor, however, is it susceptible to any rational political science. It does not fit easily into any efforts even at an international political theory. This, however, is a book of international political theory. The task of this book is to clear some pathway for those Others of the world, and the thoughtful Others within international relations; we may not, by the end of the book, understand the Falun Gong – but we may not dismiss it.

We need not set about this effort with mere seriousness. It is possible to pause at the outset for an ironic moment: for millennia before Edward Said coined the term 'Orientalism' to describe the West's misunderstanding of the Middle Eastern and Far Eastern Other, by first rendering critical aspects of that Other into Western categories of analysis and aesthetics, the Chinese had their own 'Occidentalism', and readers may wish to turn to Qing Cao's chapter in this book first, to see how much of an other they themselves are in terms of Confucian sensibilities to do with balance.

A discourse begun

Having said all that by way of preface, it should of course be acknowledged that, almost without the discipline of international relations (or IR) noticing it, a new discourse, seeking to open up the pathway alluded to above, has crept up on it since the mid-1990s; and this is to do with, not just something generalised to do with culture or multicultural study, but with methodologies of truth-saying and proving, and judging of good, that are culturally different, or different enough at first sight, to require some investigation. There is still, however, an IR response that has been to insist stubbornly upon its own credentials, shaped from the European Enlightenment and its modernism, hard-won credentials, and to marginalise alternative and wider conceptual foundations and their methodological work.

The advent of a postmodernism certainly helped to break down notions of easy universality; but the discussion of agency and its privileging of ontology above epistemology was what really allowed the stealthy crafting of a fissure inwards towards the discipline's core.[2] Nor has this been confined to the discipline's newer, methodologically expansionist zealots. Robert Cox, in a newly collected, but earlier rather unremarked, essay, cites the exemplary work of the fourteenth-century Iranian thinker, Ibn Khaldun, as a means of arguing ontology's prefiguring of epistemology.[3]

All this, however, has been slow. IR has rather reflected the grasping at a moment of security which the end of the Cold War allowed. The triumph of liberalism and individualism was made, in IR, into a discursive, though largely Kantian, critical individualism – with its anchor in a universe of defining and reciprocal moral forces. There are two things to be said here: the first is that this discursivity has not ventured far beyond Frankfurtian and other European contemporary thought; the second is, of course, the blindingly obvious fact of post-Cold War international life, and that is that there remain significant challenges to the political and intellectual hegemonies of the West, and these are located in the Middle and Far East.

The effort to point this out has a historical home in the ECPR (European Consortium for Political Research) Standing Group on International Relations conferences, particularly that in Paris in 1995. These were, in no small part, manifestations of a certain vision by John Groom, and this was recognised by an honorary doctorate from the University of Tampere in 2000. Groom sought, among other things, a certain European balance to the organisational and professional weight of the then American-dominated ISA (International Studies Association). In an effort to demonstrate a wide, if catholic, range, he sought to restrict conference workshops to three sessions each. This was honoured in the breach as much as any actuality, but the most excessive breaker of bounds – with seven sessions – was the workshop convened by Osmo Apunen and Stephen Chan, on Cultural and Textual Interpretation in International Relations; and this book derives from some of the papers presented in Paris and at the succeeding conference in Vienna in 1998, together with several new collected or commissioned contributions.

At least one of the Paris papers, 'Forget IR Theory', by Roland Bleiker, has become something of a 'classic' among younger IR dissidents. There are two points to be made at this juncture: the first is that seven sessions of twenty-one papers made a far cry from those of the first such conference, in Heidelberg in 1992, where two papers, by James Piscatori and Stephen Chan, were the only ones to attempt new (for IR) methodological pathways drawn from other cultures.[4]

Bleiker's 'classic' is republished here. For both his contributions, and the second of Chan's, the present volume has allowed, not only considerable revision, but expanded writing, over and beyond the editorial limitations of the journals where they appeared in, therefore, earlier forms. Here, they are, to borrow cinematic language, the 'director's versions', with all the cuts made by the studios restored, and new scenes added.

Chan's first paper is reproduced as it appeared in Paris and, later, in the South African journal, *Theoria*; and the second is a developed version of that which appeared in Vienna, incorporating all the sections of two differently cut editions, one of which appeared in a Finnish *festschift* to Osmo Apunen, and the other in *Millennium*. The third was written especially for this volume and seeks, in particular, to develop some of the implications of the second.

Both of Bleiker's chapters are revised and expanded versions of what appeared in issues of *Alternatives* and *Millennium*. Mehdi Mozaffari's chapter is as it appeared in Vienna and, thereafter, in *International Relations*; and Houman Sadri's chapter first appeared in the *Journal of Third World Studies*.

Xiaoming Huang presented a paper in the Apunen/Chan sessions in Paris, but his contribution here was especially commissioned, as were those of Wang Yi, Qing Cao and Hidemi Suganami. The editors of all the journals mentioned above are gratefully thanked.

A discourse within the discourse

If we are proposing the possibility of multiple composition in IR, it is not that there is any settled uniformity in the new notations and orchestrations. Indeed, there are romanticisms, classicisms, alternative modernisms, serialisms and pure cacophonies seeking their own expressions; and many of these have their very own compositional rules.

There is a challenge to all this, and it is precisely that of Steve Smith and Martin Hollis, to do with relativism, particularly cultural relativism.[5] Roland Bleiker, however, cautions against the embedded realism of any such statement – particularly the notion that there might be a realism that is also scientific; and that would, in turn, presume to be a reality. In 'Forget IR Theory', Bleiker speaks of a nostalgia within IR. It is almost as if the turn from realism was never securely accomplished. If there is not a hankering for realism itself, there is a yearning at least for security, for a sure object of study, for a site of truth. Any such site has been overlaid, if not founded upon, multiple stories that IR can no longer discern as metaphors for particular positions and interests. In any investigation of these metaphors, to which early IR also tied its hopes and dreams, the danger is in becoming entrapped in the brambles and undergrowth, in being snared, and continuing – in an affiliation of nostalgias – to live a lie. Better, Bleiker says, to forget it all and start anew. He takes the motif of forgetting from Nietzsche, although it could as easily have been taken from a Zen teacher. Like Nietzsche and a Zen master, Bleiker sees great value in, not a politics of the world, but a poetics of the world as the site for, if not investigation, then contemplation.[6] This would allow for the contradictory nature of the world – that has hitherto been distorted into the coherence of realism – and also make the primary epistemological vehicle of IR one to do with stories.

What can be done with stories? If stories are the metaphors that disguise events – that is, they relay interested accounts, self-serving interpretations – is it the role of IR to disentangle them, and thus risk becoming enmeshed in multiple undergrowths; or is it to be merely fascinated by them, seeing the world as a site of multiple truths, and congratulate itself for its clever spectatorship and voyeurism? Is IR to have merely a good time?

It is here that the contribution of Hidemi Suganami is of significance. Not only because, for the profession of IR, he incidentally shows how it is possible to use a research assessment exercise (RAE) cycle to develop and elaborate a major theme; but because his theme has a fundamental methodological ambition. In one of these articles, Suganami suggested how mechanistic was the division of explanation and understanding in Hollis and Smith's major work.[7] Between explanation and understanding, he interposed the telling of stories.[8] What about stories? How do they work? It is this methodological question that he has explored within the British RAE cycle now ending, and which is summarised in his chapter in this book.

When it comes to war, at least, Suganami claims that the act of telling stories and narratives is socialised. He observes, across cultures and times, commonalities that involve or invoke agency, nature and chance. These make possible the act of narrative.

This sounds simple at first reading but is, within IR, a significant statement. There is, in short, a commonality within difference. Not only that, here is the key that unlocks that commonality. In the anglophonic discourses, we have missed anything comparable in the declaration of a components list for a methodology of recognising how any story, and any telos, is constructed. If realism is a tissue of lies, we will know how they are told.

Of course, there is much missing here. Can narratives on ethics be as easily socialised? Can their component parts be so easily distinguished? What, for instance, are the constructions of agency? IR has had, as noted above, its own debate on agency, as have other disciplines. IR has not had, and Western disciplines in general have not had, multifarious debates on chance. There have been debates on the laws or spirit of history, and the wherewithals of structural determinisms; but there have not been, for thousands of years – as in other cultures – debates on destiny, fate, or *karma*. Not only that, the dialectical relationships between agency and destiny, and the superagent's ability almost to enter a dialogical relationship with fate, would make the Giddens proposal for a structuration seem very simple. Yet, Hindu and Buddhist cosmologies begin with the enmeshments of agency and destiny. What they propose concerns the psychological processes of agency. That is something a little beyond traditional IR discourse and, even within the new discourses, there is yet to be, for instance, a Lacanian psychoanalysis of struggle in the world. How does the Kantian subject think, after all? How does Arjuna, faced with Krishna's sermon on destiny, think? For Arjuna to live rightly, he had first to survive going crazy in the face of the immensity of fate and chance.

Is it really a proto-discourse?

We began with a pause for irony. We had better not continue without a pause for honesty. Just as IR, as it has been received, is still a crude discipline, and even its efforts to inherit some part of the Frankfurt mantle given to dyadic vulgarities, so too the new discourses within IR have essential crudities. For a start, the notion of a story always leaves 'story' undefined. Story or narrative are 'found' words; that is, we find them as a general label for a wide-ranging activity and take both that generality and wide range at face value. We would not do that for any other term with a technical composition implicit within. We have rather taken up Michael Shapiro's early critique of things driven by *telos*, and never looked back.[9] A story has thus, become anything which expresses the interests of any 'epistemic community'. The consequence of this is that all stories, from wherever they originate, are treated as having the same value. This has an essential political scientific benefit, for it confers an equality upon the stories of both East and West. Without this, and it is indeed an advance, this book would not be possible.

However, there is an entire sub-discipline of literature and linguistics called 'narratology', of which the new IR discourse on stories is acutely unaware. To a student of narratology, we are talking naiveties. This will take time to overcome, just as it took twelve years for a communitarian vision in IR to progress from Mervyn Frost's first statement to Andrew Linklater's effort at an apotheosis of this very communitarianism.[10] We have, here, not even reached the stage of Frost in 1986. Chris Brown has been threatening to write the book on culture for years, but has not done it. What we, in honesty, are doing is preparing a proto-discourse. For now, as something indicative, but also humbling, all we need intone is the linguistic work of Saussure, and its effort to deal with the signified and the signifier. In short, there is a certain problem of language, to do with the relationship between subject and object and, hence, the relationship of meaning between the two. If we were then to say that all major language groups discourse upon this *same* problem, but *differently*, because of different linguistic systems, then we have something to say about the difficulty of those which are generalised as 'stories' in IR. Moreover, if IR has a fundamental concern to do with agency and structure, between what is subjective and objective, between what is ontological and what can be called epistemological, then we are returned to *some* association with a root debate that is multifarious, because there are multifarious languages with multifarious linguistic systems. What is *common* in stories is, within IR, merely declared so. Perhaps they are so. We cannot demonstrate that they are. The new discourse, at this stage, proceeds on an assumption. However, to move IR out of the mire Bleiker so eloquently describes and denounces, we here proceed on that assumption and, indeed, impose a polemical value upon it.

An example of proto-discourse

Precisely because there is no Mervyn Frost figure in the new discourse or protodicourse, because there has not yet been the advent of a messianic Brown, and because there seem to be very few IR scholars versed in linguistics and comparative literature, and fewer with a lived sympathy for the transaction of cultures, we have included – as Part II of this book – three essays by one of the editors. The first two are a testament to the forum provided by the pan-European conferences, and were first presented in Paris and Vienna. The third, as mentioned above, seeks to develop and amplify some of the suggestivenesses of the first two.

There is also something more at stake in these essays, for they suggest not only a poetics of IR, not just a forgetting, but a remembering. William T. R. Fox, one of IR's pioneers, said that the new discipline could act in place of war. It had a mission in the world. It had to accomplish good.

One of the complaints of these essays is that, in the late twentieth century, IR – under a normative rubric – confined itself to a discussion of truth. Under this rubric, it curiously resigned itself from the responsibility of doing good. German ideal philosophy meant a retreat into Karl Jaspers's search for an ideal truth – albeit within less than ideal universities. IR having nothing to say about the atrocities of the post-Cold War world was one thing – it had by now furnished itself with a nice navel (but rather flabby abs) – but its inability to notice its greater inability to *do* anything good in the world, to alleviate and challenge that which was bad, was frankly obscene. It became a discipline of fat burghers and its leading lights became *Bürgermeisters*. ISA conferences became meat-markets and fashion shows.

Thus cut off from the world of great differences and Othernesses, IR welcomed converts and began to absorb the rudiments of more conceptual disciplines, but became, as a point of its 'maturity' at last as an academic discipline, stolidly self-satisfied. In viewing its own navel with satisfaction, it failed to notice the restricted range of even its own sophistication. If it was a Western discipline, anchored now in the preliminaries of Western philosophical thought, it was a Western thought no older than two hundred years. There was nothing in it of sustained antiquity and, thus, nothing within it to compare to those bodies of non-Western knowledge that pre-dated modernity and its young triumphs.

It is, thus, that in his second essay in this book, Stephen Chan continues an exploration of ancient Greek stories that has also been the thematic centre of his 1996–2001 RAE period.[11] It is the third essay, however, that seeks to break the greatest number of moulds. Written in aphorisms – though somewhat more elaborated than those of Nietzsche – and as poetically as possible, he hopes Bleiker, at least, will smile upon his efforts. However, what he has also done is to cite the fundamental similarities between Aristotle and Confucius; and sought to show how, in Greek thought, the use of stories – whether by Plato using Socrates as a mouthpiece, or by the great dramatists – there was an exemplary fusion of explanation, stories and understanding.

Taking both the Greek and Chinese views, not of what is right, but of what might be the righteous person, he refocuses IR's normative debate from an abstract series of notions, and locates the debate into sites of individual accountabilities – even if the formation of accounts, or excuses against accountability, is racked by the psychological and, even, Freudian guilts and slippages of the twentieth century's dementia.

The Zen of international relations

Of course the title of this book is a little naughty. In China, never mind the entirety of the East, Zen is only one aspect of Buddhism, which is, in turn, only one of a terrifyingly rich series of overlapping and interpenetrating traditions. Moreover, the idea of an intellectual clarity that is so distilled it is no longer intellectual at all, but allows a sudden intuitive insight into the structure of the universe, or one's life within the universe, is not unique to Zen. It is found within the Sufi practices of Islam; and is an intense manifestation of what, in English, is called 'epiphany'. What we are trying to do with this book, however, is to give a momentary insight, a flash, into Other views that would rewrite the foundations of IR. Xiaoming Huang's essay provides the keynote, and seeks to accomplish three primary aims. The first is to stress that, in traditional Chinese thought, the absence of dualism meant that, even in times of war, theories of realism and neorealism could not have been composed in China. The idea of a reconciliation into the natural order and hierarchy of the cosmos – the overarching of this ultimate fact – meant that an antique IR, if there had been one, could not have been based on the conflict and competition among states. Second, in a succinct but quite intense survey of contemporary IR theories, Huang draws co-relations between Zen and postmodernism – though cautiously. Third, he stresses there could not have been any settled IR theory in Chinese antiquity, because the ontology of a moving subject, that is, a subject in constant development, meant that the person as sovereign subject could never be isolated out of his or her time for any analysis to have sufficiency. Everything is change under heaven. What this means is that, within Zen, any possible beginning for IR must start, or attempt to start, with ontology.

Roland Bleiker also argues the impossibility of a neorealism in antique Chinese IR. In his famous article, considerably revised here, he also stresses the rejection of dualism and the primacy of ontology and, in particular, of an ontological intuition which can only interrogate the epistemological methods extant in the Western traditions.

Qing Cao, as mentioned at the outset, posits views of the West as Other; and Wang Yi, in his bibliographical note, provides a brief survey of Chinese theoretical thought on IR, updating the recent work of Gerald Chan and Stephen Chan's rather older (and briefer) survey.

Islamic stories and International Relations

We have included a section of the book which moves away from the metatheoretical implications of story-telling in international relations, and begins instead to explore some of the varying forms these stories assume. Beginning with Islam as a broad discursive – rather than geographical – landscape, two chapters examine discrepant accounts of how Islam can best be understood in relation to, on the one hand, the question of civilisational universality and, on the other, one of the key precepts of world politics during the Cold War: the theory and practice of non-alignment. Before moving on to consider the specific arguments offered by the authors of these chapters and their bearing on story-telling in IR, we would (by way of background) do well to dwell for a moment on the idea of the story in Islam.

As Stephen Chan indicates in his typology of states (see Chapter 5), there exist those states – such as the Islamic Republic of Iran – who seek to found their legitimacy on, as he puts it, '[a] world of text-based normativities – which may be given interpretation on literal and exegetic grounds'. It is, of course, this notion of 'text-based normativity' that brings us into the realm of the story. Forms of story-telling such as the allegorical parable are common to a number of world religions; Islam, however, is perhaps unique in terms of the authoritative significance it grants to particular forms of the story. The orthodox canon of Islam recognises two primary sources of authority and knowledge: (1) the Qur'an as the literal word of God as revealed to the Prophet Muhammad; and (2) the *Sunna*, a corpus of textual sources composed primarily of the reported sayings and doings of the Prophet during his lifetime. The example of Muhammad, the human embodiment of Islamic principles, is hence a source of authority in Islam second only to the Word itself. The most common narrative form found within the Sunna is that of the *hadith*. A hadith has two principal components. The first is the story itself, a description of what Muhammad said or did in a particular circumstance. The second part of the hadith is called an *isnad* and is best understood as the enumerated chain of transmission for a particular narrative. It takes the form of a list of names comprising all those who passed knowledge of a particular prophetic example down the ages. The last name in the list is usually that of a contemporary of the Prophet, someone who actually witnessed the purported articulation or deed. Of most interest to us is the way in which this particular story-telling practice begets the telling, recording and reading of yet more stories. The 'science of hadith' has, traditionally, been one of the most prolific sectors of Islamic learning. It consists of cataloguing and researching all of the constituent names and personalities within a hadith's isnad so as to determine the veracity of the 'story' being told about the Prophet. In this sense, biography becomes a vital component of Islamic authority. If it can be shown that an individual within the chain of transmission was of questionable character (for example, if he had been known to tell lies), then some doubt might be cast on the integrity of that particular hadith. Hence the more distant in time and space from the Prophet any hadith report is, the more difficult it is to determine the likelihood of its authenticity. It is not surprising, therefore, to find that the most widely accepted hadiths tend to have a relatively short chain of transmission tracing back to the immediate companions of the Prophet in seventh-century Arabia.

This fact goes some way towards explaining why Muhammad's original community in Medina commands a preeminent position in contemporary Muslim moral imaginaries and stories. Those able to provide the most accurate, first-hand accounts of *insan al-kamil* ('the perfect person') were granted a privileged place in the sources of canonical authority. Did Muhammad and his close followers know that in an attempt to preserve this living relationship with the Prophet their every act would be scrutinised, interpreted, reinterpreted and later codified in jurisprudential literature? Did they know that the stories told about them, as passed down through a secure chain of transmitters, would become the basis for an entire legal system? Muhammad's Medina is a memory, distant yet tangible, pulling at the modern Muslim mind like a magnet. We might invoke here Lawrence Durrell's description of Alexandria in the 1930s as 'a city half-imagined, yet wholly real'. It is a vivid model, something to be desired: the remembrance of an epoch in which anyone who had a reliable story to tell about the Prophet was assured a place in the annals of Islam.

This question of Islam's orientation to its past (and stories of its past) is addressed directly by Mehdi Mozaffari's chapter in the present volume. Pondering the question of whether a declined civilisation can be reconstructed, he is led to engage with three very different sorts of stories being told today about Islam and its relationship to the past and the future. Mozaffari defines civilisation as 'a junction between a world vision and a historical system'. He means by this the institutionalisation of a particular *Weltanschauung* within concrete political economic and military systems. The decline of any civilisation is hence caused by a rupture threatening to separate these two components. This observation leads Mozaffari to enquire as to the possible conditions for reviving a declined civilisation by affecting a reconnection of this broken link. He recognises, however, that since both stories (their form and relevance) and institutions (as historically situated material possibilities) change over time, so necessarily must the terms under which the fusion of world vision and historical system takes place. Turning to the case of Islam, which Mozaffari sees as a prime example of a declined civilisation, he goes on to identify three broad types of story being told today about how Islam can best achieve this reconciliation. The first of these – typified by 'fundamentalist' discourse – seeks a wholesale *reproduction* of Muhammad's golden Medina, leaving very little space for questioning the contemporary validity and efficacy of its form. The *communalist* approach, on the other hand, represents an attempt to reconcile aspects of Islamic discourse with elements of Western modernity, but in a formula in which Islam maintains an upper hand in the articulation of ethical imperatives. There is space for Western reason and science, but only within the limits defined by a divine morality. The third project, and the one with which Mozaffari himself seems to most identify, seeks to move beyond the Islam versus the West impasse by telling a third, and quite revolutionary, story. For these *universalists*, it is necessary to bring Islam into line with 'world-time' and integrate it into a burgeoning global civilisation. Where the reproductionists and communalists identified above would equate this universal civilisation with the West, Mozaffari argues that Muslims must move beyond seeing modernity as something that belongs to and emanates exclusively from the West. By questioning universal civilisation's Western pedigree, Mozaffari is seeking to open up spaces in this civilisation that allow for the insertion and incorporation of enriching concepts and values from Islam. It is this idea which leads him to speak not of reconstructing a singular Islamic civilisation, but rather of integrating a civilised Islam into wider universal forms of life. In this regard, telling different stories about both Islam *and* the West becomes a vital dialogical exercise.

Although perhaps the most mainstream example of IR writing in this volume, Houman Sadri's chapter on Islamic non-alignment provides us with a useful example of how Mozaffari's universalist ethos can play out in the context of international relations. Sadri takes the discourse of non-alignment – conventionally understood merely as a by-product of Cold War geopolitics – and demonstrates how the Islamic Republic of Iran articulated, and continues to articulate, an Islamic understanding of this concept. Iran, as Sadri shows, tells a very different story about non-alignment. Focusing in particular on Khomeini's terse formulation, 'neither East nor West, [only] an Islamic Republic', Sadri goes on to investigate the doctrinal foundations of an account of non-alignment that figures itself not solely as the rejection of East–West polarisation, but also as the elaboration of an alternative way in the world. The Qur'an – and Islam's Sunni orthodoxy – emphasises the importance of equilibrium and balance in relations. Iranian non-alignment, on the other hand, draws on principles – and particularly their Shi'i interpretations – which seek to mediate and respond to the presence of disharmony in a system of social relations. Sadri then draws these insights into a discussion of wider questions surrounding the meaning and relevance of non-alignment today. He shows that by refusing to define non-alignment in a limited, (anti)bipolar Cold War sense, the Iranian variant – highly amenable to reorientation as a discourse on North–South relations – has the potential to provide a new lease of life for non-alignment. It is, however, in Sadri's discussion of possible future directions for Iranian foreign policy that the link with Mozaffari's universalist, civilised Islam becomes clearest. By moving towards a non-aligned stance that accommodates (rather than vilifies) the United States, but which still draws attention to questions of hegemony and moral inconsistency in international relations, Iran has the potential to achieve something like an integration of Islamic precepts of justice into mainstream (or, in Mozaffari's terms, 'universalist') word-political discourse – but in terms that do not imply an inherent incompatibility between Islam and the West. Sadri locates the potential for this shift in the reformist discourse of recent Iranian leaders such as Rafsanjani and the president at the time of writing, Mohammad Khatami. By telling a disparate story of non-alignment, then, new possibilities for coexistence emerge – but a coexistence based not on the homogenisation of the ethico-political field in international relations, but rather on its diversification: the making of space for yet more stories to be told.

Notes

1. Rudolf Wagner, 'Political Institutions, Discourse and Imagination in China at Tiananmen', in James Manor (ed.), *Rethinking Third World Politics* (London: Longman, 1991).
2. This debate was inaugurated (somewhat unwittingly) by Walter Carlsnaes, in his essay in *International Studies Quarterly*, vol. 36 (September 1992). It was criticised by Martin Hollis and Steve Smith in the *Review of International Studies*, vol. 20, no. 3, 1994; and their position was, in turn, criticised in the same journal (vol. 22, no. 1, 1996) by Stephen Chan and Vivienne Jabri; to which Martin Hollis and Steve Smith responded in the same issue; with Stephen Chan making a final reply in that journal (vol. 24, no. 3, 1998).
3. Robert W. Cox with Timothy J. Sinclair, *Approaches to World Order* (Cambridge: Cambridge University Press, 1996), ch. 8.

4. James Piscatori's 1992 Heidelberg paper was entitled, 'Islam and International Morality: An Odd Couple?'; and Stephen Chan's was subsequently published as 'Culture and Absent Epistemologies in the International Relations Discipline', *Theoria*, vols 81/82, 1993.
5. Martin Hollis and Steve Smith, 'A Response: Why Epistemology Matters in International Theory', *Review of International Studies*, vol. 22, no. 1, 1996.
6. In 2000, Roland Bleiker has had the opportunity to devote a special issue of *Alternatives* to the question, not only of poetics, but poetry, in IR.
7. Martin Hollis and Steve Smith, *Explaining and Understanding International Relations* (Oxford: Clarendon Press, 1991).
8. Hidemi Suganami, 'Stories of War Origins: A Narrative Theory of the Causes of War', *Review of International Studies*, vol. 23, no. 4, 1997, especially p. 404.
9. Michael J. Shapiro, 'Textualizing Global Politics', in James Der Derian and Michael J. Shapiro (eds), *International/Intertextual Relations* (Lexington, Md: Lexington Books, 1989).
10. Mervyn Frost, *Towards a Normative Theory of International Relations* (Cambridge: Cambridge University Press, 1986); Andrew Linklater, *The Transformation of Political Community* (Cambridge: Polity Press, 1998).
11. The 'Hellenic' material, apart from the two essays in this volume, are Stephen Chan, 'Aspirations and Absent Epistemologies in Universalism: Towards a Multicultural Normative Theory', in Maria Lensu and Jan-Stefan Fritz (eds), *Value Pluralism, Normative Theory and International Relations* (Basingstoke: Macmillan, 2000); Stephen Chan, 'Typologies Towards an Unchained Medley: Against the Gentrification of Discourse in International Relations', in Vivienne Jabri and Eleanor O'Gorman (eds), *Women, Culture, and International Relations* (Boulder, Colo: Lynne Rienner, 1999).

Part I
Establishing a Debate

2
Western (?) Stories of War Origins[1]

Hidemi Suganami

Introduction

War is a multicausal phenomenon, not only in the oft-noted sense that a variety of factors contribute to the making of a war, but also in the perhaps less obvious sense that there are multifarious causal paths to war. Some of the more ideographically-minded are adamant, therefore, that 'the only investigation of the causes of war that is intellectually respectable is that of the unique origins...of the *particular* past wars'.[2] And even one of the more nomothetically-minded has conceded, some dissenting voices notwithstanding, that 'the hope that there are a few necessary conditions that must always be present in order for war to occur is probably not going to be fulfilled'.[3] Indeed, those factors which are commonly considered as contributory causes of war – for example, misperception, domestic instability, the 'cult of the offensive', to name but a few – are neither sufficient by themselves, nor are they even necessary to bring about a war. To the extent that these factors are deemed to have been necessary elements in causing some specific wars of the past, they must be treated as having been only *contingently* so; and there are very many contingencies resulting in the outbreak of war. None the less, it is one of the main contentions of this chapter that there are some 'family resemblances' among the narratives, or stories, of war origins.[4] The purpose of this chapter is to expound such a claim and outline some of its implications.

The approach followed here, it is important to note, is not one of generalising from a number of outbreaks of war, but one that investigates the *form* which the accounts of war origins are conventionally made to take. An attempt to generalise from a number of outbreaks of war is exemplified by Donald Kagan's *On the Origins of War*.[5] This example is not followed here because generalisation from different wars is problematic where each case yields a number of plausible causal narratives; it is probable that those who succeed in generalising, like Kagan himself, have only read or selected similar stories about different cases. Instead, the approach of this chapter has been inspired by two literary–theoretical sources. One is the writings of Hayden White, who is rightly famous for his argument that history may be narrated as a comedy, tragedy, romance, epic, or satire.[6] The other is the work of Vladimir Propp, according to whom the variety of moves made by the characters in Russian fairytales is limited in number, there are thirty-one of them at most, and these always appear in the same sequence.[7] Applying some of their insights to the war-origins literature, I will argue below that although stories of war origins, when looked at in detail, are quite diverse, such stories, taken together, are not unlimited in their variety. What reduces the variety, and what functions it serves to tell a story within the apparently delimited range are two central questions to be explored in the following. But, as a preparatory move, I want to tell a story, or a history of an idea, which is relevant to analysing the structure of narrative explanations, yet entirely neglected in the recent epistemological discussion within IR. The story – heuristic in intent – begins with an observation made by Tzevetan Todorov in his *The Conquest of America*.

A remarkable trinity

The world of Christopher Columbus apparently comprised three parts. In his journal of the third voyage, he remarked:

> I have come to believe that this is a mighty continent which was hitherto unknown. I am greatly supported in this view by reason of this great river, and by this sea which is fresh, and I am also supported by the statements of Esdras in his fourth book, the sixth chapter, which says that six parts of the world consist of dry land and one part of water. This work was approved by Saint Ambrose in his Hexameron and by Saint Augustine... Moreover I am supported by the statements of several cannibal Indians whom I captured on other occasions, who declared that there was mainland to the west of them.[8]

Commenting on this passage, Todorov observes:

> Columbus cites three reasons in support of his conviction: the abundance of fresh water; the authority of the sacred books; the opinion of

other men he has met with. Now it is clear that these three arguments are not to be set on the same level, but reveal the existence of three spheres that articulate Columbus's world: *one is natural, one divine, and the third human.*[9]

The same tripartite picture underlies Hegel's brief remark that philosophy consists in 'the speculative knowledge of God, nature, and mind'.[10] It reappears in the historian Johan Huizinga's remark that history is meaningful only in so far as we grant it a goal, 'whether the goal be thought of as set by *human will, by blind necessity, or by God's providence and continual act of creation*'.[11] It is noteworthy that Huizinga, like Hegel earlier, refers to the three domains, human, natural and divine, as though this way of classifying required no further explanation.

Huizinga's phrase, 'God's providence and continual act of creation', is, more commonly, 'divine intervention' – 'an event or circumstance which indicates divine dispensation'. And for those who do not see the need to invoke God to explain the apparently inexplicable, benign or otherwise, such an event or circumstance is no more than a matter of 'chance', or, more precisely, 'chance coincidence'.

The idea that the most natural way to give an account of the human world is to see it as affected by natural, human and chance factors is advanced by the historian Paul Veyne as follows:

[History] has no method, which means that its method is innate; in order to understand the past, it is sufficient to view it with the same eyes we use to understand the world around us or the life of a foreign people. It is sufficient to view the past in this way in order to see in it the three kinds of causes we discover as soon as we open our eyes: the nature of things, human freedom, and chance. Such are, according to the Peripatetics, and especially the Alexander of Aphrodisias, the three kinds of efficient causes that rule the sublunary world and that Wilhelm von Humboldt, in one of the finest essays ever written on history, describes as the three kinds of motivating causes of universal history.[12]

In a learned endnote to this striking passage, Veyne locates examples of this tripartite classification in the writings of Plato, Aristotle, Tacitus, St Thomas and Dante, among others.[13] To this, Veyne might have added Clausewitz, an unlikely figure perhaps, to whom, however, the phenomenon of war was 'a remarkable trinity' – of blind natural force, the play of chance, and subordination to reason as an instrument of policy.[14] He might also have added Vattel, according to whom 'the law of nations' was divisible into three kinds, 'necessary', 'voluntary', and 'arbitrary', even though here the resemblance is more terminological than substantive.[15]

We might suppose, then, there was something apparently quite natural – in the Western intellectual tradition at least – about the tripartite classification of causes and, concomitantly, the division of the world into three spheres – 'natural, human and divine', or, in its secular version, 'necessary, volitional and contingent'. This way of looking at the world and causes within it, Veyne even suggests, is 'innate', as we saw. This, of course, goes too far. As Agnes Heller notes, such a typology is 'no less an *organizing principle* of historiography than any other typology'.[16] But Heller in turn errs in implying that this principle is historiography's own. Rather, as Veyne had rightly observed in the passage cited above, the principle is followed by historians because it is already accepted in our everyday attempt to make sense of the world around us.

The tripartite classification is indeed widely used in contemporary thinking about the social world. For example, E. H. Carr incorporates this 'organizing principle' – though implicitly – in discussing historical causation in his well-known book, *What is History?*[17] The very same principle, marginally different in terminology, is also found in J. D. Singer, who has otherwise very little in common with any of the figures mentioned so far. He writes: 'All social events may be thought of as the outcome of a concatenation of some deterministic, stochastic, and voluntaristic elements'.[18]

The structure of war-origins narratives

It is very common nowadays, then, and perhaps it has been so for considerably longer, to think of a social event as an outcome of a combination of chance coincidences, mechanistic processes and volitional acts. These three items require some delineation at this stage. A 'chance coincidence' – 'co-incidence by chance' – is not an uncaused event, but a simultaneous occurrence of two or more causally independent events. A 'volitional act' means simply an intended action, not a free, unconstrained action, if ever there was one. A 'mechanistic process' is a narrative representation of the ways a segment of the world appears to us to proceed when left to its own devices. It is contrasted to a 'purposive process', in which an actor is presented as aiming to achieve a goal.[19]

Now, if it is very common to consider a social event as an outcome of a combination of these three factors, then a very commonly acceptable way to give an account of how a social event, such as the outbreak of a war, came to take place, must be to show how these factors were combined to produce the specific outcome in question. There are a number of ways in which this can be done. For example, it may be done through a 'customized' dialogue in which the person who is doing the explaining tries to answer as many questions as are raised by the enquirer in accordance with the latter's perhaps idiosyncratic set of interests. The answers given, in such circumstances, if put together afterwards, would require much editing to yield a smooth and coherent whole. Another way would be for the explainer to suggest a set of questions that he finds necessary to address in order to shed light on the causal process leading to the occurrence of the social event, order them in some systematic fashion, and answer them one by one. Then, there is the narrative way, showing how the end state came to be, beginning at the beginning wherever that might be, and going through the middle parts, in which the three factors noted interact to propel the story. 'The beginning', however, usually contains some information about the background. In addition, what W. H. Dray has aptly called 'a cross-sectional breather' would be required from time to time to supply some further background information, without which the narrative would become harder and harder to comprehend.[20]

It follows that there are four key ingredients in narrative accounts of war origins: (1) depiction of the background; (2) references to significant chance coincidences; (3) elucidation of war-conducive mechanistic processes; and (4) identification of key moves made by the major actors. It should be added here, however, that not all historical narratives give equal weight to these ingredients or necessarily make them explicit; it is possible, for example, for (2) or (3) not to be given much weight or made explicit, whereas it would be unlikely for an intelligible narrative to be constructed without explicit reference to (1) and (4). Another point to note is that the other forms of explanation just mentioned (that is, through a customised dialogue or a systematic presentation of questions and answers) would also need to give information falling in these four categories. Furthermore, when looked at in detail, it will be found that these other forms of explanation will contain a series of narrative explanations scattered in various parts of the whole explanatory enterprise.[21] At this point, I need to say a few more words about each of the four key ingredients.

The background

A first key ingredient of war-origins narratives is the explication of the background. Many kinds of information may fall under this category: geographical and demographical features of the countries involved; characteristics of the existing international system, for example, the distribution of power or alliance configurations; the governmental structures of the relevant countries, and characteristics of their foreign policy-making; the political, social, economic and military conditions of the powers concerned; national self-images, ideological motivations of the leaders and the peoples, and prevalent assumptions about the nature of international politics, diplomacy and war; the intensity of the existing rivalry and grievances; and so on.

When subjected to systematic statistical investigation, some of these characteristics, whether individually or in combination, may turn out to constitute 'correlates of war'. When giving a narrative account of the origins of a particular war, however, historians or social scientists do not necessarily mention background features, such as the ones listed above, because they are, if at all, known statistically to 'probability' the outbreaks of war. They do so to help 'intelligibility' their stories.

They decide on what to include in the background sections of their narratives in the light of their story-lines, and the level of knowledge they assume in their audiences. However, their story-lines are in turn shaped to some extent by what they see as important background conditions pertaining to the case in hand, and these may be selected on the basis of more or less well-confirmed impression or hypothesis about the sorts of circumstances of which war is a likely, as well as intelligible, consequence.

Chance coincidences

A second ingredient is reference to significant chance coincidences. By a 'chance coincidence' is meant a simultaneous occurrence of two or more events which are causally unrelated to one another.[22] Interestingly, it is largely unnoticed that our world of events is infested with chance coincidences: my neighbour's cat yawns as a leaf falls off a lime tree outside my window – by chance. But, as this imaginary example illustrates, chance coincidences mostly deserve not to be noticed, because to a large extent they are historically insignificant: they do not form part of the explanation of any particular event. There are, however, some chance coincidences which are seen to play a vital role in shaping the subsequent course of events, and some writers, often professional historians, place a great deal of emphasis on the role of chance with respect to the origins of certain wars.

For example, according to A. J. P. Taylor, Gavrilo Princip's assassination of Archduke Ferdinand and his wife in Sarajevo, which led to the outbreak of the First World War, could not have taken place without a chance coincidence: Ferdinand's car was made to halt at a corner because the chauffeur, who had not been instructed properly, took a wrong turning, and – by chance – this was the corner where Princip was at that very moment.[23] It is accepted by a number of historians that without this coincidence the Sarajevo assassination attempt would not have succeeded, and that without the assassination there would have been neither an Austrian–Serbian war, nor a world war, in the summer of 1914, even though a war might perhaps have taken place sooner or later involving roughly the same set of states as those which fought the First World War.[24]

This case may be taken to show that chance coincidences tend to be used to explain the timing of the outbreak of war where war is already highly probable. As Geoffrey Blainey rightly notes, 'an "accidental" war is more likely if the non-accidental factors are strong'.[25] Perhaps we cannot rule out the possibility, however, that various factors accumulate through a series of chance coincidences to create a war-conducive situation.

Mechanisms

A third ingredient is reference to relevant (war-conducive) mechanistic processes. A 'mechanistic process', which may be contrasted with a 'purposive process', is said to be in operation, where, for example, we are deemed to be induced to behave in a certain way because of the workings of our mind or body, or because the social environment is believed to influence us to think and act in a particular manner; or where, through the workings of the system in which our actions take place, they are taken to lead to unintended consequences.

Historians at times take such processes for granted, especially those which are familiar ones, but social scientists are often keen to draw attention to them as indispensable linkages between various key situations, events and actions. One very good example to illustrate this point is an article entitled 'Organizational Routines and the Causes of War' by an eminent American political scientist who specialises in the study of war, Jack S. Levy.[26]

Levy argues, with respect to the outbreak of the First World War, that the inflexibility of the military contingency plans, such as the Schlieffen

Plan, is insufficient by itself to explain why they were rigidly implement-
ed (where it was not optimal to do so); and that the gap which is thus
found between the preexisting plans and the actual outbreak of the war
has to be filled out by a variety of causal mechanisms. Such mechanisms
are found in the form of short and familiar stories, pointing to intelligible general tendencies, at times verging on truisms. Several examples
are contained in the following sketches based on Levy's discussion.

As one bureaucratic organisation among many, the military are compelled to seek their own autonomy and prestige. To do so, the military
may tend not to supply civilian policy-makers with full information
regarding operational tactics. As a result, civilian policy-makers are in
danger of pursuing policies not consonant with existing military plans.
In critical circumstances resulting from the pursuit of such policies, the
civilian policy-makers may be forced to become subservient to the
military to whose contingency plans no viable alternative may readily
be found. Thus having gained influence, the military may 'elevate narrow operational requirements above the needs of state policy'.[27] Years of
work in developing, revising and perfecting a plan generates a psychological commitment to it and makes improvisation difficult, even where
desirable. Furthermore, when under considerable stress, the decision-
makers may become so exhausted that they lose the normal flexibility of
their minds.[28] To cope with extreme anxiety, they may seek refuge in the
certainty of known routines, and hence in the existing plans. They may
also begin to feel, for example, that their own options are limited, forced
by the circumstances, and narrowing, while those of the adversary are
larger in number and freely chosen. Such a trend may be reinforced by
what Irving Janis has called 'the groupthink syndrome', 'a consensus-
seeking tendency which can increase resistance to policy change
through illusions of unanimity and invulnerability, moral certainty,
self-censorship, and collective rationalization'.[29] And so on.

Key actions of the major actors

A fourth ingredient, which will presently be analysed closely, is reference to key actions and inactions on the part of major actors in response
to the historical background, chance coincidences, mechanistic processes, and the actions and inactions of the other major actors, resulting
in the outbreak of war in question. But before we go on to see what
criteria are used in selecting and characterising the key moves of the
major participants, a couple of observations need to be made.

First, we should note that, in order to construct a comprehensible
narrative of the origins of any given war, it would be insufficient merely

to enumerate the key ingredients of the narrative: they must be put together to form an organic whole. They must be arranged in such a way that the narrative thereby constructed can be comprehended. But to comprehend a narrative is to be able to say what it amounts to. It is to be able to summarise the narrative so that its essence can be distilled. It is to grasp the point. This brings us to another important structural characteristic of the war-origins narratives: the narratives make the sort of point which (no doubt conventionally) is considered as an appropriate one to make, given the kind of thing which war (conventionally) is deemed to be.

Second, it is important in this connection to notice that it is chiefly through the experience of the First World War that causes of war came to be a major intellectual preoccupation of the historical profession and historical works on war origins came to proliferate.[30] Writing a self-contained book on a given war's origins *as such* is a practice familiar only since 1914; before then, origins of wars were more naturally an integral part of works on wars.[31] The historians' shift of camera angle, from war to war origins, reflects the attitudinal change among the wider public brought about by the experience of the First World War. Social scientists' interests in the causes of war are also largely a post-1914 phenomenon. War came to be seen in a more negative light than ever before, as a disaster to be avoided, a crime to be prevented, an evil to be eliminated. Given this predominantly pacificistic environment in which war origins came to be narrated as a historical theme in their own right, it is to be expected that the sort of point which is considered an appropriate one to make in writing about war origins tends to be about who or what is to blame for the outbreaks of war. And, indeed, accounts of the origins of wars are very often disputations, at times even quasi-juridical.

Such a feature of the (primarily post-1914 'Western') accounts of war origins becomes apparent when we note what sorts of questions are conventionally asked (there) about key moves of the relevant actors in constructing a story of war origins. They are questions such as the following: 'Was the invasion premeditated?' 'Was the decision to attack made in desperation, or were alternatives available to the attacker to attain its aims?' 'To what extent did the invaded country fail to deter the attack through its lack of preparedness?' 'Had the invaded country acted offensively by committing any insensitive or thoughtless acts towards the invader?' 'What were the attacker's calculations concerning intervention by a third party, and, in particular, did it act entirely thoughtlessly on this issue, or did it gamble on the third party's inaction?' 'If it did gamble, was it a reasonable thing to do in the circumstances, or was it excessively irresponsible?' 'To what extent was the third party in turn responsible for its failure to make clear, prior to the aggression, its intent to intervene in support of the victim?' And so on.

Implicit in these, and other similar, questions, which reflect a particular kind of attitude towards war, dominant most notably in the 'West' since the First World War, are certain criteria in the light of which writers conventionally characterise the types of move made by key actors in the process resulting in the outbreaks of war. Of the various moves which they are depicted as making, there are two which are necessary – 'resistance' and 'acts with belligerent intent'. The precise meaning of each of these terms will be explained presently. But before these two types of acts come to be committed, the relevant actors are likely to have made a number of other moves, and what is especially noteworthy is the fact that the criteria by which historians judge whether such moves have been committed are limited in number – only a few in fact, consisting of 'contributory negligence', 'insensitivity', 'thoughtlessness' and 'recklessness'. This relatively small number of criteria contributes to standardising the types of move the relevant actors are said to have made in the process leading to the outbreaks of wars, and this in turn contributes to creating 'family resemblances' among the stories of war origins. The claim here is much weaker than Vladimir Propp's, noted earlier, concerning Russian fairytales, but they are similar in spirit. The terms used here to characterise key actions are explained below.

Resistance

When, by an ultimatum or an open attack, state A is given by its adversary B a clear choice between immediate surrender and war, A may choose to surrender. But when, as in nearly every case, A refuses to surrender immediately, and resorts to arms in response to B's challenge, A may be said to act in 'resistance'.[32] 'Resistance', as defined here, is a broader category than 'defence' as usually understood. For we would not normally say of A that it was simply 'defending' itself against B, if A had acted offensively in the first place to provoke B's challenge. But, even in such circumstances, we would say of A that it 'resisted' B.

Acts with belligerent intent

War cannot begin where there is no resistance, but this, by definition, presupposes a state confronting its target explicitly with a choice between immediate surrender and war. Such an act is said here to be undertaken with 'belligerent intent'.

But an act with belligerent intent need not be so directly linked with an outbreak of war. As defined here, the term refers to any act motivated by clear intent, immediately or at some later stage, to force upon the opponent a choice between surrender and war. Such acts can, therefore, take place at various points in the process leading to an outbreak of war, and may take various forms, ranging from a variety of preparatory measures to an actual use of force at the start of a war. It is the presence of clear intent to engage in war that is central to the concept of acts with belligerent intent, and not their outward features, nor their temporal location *vis-à-vis* the outbreak of war.

The fact that state A performed acts with belligerent intent against state B does not entail, it is worthwhile to note, that A's war against B was aggressive, gratuitous, or premeditated. For example, the war by Britain and France against Germany in the Second World War was not aggressive – it was punitive; Japan's attack on Pearl Harbor in 1941 was not gratuitous – it was an act of desperation; and Britain's war against Argentina in 1982 was not premeditated – it had to be fought in the end.

If war cannot occur without resistance, neither can there be such a thing as an unintended war, or war without any belligerent intent, although, as is often noted, much of what happens in war is quite unintended by many participants.[33] In most cases, however, acts with belligerent intent are not performed out of the blue, but in the context of deteriorating circumstances, in which a variety of war-conductive acts have already been undertaken. 'Contributory negligence', 'insensitivity', 'thoughtlessness' and 'recklessness' are the criteria by which key actions are presented in the narrative as having been 'war-conductive'.

Contributory negligence. The first of these criteria differs from the other three just noted in that 'acts of contributory negligence' are not themselves *offensive* acts. On the contrary, a contributorily negligent act, in the context of war origins, is a failure to resort to standard countermeasures against an adversary's offensive policy, thereby unduly encouraging the adversary to take even more offensive steps, receiving harm as a result.

Insensitivity, thoughtlessness, recklessness. The remaining three criteria can be explained as follows. Suppose that state A is about to undertake what amounts to an offensive act against its adversary B, and that the act's offensiveness is noticeable to a reasonably attentive mind. If, in such circumstances, A performs the act, unaware even that B will, with good reason, consider the act to be offensive, then A can be said to act 'insensitively'. If, however, A performs the act, having noticed its offensive character, but failing to give any serious consideration to the resultant risk of war, obvious to a reasonably attentive mind, then A can be said to act 'thoughtlessly'. Finally, in deliberating whether or not to perform an offensive act, A may calculate as follows: the probability of war resulting from the act, and/or the cost of such a war, might be quite considerable; but, still, the probability and/or the cost would be tolerably low when judged in the overall context of what A could probably gain by resorting to the act, in contrast to not doing so at that time. If, on the basis of such a calculation, A carries out the offensive act, even though a reasonably prudent leader would not take such a risk, then A can be said to act 'recklessly'. This category also covers cases of controlled risk-taking: where A resorts to the offensive act, along with some softening measures to reduce the risk of escalation into war, and/or the cost of such an eventuality, speculating that the risk and/or the cost has thereby become tolerable in the overall calculation.

Sources of family resemblances

The general categories of actions, defined in terms of the above criteria, constitute a common pool such that interactions among relevant actors leading to outbreaks of war can be outlined by combinations of some or all of them. This produces family resemblances in war origins, as can readily be noted from a number of examples outlined below.

Illustrations

In the relatively simple case of the Falklands/Malvinas war of 1982, Argentina, in invading the islands, acted thoughtlessly, or perhaps recklessly, regarding potential British reactions to the Argentine resort to arms.[34] Britain, perhaps having been contributorily negligent to a small degree, now responded by sending a naval task force to the South Atlantic. In so doing, Britain appears to have calculated (not unreasonably) that the cost of failing to take military actions far outweighed the probable cost of war, which, of course, would be unnecessary if Argentina, under the threat of war, were to back down.[35] Not unnaturally, however, Argentina could not face the humiliation of defeat without a fight, but was in the end forced to withdraw.[36]

In a comparably simple case, in the Gulf War, Iraq resorted to an act with belligerent intent when it invaded Kuwait in the summer of 1990.

Kuwait, having been to some extent insensitive or thoughtless in its handling of Iraq, barely had time to register its resistance. By the following winter, however, the United States had acted with belligerent intent, and carried out a punitive war against Iraq, sanctioned by the UN and supported by other countries. Iraq resisted, but was compelled to withdraw.[37]

The origins of the Russo-Japanese War of 1904–5, though with much interesting meandering, are again reasonably straightforward in outline: Russia acted insensitively and thoughtlessly towards Japan. Exasperated, Japan became firmer in its resolve to dictate a military solution, resorting in the end to a war to challenge Russian hegemony in Manchuria and influence in Korea.[38]

The origins of the Second World War in Asia and the Pacific also involve some meandering, but the modality of the major participants' entry into the war is relatively straightforward: Japan's aggressive war against China; China's resistance; punitive measures short of war against Japan taken by the USA and other powers on the assumption that Japan would yield to the pressures; Japan's intent, in desperation, to launch a war against the USA; and the USA's resistance.[39]

The immediate origins of the Second World War in Europe, too, are relatively straightforward in outline: Germany's invasion of Poland, which was an act with belligerent intent as regards Poland, but an act of recklessness regarding the prospect of war with Britain and France; Polish resistance; the belligerent intent on the part of Britain and France, having been contributorily negligent and by now exasperated by Germany's excessively reckless provocations, to resort to a punitive war; Germany's resistance; Germany's belligerent intent to cause an aggressive war against the Soviet Union; and the Soviet resistance.[40]

The origins of the First World War are notoriously complex, but the following is one plausible outline: Austria-Hungary's ultimatum to Serbia, which was an act with belligerent intent against Serbia, and a reckless act with respect to the prospect of war with Russia;[41] Germany's support of Austria-Hungary, reflecting Germany's reckless thinking to the effect, initially, that the war could perhaps be limited to the Austrian–Serbian level, but, later, that if Germany were to have to face Russia and France, Britain would at least not enter the war immediately;[42] Russia's stage-by-stage mobilisation, which, by the time general mobilisation was ordered, became an act with belligerent intent to resort to a punitive war against Austria and a preemptive war against Germany;[43] Germany's implementation of the Schlieffen Plan, which was an act with belligerent intent against Belgium, France and Russia;

resistance by Belgium and France; and, finally, Britain's resort to a punitive war against Germany.

It is important to note here that the above illustrations are presented only as plausible, or standardly accepted, outlines of the several cases. We would expect there to be contending versions. But other interpretations would not be so radically different. They would not do away with the criteria for selecting and characterising key actions discussed here; or so this chapter asserts for further testing.[44] According to my study so far, the historical illustrations presented above, and their likely variants, do indicate that there are certain family resemblances among the stories of war origins. Similarities crop up and disappear as we compare different cases (or stories about them) at a certain level of generality in terms of key actions which are presented in the narratives as having contributed to the outbreaks of war. Can the same point be made about war- origins narratives with respect to their other ingredients: background conditions, war-conducive mechanisms and chance coincidences?

Other sources

As far as war's background conditions are concerned, a particular combination of factors, with all the relevant details, constituting a background to a given war, in a story of its origins, is of course unique to that story. Under certain general descriptions, however, some conditions constituting the background with respect to one case may find their equivalent in a number of other cases: for example, multipolarity, or the presence of a relatively large number of decision-making centres, in a crisis situation;[45] the lack of civilian control of the military;[46] and so on. As in the case of key actions, there might perhaps be a common pool of general features such that background conditions of particular wars are its subsets in concrete forms. The same point can be made with respect to war-conducive mechanisms. If so, backgrounds and mechanistic processes may also contribute, to some extent, to family resemblances among stories of war origins.

By contrast, it would be difficult to see how family resemblances might ever emerge among war-origins narratives if we compared them with respect to the element of chance coincidences. Under relevantly detailed descriptions, they play critical parts in some stories of war origins. Yet, it is difficult to visualise a common pool, comprising types of chance coincidences such that – as in the case of background conditions or war-conducive mechanisms – those relevant to particular wars are the subsets, in concrete forms, of the entire pool.

Indispensable categories, dispensable categorisations

It is worth emphasising here that criteria for characterising key actions have not been invented for the sake of forcing similarities to emerge from what are after all very diverse stories of the origins of wars. These criteria appear to be conventionally employed by anyone who tries to give an account of government interactions ending in war. A parallel case, however, cannot be made with respect to background conditions, war- conducive mechanisms, or chance coincidences. This point deserves a brief discussion.

As far as background conditions and war-conducive mechanisms are concerned, it is of course possible to classify them, and their subdivisions are often accorded some conventional labels. For example, P. M. H. Bell divides the background to the Second World War in Europe into 'ideological', 'economic' and 'strategic' factors.[47] Kenneth Waltz's well-known tripartite scheme, reflecting a conventional view of world political order, may also be used in sorting out background or mechanistic factors.[48] Such classificatory schemes, well accepted though they may be, are not, however, integral to our understanding of background conditions or war-conducive mechanisms. No particular scheme of classification concerning such factors is indispensable to our understanding of them.

As far as chance coincidences are concerned, no classificatory scheme is even conceivable which is conventional or appropriate. This is because chance coincidences, so long as they are accepted as such, do not require us to make sense of them. The fact that two events occurred simultaneously by chance becomes incorporated into our story without requiring us to understand what sort of fact that was. Indeed, this question does not appear to make any sense (although, admittedly, some cultures do try to make sense of what to 'us' appear as chance coincidences not requiring any further explanation).[49]

The situation is manifestly different with respect to key actions of the narrative. Here we need to understand what sort of act was committed by a relevant actor, in order to be able to incorporate it, as a significant element, into our narrative. And in answering this question, it appears, we make use of the criteria identified, and the resultant categories, indispensably. Their indispensability is nowhere more apparent than where historians disagree about the origins of particular wars. Typically, the disputes are conducted in terms of the categories (and their subdivisions, such as 'premeditation'). For example, controversies concerning the origins of the First World War in Europe are mainly about whether the Imperial German government had premeditated a Continental war.[50] And disputes about the origins of the Second World War in Europe are mainly about whether Hitler was acting recklessly, and how much, if any, weight should be given to contributory negligence on the part of Britain and France. Such controversies take on a quasi- juridical quality because the categories used to characterise relevant actions are, as will have been noticed, themselves quasi-juridical.[51]

Concluding remarks

In this chapter, I have tried to demonstrate a number of interrelated points: (1) there is a well-established conventional way of seeing how, in the social world, an event came to take place; (2) this pays attention to three kinds of causative factors: volitional, mechanistic and chance coincidental; (3) correspondingly, in explaining the occurrence of an event in the social world it is conventional to take these three kinds of factors into account; (4) such an explanation need not take a narrative form, but narrative explanations are in fact common, and will also be found scattered in various parts of other forms of explanatory enter-prise; (5) in giving a narrative explanation of the occurrence of an event in the social world, attention will also be paid to 'background condi-tions'; (6) so that, for example, in explaining the origins of a particular war, the narrative will take into account the background, chance coin-cidences, war-conductive mechanisms and key actions of the major participants; (7) narratives of war origins are standardised in outline particularly because of the ways key actions of the major participants are identified and characterised; (8) a set of quasi-juridical criteria are used for this purpose, and these are what I have called 'acts with belli-gerent intent', 'resistance', 'contributory negligence', 'insensitivity', 'thoughtlessness' and 'recklessness'; (9) it follows from this that the point of such a narrative is quasi-juridical, aiming to establish who or what, if any, was to blame for the occurrence of a particular war; and (10) this is understandable when we realise that the war-origins litera-ture emerged in the aftermath of the First World War as an integral part of the rise of the pacificistic attitude, according to which war is a crime, a disaster, or an evil, which must at least be controlled if it cannot be eliminated.

   This is my story of the war-origins stories, which immediately raises an intriguing question: how far beyond the pacificistic 'West' does this story apply? More specifically, to the extent that non-pacificistic cul-tures address the question of how particular wars came to be fought (even though war-origins literature may not thrive as a genre in such cultures), are the answers given in such cultures similar to the ones nowadays commonly encountered in standard historical works in 'the West' upon which the foregoing analysis has been based? I am intrigued, but do not know the answer. There is, of course, a related question of how far, even in 'the West', narratives are offered to explain the origins of wars in ways that are different from what I have been arguing to be a standard fashion. To this, my answer is that I have yet to come across exceptions in my study of contemporary writings specifically aimed at explaining how particular wars came to be fought.

Another question which may be raised is an application to the war-origins issue of a familiar, more general, question: if a culture, different from 'ours', explains the origins of a particular war in a manner different from how 'we' would find appropriate, how would it be possible to choose between them? But this question is not a very helpful one in the absence of a concrete example; and, when confronted with an example, there is no alternative but to consider how a dialogue might be developed between the proponents of different explanations about the same event, bearing in mind that there would be no conflict between different explanations unless they were of the same event under the same description. Of course, cultural differences may be so wide between the two societies that the same event even under the same description, such as 'war' or 'the starting of a war', may have quite different meanings for them. In such cases, however, the question of how to choose between different explanations of war origins would not be particularly significant. It would, in such cases, be more worthwhile to investigate the sources and consequences of different conceptualisations about the nature and role of war in their respective societies.

Leaving aside the intercultural issue, which is best discussed with reference to specific cases, there remains one question that may be touched on here: what are the functions of war-origins narratives formulated in the ways apparently standard in 'the West'? There is no doubt that the primary objective of such a narrative is to explain, or to solve some puzzles about the event such that our understanding or grasp of the event, and of the world as a whole, is rendered somewhat more comprehensive and coherent than before the explanation was given. Whether or not our understanding of a past event is useful in some way is a separate issue. It will certainly function as a practical reminder – perhaps not much more than that. But, in any case, we or very many of us do have an urge to be told or find out about the past. This is understandable given that our very existence as a person within a society is sustained by our autobiographical grasp, our understanding of how we have been related to those with whom we interact, and historical knowledge claims about our society.[52] To satisfy our historical curiosity, then, is a basic function of historical narratives. In the case of the war-origins literature more specifically, the way in which we want to satisfy our curiosity appears to be normatively driven – we want to find out who did the wrong thing, what went wrong, or what was bad about the set-up which produced the war. Historians would not necessarily agree, but it would not be a bad thing for there to be a constant possibility of revising existing views – which, of course, is never the same as saying that history is as we like it to be. 'All history is tendentious, and if it were not tendentious nobody would write it', remarked R. G. Collingwood. He went on to add: 'Great history, however, is never merely tendentious'.[53]

Notes

1. This chapter is based on a series of works I published between 1996 and 1999: *On the Causes of War* (Oxford, 1996); 'Stories of War Origins: A Narrativist Theory of the Causes of War', *Review of International Studies*, vol. 23, 1997, pp. 401–18; 'Narratives of War Origins and Endings: A Note on the End of the Cold War', *Millennium: Journal of International Studies*, vol. 26, 1997, pp. 631–49; 'Agents, Structures, Narratives', *European Journal of International Relations*, vol. 5, 1999, pp. 365–86. By 'war' I have in mind standard interstate wars.
2. A. Seabury and A. Codevilla, *War: Ends and Means* (New York, 1989), p. 50; emphasis in original.
3. J. A. Vasquez, *The War Puzzle* (Cambridge, 1993), p. 48. Compare B. Bueno de Mesquita, *The War Trap* (New Haven, Conn. 1981).
4. For the idea of family resemblances, see L. Wittgenstein, *Philosophical Investigations*, tr. G. E. M. Anscombe (Oxford, 1968), sections 66 and 67.
5. (London, 1995).
6. H. White, *Metahistory: The Historical Imagination in Nineteenth-Century Europe* (Baltimore, Md, 1973); *Tropics of Discourse* (Baltimore, Md, 1978); *The Content of the Form: Narrative Discourse and Historical Representation* (Baltimore, Md, 1987).
7. V. Propp, *Morphology of the Folktale*, 2nd edn, tr. Laurence Scott, rev. and ed. Louis A. Wagner (Austin, Tex., 1968).
8. Tzevetan Todorov, *The Conquest of America: The Question of the Other*, tr. Richard Howard (New York, 1984), p. 14.
9. Ibid.; emphasis added.
10. G. W. F. Hegel, *Philosophy of Right*, tr. T. M. Knox (Oxford, 1952), p. 8.
11. Johan Huizinga, 'The Idea of History', in Fritz Stern (ed.), *The Variety of History: From Voltaire to the Present* (New York, 1973), pp. 290–303 at p. 293; emphasis added.
12. Veyne, *Writing History: Essays on Epistemology*, tr. Mina Moore-Rinvolucri (Manchester, 1984), p. 105.
13. Ibid., p. 307, n. 18.

14. Carl von Clausewitz, *On War*, ed. and tr. by M. Howard and P. Paret (Princeton, NJ, 1976), p. 89.

15. Emmerich de Vattel, *The Law of Nations* (1758 edn), extracted in M. G. Forsyth *et al.* (eds), *The Theory of International Relations: Selected Writings from Gentili to Treitschke* (London, 1970), pp. 89–125, Preface.

16. Agnes Heller, *A Theory of History* (London, 1982), p. 173.

17. (Harmondsworth, 1964), ch. 4.

18. J. D. Singer, 'The Historical Experiment as Research Strategy in the Study of World Politics', in J. D. Singer (ed.), *The Correlates of War* (New York, 1979), Vol. 1, pp. 175–96, at p. 184.

19. 'Mechanistic processes' are narrative representations in the sense that what we present as mechanistic processes are narrative representations. As to what goes on in the world, independently of our representations, when what we so represent goes on, I tentatively plead ignorance. It is tempting to suggest that some sort of necessitation is going on, but since such necessitation cannot be experienced directly by our senses, the world in which it can be said to go on is not what we call the empirical world. Perhaps the empirical world is a portion of the world, another part of which we cannot experience but understand (or make sense of through representation), yet another part of which we can perhaps neither experience nor (as yet) understand.

20. W. H. Dray, 'On the Nature and Role of Narrative in Historiography', *History and Theory*, vol. 10 (May, 1971) pp. 153–71, at p. 155.

21. See, for example, James Joll, *The Origins of the First World War* (London, 1984).

22. See W. Kneale, *Probability and Induction* (Oxford, 1949), pp. 114–17; E. H. Carr, *What is History?*, pp. 98–100.

23. A. J. P. Taylor, 'In Defence of Small Nations', *The Listener*, no. 98 (August 1977), pp. 138–40, at p. 128.

24. S. B. Fay, *The Origins of the World War*, 2 vols, 2nd edn (New York, 1930), Vol. 2, p. 53; L. Albertini, *The Origins of the War of 1914*, tr. and ed. I. M. Massey, 3 vols (London, 1952–7), Vol. 2, p. 38; A. J. P. Taylor, 'Accident Prone, or What Happened Next', *Journal of Modern History*, vol. 49, 1977, pp. 1–8, at p. 10.

25. G. Blainey, *The Causes of War*, 3rd edn (London, 1988), p. 142.

26. See *International Studies Quarterly*, vol. 30, 1986, pp. 193–222.

27. Ibid., p. 208.

28. Ibid., p. 213.

29. Ibid., p. 214.

30. M. Howard, 'Causes of Wars', in his *The Causes of Wars and Other Essays* (London, 1983), pp. 7–22, at pp. 8–9.

31. See, for example, A. W. Kinglake, *The Invasion of the Crimea: Its Origin, and an Account of its Progress Down to the Death of Lord Raglan*, 6th edn (Edinburgh, 1877).

32. Immediate surrender seems rare. One notable case is Denmark's decision to surrender at 6 a.m. on 9 April 1940, only two hours after the German invasion. The Danish army resisted, however, while the government met to decide when and how to surrender. I am indebted to Tonny Knudsen of Aarhus for this information.

33. See Blainey, *Causes of War*, p. 292.

34. L. Freedman and V. Gamba-Stonehouse, *Signals of War: The Falklands Conflict of 1982* (London, 1990), pp. 142, 323.

35. Ibid., p. 124.
36. Ibid., p. 143.
37. See L. Freedman and E. Karsh, *The Gulf Conflict 1990–1991: Diplomacy and War in the New World Order* (Princeton, NJ, 1993).
38. See I. Nish, *The Origins of the Russo-Japanese War* (London, 1985).
39. A. Iriye, *The Origins of the Second World War in Asia and the Pacific* (London, 1987).
40. See P. M. H. Bell, *The Origins of the Second World War in Europe* (London, 1986).
41. See S. R. Williamson, *Austria-Hungary and the Origins of the First World War* (London, 1991), pp. 190 ff.
42. See J. S. Levy, 'Preferences, Constraints, and Choices in July 1914', in S. E. Miller *et al.* (eds), *Military Strategy and the Origins of the First World War* (Princeton, NJ, 1991), pp. 226–61.
43. See L. C. F. Turner, 'The Russian Mobilization in 1914', *Journal of Contemporary History*, vol. 3, 1968, pp. 65–88.
44. For example, David Campbell's radically revisionist work, *Politics without Principle: Sovereignty, Ethics, and the Narratives of the Gulf War* (Boulder, Colo, 1993), stays within the narrative structures of war origins presented here.
45. See Kenneth Waltz, *Theory of International Politics* (Reading, Mass., 1979), p. 171.
46. See J. Snyder, 'Averting Anarchy in the New Europe', *International Security*, vol. 14, 1990, pp. 5–41, at pp. 18–19.
47. Bell, *Origins of the Second World War in Europe*, Part 2.
48. See Waltz, *Man, the State and War: A Theoretical Analysis* (New York, 1957).
49. See, for example, E. E. Evants-Pritchard, *Witchcraft, Oracles, and Magic among the Azande* (Oxford, 1976), esp. ch. 2.
50. See F. Fischer, *War of Illusions: German Policies from 1911 to 1914*, tr. Marian Jackson (London, 1975); Levy, 'Preferences, Constraints, and Choices'.
51. These categories have been worked out over a number of years by going back and forth between legal writings and historical works on war origins. The categories found in legal sources supplied the prototypes, but were repeatedly modified in the course of reading and rereading historical works on war origins. The legal sources consulted include: Aquarius (pseudonym), 'Causation and Legal Responsibility', *South African Law Journal*, vol. 62, 1945, pp. 126–45; H. L. A. Hart and T. Honore, *Causation in the Law*, 2nd edn (Oxford, 1985); J. C. Smith and B. Hogan, *Criminal Law*, 7th edn (London, 1992).
52. See David Carr, *Time, Narrative, and History* (Bloomington, Ind., 1986).
53. Collingwood, *The Idea of History*, rev. edn, ed. Jan van der Dussen (Oxford, 1994), pp. 398–400.

3
Forget IR Theory[1]

Roland Bleiker

> Tell me, draftsman of the desert,
> Surveyor of the sinking sands:
> Is the unrestraint of lines
> Really stronger than the blowing winds?[2]

Stories, so we are told by prevailing social science wisdom, are not part of international relations (IR) scholarship. Stories belong to the realm of fiction, not the domain of fact. And yet, stories freely whizz in and out of IR. Indeed, if we look more carefully, IR appears as nothing but a set of narratives that provide us with meaning and coherence. Consider how critical scholars increasingly portray the *locus classicus* of IR – the state, that is – not only as an institution, but also, and primarily, as a series of stories. These stories, Michael Shapiro points out, are part of a legitim-isation process that highlights, promotes and naturalises certain political practices and the territorial context within which they take place. Taken together, these stories provide the state with a sense of identity, coher-ence and unity. They create boundaries between an inside and an out-side, between a people and its Others. But by virtue of what they are and do, state-stories also exclude, for they seek 'to repress or delegitimise other stories and practices of identity and space they reflect'.[3]

Of course, the prevailing IR stories have not gone unchallenged. Since the early 1980s, IR has come under harsh criticism. We have heard not only of state-centrism, but also of masculine values, structural determin-ism, ethnocentrism, positivism, and, indeed, of the refusal to engage altogether in epistemological debates.[4] And yet, orthodox approaches to IR appear surprisingly resilient, or so at least they present themselves. Many IR scholars who occupy key positions in the Western academy, particularly in North America, unwaveringly pursue the same research agendas. They reaffirm the realist dilemmas that allegedly arise from the anarchical character of the international system, contemplate the role of regimes and international institutions, or revisit one more time the issue of absolute versus relative gains.[5] What accounts for this surprising resilience of entrenched IR stories? Are prevalent realist and liberal stories simply more convincing than others?

The power to tell stories is the power to define common sense. Prevalent IR stories have been told for so long that they no longer appear as stories. They are accepted as fact, for their metaphorical dimensions have vanished from our collective memories. We have become accustomed to our distorting IR metaphors until we come to lie, as Nietzsche would say, 'herd-like in a style obligatory for all'.[6] As a result, dominant IR stories have successfully transformed one specific interpretation of world political realities, the realist one, into reality *per se*.[7] Realist perceptions of the international have gradually become accepted as common sense, to the point that any critique against them has to be evaluated in terms of an already existing and objectivised world view. There are powerful mechanisms of control precisely in this ability to determine meaning and rationality. 'Defining common sense', Steve Smith argues, 'is the ultimate act of political power.'[8] It separates the possible from the impossible and directs the theory and practice of international relations on a particular path.

The prime objective of this essay is to challenge prevalent IR stories. The most effective way of doing so, the chapter argues, is not to critique these stories, but to forget them, to tell new stories about world politics – stories that are not constrained by the boundaries of established and objectified IR narratives. Such an approach diverges from many critical engagements with world politics. Most challenges against dominant IR stories have been advanced in the form of critiques. While critiquing orthodox IR stories remains an important task, it is not sufficient. Exploring the origin of problems, in this case discourses of power politics and their positivist framing of political practice, cannot overcome all the existing theoretical and practical dilemmas. By articulating critique in relation to arguments advanced by orthodox IR theory, the impact of critical voices remains confined within the larger discursive boundaries that have been established through the initial framing of debates. A successful challenge of orthodox IR stories must do more than merely critique their narrow and problematic nature. To be effective, critique must be supplemented with a process of *forgetting the object of critique*, of theorising world politics beyond the agendas, issues and terminologies that are preset by orthodox debates. Indeed, the most powerful potential of critical scholarship may well lie in the attempt to tell different stories about IR, for once these stories have become validated, they may well open up spaces for a more inclusive and less violence-prone practice of world politics.

Healed is who forgot: towards a tabula rasa of the consciousness

To forget orthodox IR theory is not to ignore the IR practices that have framed our realities. Countless events of the past, such as the Holocaust, cannot and should not be simply chased out of our collective memory. Neither does forgetting amount to turning a blind eye towards the violent nature that characterises present world politics. Forgetting is not only a negative process, a neglecting and overlooking, but also a necessary part of our existence, something we often do without being aware of it. Jeanette Winterson:

> They say that every snowflake is different. If that were true, how could we go on? How could we ever get up and off our knees? How could we ever recover from the wonder of it? By forgetting. We cannot keep in mind too many things. There is only the present and nothing to remember.[9]

The task, then, becomes one of turning forgetting from a selective, arbitrary and unconscious constitution of things past into an active, conscious and more inclusive process. Instead of perpetuating IR nostalgia, seeking comfort and security in the familiar interpretation of long-gone epochs, even if they are characterised by violence and insecurity, conscious forgetting opens up possibilities for a dialogical understanding of our present and past. It refuses to tie future possibilities to established forms of life. Rather than further entrenching current IR security dilemmas by engaging with the orthodox stories that continuously give meaning to them, forgetting tries to escape the vicious circle by which these stories serve to legitimise and objectivise the very discourses that have given rise to them. Forgetting becomes an instrument of dialogue and inclusion. It is a process that reorients our memories. Forgetting is an essential element of remembering or, seen from Milan Kundera's reversed perspective, 'remembering is a form of forgetting'.[10]

How, then, are we to start forgetting orthodox IR theory? Nietzsche is a good entry point. His work can serve as a stepping stone, a source to provoke thought before it too has to be forgotten in order not to turn into a new orthodoxy. The process of forgetting, for Nietzsche, is a process of healing:

> Only now do I believe you healed:
> for healed is who forget.[11]

A human being who is unable to forget, Nietzsche says, would be doomed, would 'no longer be able to believe in himself, would see everything flow apart in turbulent particles'. Forgetting, then, is not only normal, it is essential. 'All actions requires forgetting.'[12] Nietzsche ended up with this position by dealing with a set of methodological dilemmas similar to those entailed in the attempt to forget IR theory. The need to forget emerges from recognising the problematic links that are commonly drawn between cause and effect. Such a duality, Nietzsche claims, probably never existed. We merely establish arbitrary links between things that we consider important, isolate a few pieces out of a continuum of complex and intertwined events. This is why it is futile to search for a causal origin in this web of human life and to think we could somehow ground a better world on this form of flawed insight. 'How foolish it would be', Nietzsche claims, 'to suppose that one only needs to point out this origin and this misty shroud of delusion in order to *destroy* the world that counts for real, so-called "reality."'[13]

Nietzsche's scepticism towards grounding critique in an investigation of the origins of things is important. It is one of the reasons why some consider his work as the conceptual turning point from modernity to postmodernity.[14] Nietzsche's own words may explain best the importance of forgetting for a critique of orthodox IR:

> Why is it that this thought comes back to me again and again and in ever more varied colours? – that *formerly*, when investigators of knowledge sought out the origin of things they always believed they would discover something of incalculable significance for all later action and judgement, that they always *presupposed*, indeed, that the *salvation* of man must depend on *insight into the origins of things*, but . . . [t]he more insight we possess into an origin the less significant does the origin appear: while *what is nearest to us*, what is around us and in us, gradually begins to display colours and beauties and enigmas and riches of significance of which earlier mankind had not an inkling.[15]

By observing why Nietzsche ended up with this position I will explore the 'riches of significance' that could emerge once we liberate IR theory from the compulsion to link the search for peace with exploring the origins of present dilemmas in world politics. I will then retrace Nietzsche's next step, an engagement with what he calls 'active forget-fulness', as a way of thinking that enables 'a tabula rasa of the conscious-ness', that makes room for new things, new thoughts and new stories about world politics.[16]

Critique of IR between genealogies and active forgetfulness

Before exploring the potentials and limits of forgetting IR theory, it is necessary to outline how forgetting interacts with the process of cri-tique. The latter has become a well-applied practice in the study of world politics. In an attempt to open up what Jim George called 'thinking space',[17] alternative approaches to IR have reread and rewritten the discipline's present and past. They have challenged prevalent IR stories. They have deconstructed orthodox IR, listened to repressed voices and scrutinised why we have ended up where we are today. It is not my task here to summarise these diverse and highly complex attempts. A few examples, however, reveal a common theme. James Der Derian rereads the history of diplomacy, for, as he argues, its contemporary practices cannot be understood without knowledge of its origins.[18] Jim George surveys the evolution of classical approaches to IR, trying to demon-strate how they have entrenched an unusually narrow and problematic interpretation of global politics.[19] David Campbell scrutinises how United States foreign policy produced and reproduced a specific form of political identity.[20] Jean Elshtain goes back in IR time and observes how patriarchal discourses have assigned women the task of life givers, and men the one of life takers, despite empirical cases that confound these assignments.[21] Christine Sylvester revisits the three discipline-defining IR debates and ruminates about the consequences that are entailed in their failure to take gender issues and feminist theorising into account.[22] R. B. J. Walker, Jens Bartelson, Cindy Weber and Michael Shapiro have in one way or another scrutinised how centuries of modern political dis-courses have shaped the concept of sovereignty and entrenched rigid boundaries between domestic and international spheres.[23] Bradley Klein analyses how strategic studies have continuously narrowed down dis-cussions of security issues.[24] Various scholars have also drawn attention to aspects of culture, to the ethnocentric dimensions of IR theory.[25]

These examples, presented here in an oversimplified and selective way, reveal a common theme in critical IR scholarship: the quest to find out where the ideas and underlying principles that influence our life emanated from, the desire to reveal how the dilemmas of contemporary world politics are not immutable, but part of a historically constructed system of exclusion. Many of these attempts to scrutinise the historical origins of the present take the form of genealogies, a method of critique that is associated with Nietzsche. But did Nietzsche not throw up his hands and warn of searching for the origin of things? An interpretative essay by Michel Foucault sheds light on this seemingly paradoxical issue. Drawing attention to terminological subtleties of the German language, Foucault illustrates that the key issue revolves around what sort of origins one searches for, how one embarks upon and presents this task. Nietzsche strongly condemns the quest to discover an *Ursprung*, the term he uses in the above-quoted passages. Such a quest is futile and dangerous for it attempts to uncover an authentic essence in things, some form of original meaning, a site of truth.[26] By doing so, this quest excludes everything that does not fit into the particular interpretation that is imposed upon a complex set of past and present events. The task of genealogies is radically different and much better captured by the terms *Herkunft* and *Entstehung*, which are also translated as 'origin' into French (and English). These terms do not indicate a search for a telos in history, an authentic starting point, a source to which everything can be traced back. Genealogies, by contrast, focus on the process by which we construct origins and give meaning to our past. They read multiplicity into history, disturb what was taken as immobile, fragment what was considered unified.[27] Genealogies focus on revealing subtle systems of subjection, plays of power. Nietzsche demonstrates this approach when, searching for the origin (*Herkunft*) of moral prejudices, he argues that

> we need a *critique* of moral values, *the value of these values themselves must first be called in question* – and for that there is needed a knowledge of the conditions and circumstances in which they grew, under which they evolved and changed.[28]

Genealogies will always remain necessary. To reach a critical understanding of IR, we need to known how we have arbitrarily constructed the present – what and who was left out on the way. We need to scrutinise the stories that have been told about the past, and those many others which were silenced.

But the issue does not end here. Gaston Bachelard, the French scientist-turned-poet, is sceptical of the search for origins, and he does not reserve this scepticism to essentialist endeavours. Bachelard questions more broadly why we should continue to judge all things by the source, by the cause, in short, by the antecedents. This approach, he argues, emerged from a desire for spiritual monotony and leads to closed rationalities.[29] Feminist authors have been trying to deal with these dangers almost ever since a feminist consciousness emerged. They know that revisiting the classics, even if done critically, still amounts to glorifying the male authors who were responsible for setting up patriarchal systems of exclusion in the first place. Consider, for example, how women writers during the Romantic period displayed a clear distrust towards canonical knowledge. They refused to even engage with dominant Romantic themes, such as the masculine search for a visionary freedom beyond the confines of the state or the affirmation of an omnipotent and autonomous Self. Nineteenth-century women Romantics, instead, were concerned with patriarchal constraints that had been imposed upon them. They employed the novel as a site of contestation, expressing the manners in which their female subjectivities were intertwined with and confined by concrete daily concerns, linked to such issues as family, community, or female bodies. For instance, Margaret Fuller, a contemporary of Thoreau and Emerson, draws attention to the social construction of femininity and masculinity, to the ways in which men are allegedly unable to think truly emancipatory thoughts because they are 'under the slavery of habit'.[30]

What actually are the habits and conventions of IR? Which stories have we remembered? How do we recognise them, deal with them, forget them? Why not start with the site where habits and stories have become objectified: the academic discipline of IR?

Doorkeepers of IR

Before the Law stands a doorkeeper. To this doorkeeper there comes a man from the country and prays for admittance to the Law. But the doorkeeper says that he cannot grant admittance at the moment... Since the gate stands open, as usual, and the doorkeeper steps to one side, the man stoops to peer through the gateway into the interior. Observing that, the doorkeeper laughs and says: 'If you are so drawn to it, just try to go in despite my veto. But take note: I am powerful. And I am only the least of the doorkeepers. From hall to hall there is one doorkeeper after another, each more powerful than the last. The third doorkeeper is already so terrible that even I cannot bear to look at him.'[31]

The doorkeepers of IR are those who, knowingly or unknowingly, make sure that the discipline's discursive boundaries remain intact. Discourses, in a Foucaultian sense, are subtle mechanisms that frame our thinking process. They determine the limits of what can be thought, talked and written of in a normal and rational way. In every society the production of discourses is controlled, selected, organised and diffused by certain procedures. They create systems of exclusion that elevate one group of discourses to a hegemonic status while condemning others to exile. Although the boundaries of discourses change, at times gradually, at times abruptly, they maintain a certain unity across time, a unity that dominates and transgresses individual authors, texts or social practices. They explain, to come back to Nietzsche, why 'all things that live long are gradually so saturated with reason that their origin in unreason thereby becomes improbable'.[32]

Academic disciplines are powerful mechanisms that direct and control the production and diffusion of discourses. They establish the rules of intellectual exchange and define the methods, techniques and instruments that are considered proper for the pursuit of knowledge. Within these margins each discipline recognises true and false propositions based on the standards of evaluation it established to assess them.[33]

It is not my intention here to provide a coherent account or historical survey of the exclusionary academic conventions that have been established by the discipline of IR.[34] Instead, I want to illustrate the process of disciplining thought by focusing on an influential monograph by three well-placed academics, Gary King, Robert O. Keohane and Sidney Verba. By outlining the methodological rules about how to conduct good scholarly research, they fulfil important and powerful doorkeeping functions. These functions emerge as soon as the authors present their main argument, that 'qualitative' and 'quantitative' research approaches do not differ in substance for both can (and must be) systematic and scientific.[35] One does not need to be endowed with the investigating genius of a Sherlock Holmes to detect positivist traits in these pages. One easily recognises an (anti)philosophical stance that attempts to separate subject and object, that believes the social scientist, as detached observer, can produce value-free knowledge. Such a positivist position assumes only that which is manifested in experience, which emerges from observing 'reality', of deserves the name knowledge. All other utterances have no cognitive and empirical merit, they are mere value statements, normative claims, unprovable speculations.[36] Indeed, if the doorkeepers did not inform us that their methodological suggestions emerged from years of teaching a core graduate course at one of North America's foremost research institutions, one could easily mistake their claims as parodies of positivism. We are told that the goal of research is 'to learn facts about the real world' and that all hypothesis 'need to be evaluated empirically before they can make a contribution to knowledge'.[37]

Which facts? Whose 'real' world? What forms of knowledge?

The discursive power of academic disciplines, George Canguilhem argues, works such that a statement has to be 'within the true' before one can even start to judge whether it is true or false, legitimate or illegitimate.[38] Hence, the doorkeepers inform us that what distinguishes serious research about the 'facts' of the 'real world' from casual observation is the search for 'valid inferences by the systematic use of well-established procedures of inquiry'.[39] Such procedures not only suggest on what grounds things can be studied legitimately, but also decide what issues are worthwhile to be assessed in the first place. In other words, a topic has to fulfil a number of preliminary criteria before it can even be evaluated as a legitimate IR concern. The criteria of admittance, the doorkeepers notify us, are twofold. A research topic must 'pose a question that is "important" in the real world' and it must contribute to the scholarly literature by 'increasing our collective ability to construct verified scientific explanation of some aspect of the world'.[40]

The doorkeepers of IR remind the women and men from the country who pray for admittance to the temple of IR that only those who abide by the established rules will gain access. Admittance cannot be granted at the moment to those who are eager to investigate the process of knowing, to those who intend to redraw the boundaries of 'good' and 'evil' research, or to those who even have the audacity of questioning what this 'real world' really is. The warning is loud and clear: 'A proposed topic that cannot be refined into a specific research project permitting valid descriptive or causal inference should be modified along the way or abandoned.'[41] And if you are drawn to the temple of IR after all, the doorkeepers laugh, then just try to go in despite our veto. But take note, we are powerful and we are only the least of the doorkeepers, for ultimately all research topics that have no 'real-world importance' will run 'the risk of descending to politically insignificant questions'.[42] Or could it be that these allegedly unimportant research topics need to be silenced *precisely because they run the risk of turning into politically significant questions*?

The dominant IR stories that doorkeeping functions uphold are sustained by a wide range of discipline-related procedures, linked to such aspects as university admittance standards, teaching curricula, examination topics, policies of hiring and promoting teaching staff, or publishing criteria determined by the major journals in the field. At least the doorkeepers of IR have not lost a sense of (unintended) irony. They readily admit that 'we seek not dogma, but disciplined thought'.[43]

Academic disciplines discipline the production of discourses. They have the power to separate rational from irrational stories. They force the creation and exchange of knowledge into preconceived spaces, called debates. Even if one is to engage the orthodox position in a critical manner, the outcome of the discussion is already circumscribed by the parameters that had been established through the initial framing of debates. Thus, as soon as one addresses academic disciplines on their own terms, one has to play according to the rules of a discursive 'police' which is reactivated each time one speaks.[44]

The politics of writing IR

How is one to proceed in the face of such disciplinary power? How can one resist the arguments, debates and categories of IR as a discipline, defy its entrenched and constraining intellectual rules of conduct? How can one start not with canonical knowledge, but, as standpoint feminists suggest, with the improbable, the subjugated elements of society, the margins of discursive practices?[45] In short, how can one tell different stories about world politics? Does the solution simply lie in crossing disciplinary boundaries to explore themes other than prescribed by orthodox IR? But this is easier said than done. And once embarked upon this path, how is one to avoid the creation of new orthodoxies?

There is no panacea for the process of forgetting the object of critique. My suggestions here focus on only one aspect of this intricate process, an aspect that contains both constraining and enabling elements: the role of language. In some ways, this chapter thus deals with methodological concerns, with what conventionally is considered form, rather than substance. Yet, the manner in which we approach, think, conceptualise and formulate IR has a significant impact on how it is practised. Language frames politics. Form turns into substance.

An essay cannot possibly be exhaustive in outlining the role that language plays in attempts to forget orthodox IR stories. Discussions on language have played a crucial role in twentieth-century thought. This is particularly the case in philosophy and feminist theory, where hardly any author would not claim to have made the 'linguistic turn', the admission that knowledge of 'reality' is always pre-interpreted by the language that we employ to assess and express it. In my effort to illustrate the importance of this debate to wor(l)d politics I will focus primarily on some contributions that have emerged in the wake of Nietzsche's work.

Languages, in Nietzsche's view, are built upon a set of prejudices that are expressed via metaphors; selectively filtered images of objects and impressions that surround us. Languages are more than just mediums of communication. They represent the relationship between people and their environment. They are part of a larger discursive struggle over meaning and interpretation, an integral element of politics. Yet, the process of neglecting that we are all conditioned by decades of linguistically entrenched values largely camouflages the system of exclusion that is operative in all speech forms. The following passage illustrates well the extent to which language and social practice are intertwined:

> This has given me the greatest trouble and still does: to realise that what things *are called* is incomparably more important than what they are. The reputation, name, and appearance, the usual measure and weight of a thing, what it counts for – originally almost always wrong and arbitrary, thrown over things like a dress and altogether foreign to their nature and even to their skin – all this grows from generation unto generation, merely because people believe in it, until it gradually grows to be part of the thing and turns into its very body. What at first was appearance becomes in the end, almost invariably, the essence and is effective as such.[46]

Ideas become objectified because reality and dominant discursive practices merge to the point that the links between them vanish from our collective memories. George Orwell's fictional world provides a perfect illustration for this subjugating power of languages. Consider how Oceania introduced Newspeak to accommodate its official ideology, Ingsoc. New words were invented and undesirable ones either eliminated or stripped of unorthodox meanings. The objective of this exercise was that 'when Newspeak had been adopted once and for all and Oldspeak forgotten, a heretical thought – that is, a thought diverging from the principles of Ingsoc – should be literally unthinkable'.[47] By then history would be rewritten to the point that even if fragments of documents from the past were still to surface, they simply would be unintelligible and untranslatable.

We find similar dynamics at work in the more 'real' (but equally Orwellian) IR world of defence intellectuals. Carol Cohn demonstrates how the particular language that they employ not only removes them from the 'reality' of nuclear war, but also constructs a new world of abstraction that makes it impossible to think or express certain concerns related to feelings, morality, or simply 'peace'. The consequences, Cohn rightly stresses, are fateful because the language of defence intellectuals has been elevated to virtually the only legitimate medium of debating security issues.[48] Noam Chomsky provides another example of the links between language and politics. He argues that mainstream discourses linguistically presented the 'involvement' in Vietnam such that the actual thought of an American 'aggression' or 'invasion' was unthinkable, and this despite plenty of readily available evidence in support of such an interpretation.[49] The same linguistic dynamic of exclusion is at work in IR theory, where the dominant realist language renders discussions of epistemology virtually impossible. Consider how Robert Gilpin criticises the post-structuralist language of Richard Ashley by declaring entirely unintelligible his claim that 'the objective truth of the discourse lies within and is produced by the discourse itself'.[50] The concepts used in this sentence not only make perfect sense to any critical social theorist, but may well be essential for the articulation of an epistemological critique. Yet, read through the Newspeak of scientific realism, the very idea of epistemological critique is a heretic thought and the sentence thus becomes simply untranslatable. Not surprisingly, Gilpin admits that he frequently was unable to follow Ashley's argument. The language of realism has rendered any challenge to its own political foundations unthinkable.

How is it possible to escape this encroaching function of language? How can one turn language from a practice of exclusion to one of inclusion? Is it enough, as Nietzsche suggests, 'to create new names and estimations and probabilities in order to create in the long run new "things"'?[51] Of course not. We must be careful not to get trapped in a linguistic idealism which suggests that the world can only exist because it is perceived by our mind, that objects outside this mental sphere have no qualities of their own. Carol Cohn knows that the world would not change miraculously overnight if defence intellectuals were to use the term 'mass murder' instead of 'collateral damage'.[52]

Nietzsche played a crucial historical role in having connected philosophical tasks with radical reflections on language.[53] Yet, his views on language must be supplemented with more recent contributions, particularly those made in the wake of the later Wittgenstein. As opposed to Nietzsche, Wittgenstein no longer considers language as a representation of 'reality', not even a distorted one. For him language 'is part of an activity, a form of life'.[54] A pure Nietzschean attempt to simply 'create new words . . . to create . . . new things' would go astray in a futile search for a perfect language and, by doing so, fall back into the logical positivism from which the later Wittgenstein so carefully tried to escape.

Not all forms of speaking and writing constitute 'reality' in the sense that they give rise to a set of political practices that are then legitimised and objectivised. The point is, rather, to investigate why certain language games become dominant, how they have framed our political realities and how alternative forms of thinking and speaking may reframe these realities. But this process of reframing is delicate, especially if one accepts a Wittgensteinian position that languages are forms of life rather than representations of the world. Because there is no direct and logical correspondence between words and their meaning, a spear heading into unexplored linguistic terrains can only be socially meaningful if it stretches the rules of existing language games while never losing sight of the ways in which these language games constitute and are constituted by concrete forms of life. Thus, the transformative capacity of languages is unleashed only through a long process. But this does not contradict the claim that languages are important sites of political practice, sites where realities are formed, reformed, legitimised and objectivised.

Writing dissent I: disenchanting the concept

I illustrate my engagement with the linguistic aspects of forgetting and remembering IR stories through Theodor W. Adorno's reading of Nietzsche. I have chosen Adorno because he epitomised both the strengths and dangers of this approach. Adorno recognises that even before dealing with specific speech contents, languages mould a thought such that it gets drawn into subordination even where it appears to resist this tendency.[55] Hence, *if challenges to orthodoxy and attempts to open up thinking space are to avoid being absorbed by the dominant discourse, then they must engage in a struggle with conventionally recognised linguistic practices*, or at least with the manner in which these practices have been constituted. *The form of writing becomes as important as its content.*

Critique of society cannot be separated from *Sprachkritik*, critique of language. In making this assumption, Adorno follows a well-carved-out path. The linguist Fritz Mauthner already considered *Sprachkritik* as 'the most important task of thinking humanity' and the poet Paul Valéry probably captured its objective best when claiming that 'the secret of well-founded thinking is based on suspicion towards language'.[56] From this perspective the first step in any process that tries to escape the controlling power of orthodox IR theory entails paying close attention to its linguistic practices. The usage of concepts is Adorno's starting point.

To talk of IR, or of anything for that matter, we need to employ concepts to express our ideas. Yet, concepts can never entirely capture the objects that they are trying to describe. A concept is always a violation, an imposition of static subjectivity upon complex, interconnected and continuously changing phenomena. Nietzsche was already aware that 'all concepts in which an entire process is semiotically concentrated elude definition: only that which has no history can be defined'.[57] What Nietzsche emphasised in a historical manner, Adorno illustrates through a contemporary example. He shows how the judgement that one is free depends on the concept of freedom. But this concept is both less and more than the object or subject it refers to.[58] It is less because it cannot adequately assess the complexities of the individual's expectations and the contexts within which he or she seeks freedom. It is more because it imposes a particular interpretation of freedom upon and beyond the conditions of freedom sought after at a particular time and place. Thus, Adorno argues that 'the concept of freedom always lags behind itself. As soon as it is applied empirically it ceases to be what it claims it is.'[59] Here, again, we hear the echo of Nietzsche, who already claimed that liberal institutions cease to be liberal as soon as they are established, that, as a result, 'there is nothing more wicked and harmful to freedom than liberal institutions'.[60]

Acknowledging and dealing with the political dimensions of concepts is essential in the effort to defy the doorkeeping power of orthodox IR. There are at least two ways through which one can subvert the delineation of thinking space imposed by orthodox definitions of IR concepts. First, one can appropriate and open up the meaning of existing concepts. This strategy was demonstrated in political practice by German- and English-speaking gay/lesbian activists, who transformed the terms '*schwul*' and 'queer' from derogative and discriminatory expressions to positively imbued assertions of identity that create possibilities for more inclusive ways of thinking and acting.[61] In almost diametrically opposed terrains we find Australia's preeminent poet, Les Murray, trying to reshape and devilify the term 'redneck'.[62] Closer to the 'realities' of IR, we can observe struggles over the meaning of such concepts as 'state', 'anarchy', 'hegemony', 'diplomacy', 'security' and 'ethics'. Consider, for instance, the concept of 'power'. Some traditional realists view(ed) it, to simplify things a bit, as 'man's control over the minds and actions of other men'.[63] In this phallocentric definition, power is the capacity to act, something someone (a man!) has and others do not. But diverging opinions pressed for a more broad conceptualisation, one that is also linked to functions of consent and legitimacy. Others again view power as a complex structure of actions that permeate every aspect of society, not simply a subjugating force, but at least as much an enabling opportunity.[64]

Besides appropriating the constituted meaning of existing concepts one can open up possibilities for more inclusive ways of theorising and acting by resorting to an altogether new way of conceptualising. Orthodox IR concepts are then simply left behind, filed *ad acta* as relics of a past way of thinking that is no longer adequate to deal with an increasingly complex and interwined sphere of contemporary life. But how do we prevent new concepts from imposing their own subjectivities?

No concept will ever be sufficient, will ever do justice to the object it is trying to capture. The objective then becomes to conceptualise thoughts such that they do not silence other voices, but coexist and interact with them. Various authors have suggested methods for this purpose, methods that will always remain attempts without ever reaching the ideal state that they aspire to. We know of Mikhail Bakhtin's dialogism, a theory of knowledge and language that tries to avoid the excluding tendencies of monological thought forms. Instead, he accepts the existence of multiple meanings, draws connections between differences, and searches for possibilities to establish conceptual and linguistic dialogues among competing ideas, values, speech forms, texts, validity claims and the like.[65] Jürgen Habermas attempts to theorise the preconditions for ideal speech situations. Communication, in this case, should be as unrestrained as possible, such that 'claims to truth and rightness can be discursively redeemed',[66] albeit, one should add, through a rationalism and universalism that is violently anti-Bakhtinian and anti-Adornian. Closer to the familiar terrain of IR we find Christine Sylvester's feminist method of empathetic cooperation, which aims at opening up questions of gender by a 'process of positional slippage that occurs when one listens seriously to the concerns, fears, and agendas of those one is unaccustomed to heeding when building social theory'.[67] But how does one conceptualise such attempts if concepts can never do justice to the objects they are trying to capture?

The daring task is, as we know from Adorno, to open up with concepts what does not fit into concepts, to resist the distorting power of reification and return the conceptual to the non-conceptual. This disenchantment of the concept is the antidote of critical philosophy, it impedes the concept from developing its own dynamics and from becoming an absolute in itself.[68] The first step towards disenchanting the concept is simply refusing to define it monologically. Concepts should achieve meaning only gradually, in relation to each other. Adorno even intentionally uses the same concept in different ways in order to liberate it from the narrow definition that language itself had already imposed on it.[69] That contradictions could arise out of this practice does not bother Adorno. Indeed, he considers them essential.

One cannot eliminate the contradictory, the fragmentary and the discontinuous. Contradictions are only contradictions if one assumes the existence of a prior universal standard of reference. What is different appears as divergent, dissonant and negative only as long as our consciousness strives for a totalising standpoint, which we must avoid if we are to escape the reifying and excluding dangers of identity thinking.[70] Just as reality is fragmented, we need to think in fragments. Unity then is not to be found by evening out discontinuities. Contradictions are to be preferred over artificially constructed meanings and the silencing of underlying conflicts. Thus, Adorno advocates writing in fragments, such that the resulting text appears as if it always could be interrupted, cut off abruptly, any time, any place.[71] He adheres to Nietzsche's advice that one should approach deep problems like taking a cold bath, 'quickly into them and quickly out again'.[72] The belief that one does not reach deep enough this way, he claims, is simply the superstition of those who fear cold water. But Nietzsche's bath has already catapulted us into the vortex of the next linguistic terrain of resistance, the question of style.

Writing dissent II: thoughts on the substance of form

Conventional wisdom holds that good writing is concise, clear and to the point. Orthodox IR wisdom, as a result, dismisses the unusual writing style of postmodern dissidents as nothing but needless jargon, assaults on language,[73] a rambling and conceptual menace that is employed 'not to reinforce argument, but to compensate for the lack of it'.[74]

We easily forget, of course, that the language of realism only appears clear because we have acquired familiarity with it. Abstract realist concepts like 'unit', 'actor', 'system', 'regime', 'realpolitik', 'dependent/ independent variable' and 'relative/absolute gains' are not clear and intelligible by some objective standard, but only because they have been rehearsed time and again as part of a system of shared meanings that channels our thinking into particular directions. By contrast, the allegedly faddish and rambling concepts of postmodern scholarship, like 'genealogy', 'foundationalism', 'reification', 'logocentrism' or 'incommensurability' only appear dissonant because they diverge from or subvert the linguistic conventions that legitimise dominant discursive practices. But this is only the beginning. Nietzsche and Adorno suggest that the question of style reaches much further.

Clear language is domination. It imposes closure. Even if it is critical, an argument presented in a straightforward writing style can, at best, articulate an alternative position and replace one orthodoxy with another one. It is unable to open up thinking space. Or so at least claims Adorno. In defiance of all Cartesian methodological rules, he rejects as dangerous the proposition that one ought to move from the simple to the complex and that one must demonstrate clearly and explicitly each step that leads up to the articulation of a particular utterance.[75] Adorno justifies this unusual position with the argument that the true value of a thought is measured according to its distance from the continuities of orthodox knowledge. This is to say that the closer a thought gets to the generally accepted standards of writing and representing, the more it loses its dialectical and antithetical function. Hence Adorno attempts to open up thinking space by writing in an unusual style, unusual in word choice, concept usage, syntax, sentence flow and many other aspects.[76] Style is the key to Adorno's thought. It leads him to a position where, expressed in Terry Eagleton's disapproving voice, every sentence is 'forced to work overtime: each phrase must become a little masterpiece or miracle of dialectics, fixing a thought in the second before it disappears into its own contradictions'.[77]

It is not my intention to endorse Adorno's provocative and controversial position on language. The difficulty of his style renders virtually impossible any form of emancipatory politics. As long as a critical text is only accessible to a small circle of intellectuals who invest the time to decipher it, solve its puzzles and explore its contradictions, critical knowledge will continue to reside in the margins. Adorno also comes dangerously close to forms of linguistic idealism and heroic avant-garde elitism. By trying to free himself from the forces of totalising thought, he paradoxically runs the risk of falling back into the positivist dangers that the later Wittenstein so vehemently warned of. Adorno's approach to style implies, much like the early Wittgenstein, that ordinary language is insufficient, in need of correction.

The point is not to search for a more perfect representation of reality, but to acknowledge that language games are an integral part of politics. Thus, while rejecting Adorno's futile search for perfect expression I accept the importance of the issue that feeds his dilemma, namely the recognition that writing style and language in general are intrinsically linked to politics. In this sense Adorno clearly demonstrates the dangers of claiming that issues of style have no substantive dimension, a position expressed, for example, in the doorkeeping argument that 'differences between quantitative and qualitative traditions are only stylistic and are methodologically and substantively unimportant'.[78]

Writing styles are issues of substance, sights of contestation. Any approach that attempts to resist the enroachment of thought by dominant and monological discursive practices must grapple with the question of style.

There are, of course, many ways of stylistically resisting impositions by systems of shared meaning. I have already mentioned Nietzsches and Adorno's preference for writing in fragments to avoid silencing conflicts and evening out contradictions. Indeed, Nietzsche's resort to aphorisms and his particular writing style in general are often considered to be the most important substantive contribution of his work. We know of Zarathustra, who constantly asserts things just to deconstruct them a few pages later, to the point that Thomas Mann, Giorgio Colli and many others argued that to take Nietzsche literally is to be lost, for 'he said everything, and the opposite of everything'.[79] The key to Nietzsche does not lie in his viewpoints, but in the style through which he opened up thinking space and celebrated diversity.

The resort to dialogues is another, more direct way of accepting fragmentation and resisting monological constructions. Tom Stoppard writes plays because dialogue is the most respectable way of contradicting himself, an insight that has not gone unnoticed among some IR scholars, who tentatively started to Stoppardise the discipline.[80] Instead of exploring all of the various stylistic forms of dissent, I illustrate their functioning by paying slightly more attention to one, usually thought to be the most esoteric of all – poetry.

The potential of a poetic rethinking of world politics

Poetry has the potential of subverting and unsettling the encroachment of dominant IR stories, for it arguably is the most radical way of stretching, even violating the stylistic, syntactic and grammatical rules of linguistic conventions. Poetry revolves, much like Adorno's *Sprachkritik*, around the substance of form. Or so at least claims the influential voice of Paul Valéry. He separates poetry from prose and stresses that in the latter form is not preserved. It disappears as soon as it has fulfilled its purpose. Once you have understood the content of my speech, Valèry illustrates, the form of my speech becomes meaningless, it vanishes from your memory. The form of the poem, by contrast, does not vanish after its usage. It is an integral part of speech, designed to rise from its ashes.[81]

The poem is not able to escape the constraints of language, but it makes these constraints its *raison d'être*. Poetry is *Sprachkritik* at its most self-conscious existence. Indeed, the attempt to stretch language games is probably the single most important defining characteristic of poetry. A poem is a conscious transgression of existing linguistic conventions, a protest against an established language game and the system of exclusion that are embedded in it. In this sense poetry sets itself apart from prose because it negates, not by chance or as a side effect, but because it cannot do otherwise, because that is what poetry is all about.[82] A poet renders strange that which is familiar and thus forces the reader to confront that which he or she habitually has refused to confront. For Kristeva, poetic language disturbs, transgresses rules, fractures meaning. In doing so it 'breaks up the inertia of language habits' and 'liberates the subject from a number of linguistic, psychic, and social networks'.[83]

Illustrating the power of poetry to redescribe reality is no easy task, for poetry is not about this or that argument, this or that idea. It is about searching for a language that provides us with different eyes, different ways of perceiving what we already know; it is about unsettling, making strange that which is familiar, about opening up thinking space and creating possibilities to act in more inclusive ways. No isolated citation will ever do justice to this objective. Only an extended lecture of poetry can succeed in stretching the boundaries of our mind. But for the more limited purpose of this chapter, an example will have to suffice. 'The Pupil', a poem written by Jayne-Ann Igel, expresses aspects of the transition from the Cold War to a new international order. Igel is one of the East German poets who, during the 1980s, actively engaged in a critique of the dominant language in order to create thinking space in a suffocating society. His/her poem deals not so much with the obvious forms of repression that existed at the time, but with more subtle and far more powerful aspects of discursive domination:

> was i caught forever, as i learned their language, my
> voice a bird-squeak, keeping me under their spell; they held
> me near the house like a vine, whose shoots they clip
> ped, so that they do not darken the rooms

and close to the wall of the house i played, under the light
of drying sheets, the fingers pierced through the plaster, i
did not want to miss the personified sound of my name, which
smelled like urine; those who carried my name in their mouth,
held me by the neck with their teeth[84]

Needed: *Sprachkritik*, a radical critique of language that pierces through the plaster of the ruling philosophy, breaks its spell, slips away from the linguistic teeth drilled into one's neck. Needed: a language that is not a vine, confined to the wall of the house and constantly trimmed, but a free-standing and freely growing tree, pushing its branches up into the open sky.

Igel's poem not only captures this objective in content, but also in form. In a societal context (East Germany of the 1980s) of strong ideological dogmatism and strict behavioural rules, her poem purposely violates a number of existing linguistic conventions. For example, she starts off with a question ('was i caught forever, as i learned their language') but refuses to close this question with an appropriate question mark. One is inevitably thrown into a continuous questioning mood, a permanent state of suspense that lasts until the end of the poem. This sense of suspense is accentuated by the fact that Igel fuses sentences with commas, semi-colons or a simple 'and' where they normally would be terminated with a period. Indeed, the suspense of the initial question even goes beyond the end of the poem for Igel refuses to close it with any sort of punctuation. The question 'was i caught forever, as i learned their language' echoes long after the last word is read. Moreover, her poem entirely disregards the German linguistic convention of capitalising nouns – a subversive act my English translation is unable to convey, except maybe through the refusal to capitalise 'I' and the first word of the poem.

The breaking free, the forgetting that a poem like 'The Pupil' does, is a form of remembering. It illustrates how poetry can be a way of coming to terms with history, a search for more inclusive ways of looking at the constitution of things present and past. Poetry, then, fulfils the task of a critical memory, it assures a presence beyond death and beyond the current, historically delineated moment.[85]

Poetry remains the most underrated and unexplored approach to reconceptualising wor(l)d politics. We know of some attempts that successfully stretched the boundaries of IR language.[86] But such efforts remain rare. We need more of them, not to search for beauty or a more perfect representation of reality, but simply to be able to speak again, to walk through the silence that orthodox IR language has imposed on its community of scholars. Poetry addresses this difficult issue. How to speak in a language that has structurally excluded women, the Other, anybody and anything that cannot be identified with the speaking (realist/liberal) subject? How to speak in a language that has historically evolved from the centre of the world, first from the British colonial Empire, then from the vantage point of American hegemony, and now as the new lingua franca of international political, economic and cultural interactions? How to express those silenced voices, those worlds that lie beyond the linguistic zone of exclusion that the global dominance of English has established? How to decentre the centre through the language of the centre? Poetry can show us ways of dealing with these important and difficult issues, with the 'reconstruction of the world through words',[87] with how 'the mortal ones can learn, once more, how to live in language'.[88]

The radically different viewpoints that a poetic image illuminates may not always be directly translatable into clear-cut policy recommendations, but they have the potential to contribute immensely by bringing into a dialogical realm many of the repressed voices, perspectives and emotions that otherwise may never reach the prose-oriented theorists and practitioners of contemporary wor(l)d politics. Poetry can bring about a slow transformation of discursive and linguistic practices that gradually open up spaces for more inclusive ways of perceiving and practising IR. Forget. Listen. Feel. For(to)get a new angle on IR. Derek Walcott:

> It was in winter. Steeples, spires
> congealed like holy candles. Rotting snow
> flaked from Europe's ceiling. A compact man,
> I crossed the canal in a gray overcoat,
> on one lapel a crimson buttonhole
> for the cold ecstasy of the assassin.
> In the square coffin manacled to my wrist:
> small countries pleaded through the mesh of graphs,
> in treble-spaced, Xeroxed forms to the World Bank
> on which I had scrawled the one world, MERCY.[89]

The need to disturb slack and sleeping senses

Poetry, disenchanted concepts, aphorisms and dialogue are only examples of stylistic devices that can be employed to forget, to resist the discursive domination of orthodox IR theory. Yet, all of the above examples have one aspect in common, they are political, they *disturb*, and they fulfil an important function by doing so. We are all trained to read, think and write in certain ways. To transgress the limits of these habits is unsettling.

If readers are to break free from the subtle repression that the dominant discourse disguises through its linguistic practices, they have to struggle with a text, grapple for the meaning of words, and be torn away, sometimes painfully, from a deeply entrenched form of communicative subjugation. If readers are to come to terms with their own prejudices, a text must challenge, puzzle, shake, uproot, even frustrate and torment them. Slack and sleeping sense, Zarathustra proclaims, 'must be addressed with thunder and heavenly fireworks'.[90] Some authors who defy orthodox IR wisdom are well aware of this necessity. David Campbell, for example, refuses to identify democracy with a fixed and objective set of institutional practices. Instead, he defines it as an ethos, a promise, something that disturbs, challenges, problematises and constantly is in the process of becoming.[91]

The extent to which the disturbing function of dislocating meanings entails political and moral dimensions is not only evident in the attitude of 'disturbers', but also in the reaction of IR doorkeepers. Consider how they provide a warm welcome to feminists who want to locate women empirically in the international spheres, even to those who intend to theorise from women's disadvantaged standpoints.[92] The situation changes dramatically when feminists start to deconstruct the very foundation of these standpoints, problematise the category of women, and attempt to reveal the underlying power dynamics of patriarchy. In this case, doorkeepers are not content with delivering a word of caution. They immediately and violently shut all IR doors. Pursuing this postmodern path, they warn, would fragment epistemology, deny the possibility of social science, and lead to 'an intellectual and moral disaster'.[93] In the USA, key doorkeepers similarly shield the discipline of IR from postmodern challenges, for such work is 'pretentious, derivative and vacuous, an Anglo-Saxon mimesis of what was already, in its Parisian form, a confused and second-rate debate'.[94] This hostility confirms above all the political dimension entailed in epistemological critique, a phenomenon that is, of course, not new or limited to postmodern challenges, but inherent to all processes of unsettling. Max Horkheimer observed already half a century ago that widespread hostility emerges as soon as theorists fail to limit themselves to verifying facts and ordering them into familiar categories

– categories which are indispensable for the sustenance of entrenched forms of life.[95]

Against conclusions

A topic that deals with the struggle over meaning and interpretation does not easily lend itself to a conclusion. There is no essence that crystallises, that can be wrapped up in a few succinct points or be classified neatly into existing categories. Language is never adequate to express social dynamics, especially if they touch upon the very issue of language. Conclusions are illusions, for debates about language will never come to an end. They will always constitute sites of contestation that an author cannot, or at least should not, circumvent.

A critical author must, on the one hand, defy the language of the dominant discourse in order not to get drawn into its powerful linguistic vortex and, on the other hand, articulate alternative thoughts such that they are accessible enough to constitute viable tools to open up dialogical interactions. This can, of course, only be achieved if alternative knowledge can break out of intellectual obscurity, if it can reach and change the minds of most people. However, a text that breaks with established practices of communication to escape their discursive power has, by definition, great difficulties in doing this. Nietzsche was well aware of this inevitable dilemma. Zarathustra is constantly torn back and forth between engaging with people and withdrawing from them. The masses fail to comprehend his attempts to defy herd instincts and problematise the unproblematic. 'They do not understand me; I am not the mouth for these ears', he hails. 'Must one smash their ears before they learn to listen with their eyes?'[96] At times he appears without hope: 'what matters a time that "has not time" for Zarathustra?... why do I speak where nobody has *my* ears? It is still an hour too early for me here.'[97] Succumbing to the power of language, Zarathustra returns to the mountains, withdraws in the solitude of his cave. But thoughts of engaging with humanity never leave him. He repeatedly climbs down from his cave to the depths of life, regains hope that monological discourses will give way to dialogue, that the herds will understand him one day. 'But *their* hour will come! And mine will come too! Hourly they are becoming smaller, poorer, more sterile – poor herbs! poor soil! and *soon* they shall stand there like dry grass and prairie – and verily, weary of themselves and languish even more than for water – for *fire*.'[98]

Dissident scholarship will not immediately incinerate the dry grass of orthodox IR prairies. Fire-fighters are holding off the blaze. Discourses live on and appear reasonable long after their premises have turned into anachronistic relics. More inclusive ways of theorising and living world(s) politics cannot surface over night. There are no quick solutions, no new paradigms or miraculous political settlements that one could hope for. Changing the practice of IR is a long process, saturated with obstacles and contradictions. Zarathustra knows that. It is in our daily practices of speaking, of forgetting and remembering that slow transformative potentials are hidden. The great events in history, he claims, 'are not our loudest but our stillest hours. Not around the inventors of new noise, but around the inventors of new values does the world revolve; it revolves *inaudibly.'*[99]

The inaudible character of these transformative potentials does not make them any less real. The systems of domination and the possibilities for change that are embedded in language are as real as the practices of realpolitik. They effect the daily lives of people as much as the so-called 'real-world issues' of orthodox IR. *Language is politics disguised.* Taking this dynamic seriously means that one can no longer simply 'sidestep many issues in the philosophy of social science as well as controversies about the role of postmodernism, the nature and existence of truth, relativism, and related subjects'.[100] One can no longer avoid questions of ethics and responsibility by hiding behind the language of realism and the inevitability of power politics. One can no longer blow the trumpet of anti-positivism while advising at the same time to focus only on 'questions of fact', without being 'goaded into taking seriously problems about words and their meanings'.[101] Any scholar who is concerned with the inevitable impact of theorising on daily practices of wor(l)d politics must take seriously questions about words and their meanings. Rhetoric and dialogue are needed, not scientific rigidity.

While acknowledging the continuous importance of genealogical critique, of deconstructing IR, I suggested that efforts should not stop at this point. Critique must be supplemented with a process that forgets the object of critique. The above-presented conceptual and stylistic strategies for opening up dominant and monological discursive practices constitute only illustrative examples. Doorkeeping functions emerge everywhere, and so do potentials to avoid them. Hence, my suggestions should not be read as ready-made solutions or endorsements of particular writing styles and forms of conceptualising. They are, above all, meant to demonstrate the crucial and unavoidable political function that language plays in the theory and practice of wor(l)d(s) politics.

Many of my methodological arguments have been derived from a reading of Nietzsche's work. Nietzsche, of course, is not unproblematic. We know of his Eurocentrism, his disregard for economic factors and his alleged anti-Semitism. We observe in his pages a strange oscillation between apparent feminist arguments and violent expressions of misogyny. There are dangers in such an approach even if, as Jacques Derrida suggests, this very congruence is rigorously necessary for Nietzsche's deconstructive enterprise.[102] To keep the dialectical and dialogical process running, we must forget Nietzsche as much as we must forget IR theory. This is not to say that we should forget the insight that Nietzsche provided or turn a blind eye towards realist practices of exclusion, but to acknowledge the need to see beyond them in order not to entrench present or future forms of canonical knowledge. Only a constant dialectical process of disturbing and rethinking can maintain hope for a dialogical understanding among peoples and prevent critical approaches to wor(l)d(s) politics from eventually turning into new orthodoxies.

Notes

1. This is a revised version of an essay that originally appeared in *Alternatives: Social Transformation and Humane Governance*, no. 4, Dec. 1998, pp. 471–97. Some aspects, most notably the linguistic dimensions of the interaction between language and global politics, are explored in more detail in my *Popular Dissent, Human Agency and Global Politics* (Cambridge: Cambridge University Press, 2000).
2. Osip Mandelstam, 'Ottave', in A. C. Todd and M. Hayward (eds), *Twentieth-Century Russian Poetry* (London: Fourth Estate, 1993), p. 105.
3. Michael Shapiro, 'Sovereign Anxieties', in E. Lee and W. Kim, *Recasting International Relations Paradigms* (Seoul: Korean Association of International Studies, 1996), p. 212. See also his *Violent Cartographies: Mapping Cultures of War* (Minneapolis: University of Minnesota Press, 1997) and William Connolly, *Identity/Difference: Democratic Negotiation of Political Paradox* (Ithaca, NY: Cornell University Press, 1991), p. 207.
4. For reviews see Chris Brown, '"Turtles All the Way Down": Anti-Foundationalism, Critical Theory, and International Relations', *Millennium*, vol. 23, no. 2, 1994, pp. 213–36; Jim George, 'Of Incarceration and Closure: Neo-Realism and the New/Old World Order', in *Millennium*, vol. 22, no. 2, 1993, pp. 197–234; and Sankaran Krishna, 'The Importance of Being Ironic: A Postcolonial View on Critical International Relations Theory', in *Alternatives*, vol. 18, 1993, pp. 385–417; Steve Smith, 'The Self-Images of a Discipline: A Genealogy of International Relations Theory', in Ken Booth and Steve Smith, *International Relations Theory Today* (University Park: The Pennsylvania State University Press, 1995); Christine Sylvester, *Feminist Theory and International Relations in a Postmodern Era* (Cambridge: Cambridge University Press, 1994).
5. A recent representative example of this tendency is D. A. Baldwin (ed.), *Neorealism and Neoliberalism: The Contemporary Debate* (New York: Columbia

. University Press, 1993), a collection of essays by eminent scholars who claim to 'pick up' where an earlier work ended: Robert O. Keohane (ed.), *Neorealism and its Critics* (New York: Columbia University Press, 1986). Yet, while Keohane's volume still contained two critical essays (by R. W. Cox and R. K. Ashley), Baldwin's sequences is entirely cleansed of dissident voices and in many ways returns to agendas that dominated IR more than a decade ago.

6. Friedrich Nietzsche, 'Über Warheit und Lüge im aussermoralischen Sinn', in *Erkenntnistheoretische Schriften*, ed. J. Habermas (Frankfurt: Suhrkamp, 1968/ 1872), p. 103.

7. See Jim George, *Discourses of Global Politics: A Critical (Re)Introduction to International Relations* (Boulder, Colo: Lynne Rienner, 1994), p. x; Richard Ashley, 'The Poverty of Neorealism', in *International Organization*, vol. 38, no. 2, 1984 pp. 225–86; Steve Smith, 'Positivism and Beyond', in S. Smith, K. Booth and M. Zalewski (eds), *International Theory: Positivism and Beyond* (Cambridge: Cambridge University Press, 1996), pp. 11–44.

8. Smith, 'Positivism and Beyond', p. 13.

9. Jeanette Winterson, *The Passion* (London: Penguin, 1987), pp. 42–3.

10. Milan Kundera, *Testaments Betrayed*, tr. L. Asher (New York: HarperCollins, 1995), p. 128. This is also the reason why Jean Baudrillard argues, implicitly, that those who have understood Foucault's work have already 'forgotten' him. See Baudrillard's *Oublier Foucault* (Paris: Editions Galilée, 1977).

11. Nietzsche, 'Zwiegespräch', in *Gedichte*, ed. R. Kray and K. Riha (Frankfurt: Insel Taschenbuch, 1994), p. 54: 'Jetzt erst glaub ich dich genesen: / Denn gesund ist, wer vergass.'

12. Nietzsche, *Unfashionable Observations*, tr. R. Gray (Stanford, Calif.: Stanford University Press, 1995), p. 89

13. Nietzsche, *The Gay Science*, tr. W. Kaufmann (New York: Vintage Books, 1882/ 1974), pp. 121–2, 169–173.

14. As, for example, Jürgen Habermas, *Der philosophische Diskurs der Moderne* (Frankfurt: Suhrkamp, 1985), pp. 104–29; Wolfgang Welsch, 'Postmoderne: Genealogic und Bedeutung eines umstrittenen Begriffes', in P. Kemper (ed.), *Postmoderne oder der Kampf um die Zukunft* (Frankfurt: Fischer Taschenbuch, 1988), p. 12.

15. Nietzsche, *Daybreak: Thoughts on the Prejudices of Morality*, tr. R. J. Hollingdale (Cambridge: Cambridge University Press, 1881/1982), pp. 43–4.

16. Nietzsche, cited in Gayatri Chakravorty Spivak, 'Translator's Preface' to J. Derrida, *Of Grammatology* (Baltimore, Md: The Johns Hopkins University Press, 1967/1976), p. xxxii.

17. George, 'International Relations and the Search for Thinking Space: Another View of the Third Debate', *International Studies Quarterly*, vol. 33, no. 3, 1989, pp. 269–79.

18. Der Derian, *On Diplomacy: A Genealogy of Western Estrangement* (Oxford: Basil Blackwell, 1987).

19. George, *Discourses of Global Politics: A Critical (Re)Introduction to International Relations* (Boulder, Colo: Lynne Rienner, 1994).

20. David Campbell, *Writing Security: United States Foreign Policy and the Politics of Identity* (Manchester: Manchester University Press, 1992).

21. Jean Elshtain, *Women and War* (New York: Basic Books, 1987).

22. Sylvester, *Feminist Theory and International Relations*.

23. R. B. J. Walker, *Inside/Outside: International Relations as Political Theory* (Cambridge: Cambridge University Press, 1993); Jens Bartelson, *A Genealogy of Sovereignty* (Cambridge: Cambridge University Press, 1995); Cynthia Weber, *Simulating Sovereignty: Intervention, the State and Symbolic Exchange* (Cambridge: Cambridge University Press, 1995); Shapiro, *Violent Cartographies*.

24. Bradley Klein, *Strategic Studies and World Order: The Global Politics of Deterrence* (Cambridge: Cambridge University Press, 1994).

25. Dominique Jacquin-Berdal, Andrew Oros and Marco Verweij, *Culture in World Politics* (London: Macmillan, 1998); Yosef Lapid and Friedrich Kratochwil (eds), *The Return of Culture in IR Theory* (Boulder, Colo: Lynne Rienner, 1996); R. B. J. Walker (ed.), *Culture, Ideology and World Order* (Boulder, Colo: Westview Press, 1984).

26. Michel Foucault, 'Nietzsche, Genealogy, History', tr. D. F. Bouchard and S. Simon, in P. Rainbow (ed.), *The Foucault Reader* (New York: Pantheon Books, 1971/1984), pp. 77–80.

27. Ibid., pp. 80–3.

28. Nietzsche, *On the Genealogy of Morals*, tr. W. Kaufamann and R. J. Hollingdale (New York: Vintage Books, 1877/1967/1989), p. 20.

29. Gaston Bachelard, *L'Engagement Rationaliste* (Paris: Presses Universitaires de France, 1972), p. 12.

30. Margaret Fuller, 'Women in the Nineteenth Century', in *The Essential Margaret Fuller*, ed. J. Steele (New Brunswick, NJ: Rutgers University Press, 1992), p. 312. See also Meena Alexander, *Women in Romanticism* (London: Macmillan, 1989), pp. 1–17; and Anne K. Mellor, *Romanticism and Gender* (New York: Routledge, 1993), pp. 2–11.

31. Franz Kafka, *The Penal Colony: Stories and Short Pieces*, tr. W. and E. Muir (New York: Schocken Books, 1948/1970), p. 148.

32. Nietzsche, *Daybreak*, p. 9. For a detailed discussion of discourses see Michel Foucault, *L'Archéologie du Savoir* (Paris: Gallimard, 1969), esp. pp. 166–73, 181–3.

33. Foucault, *L'Ordre du Discours* (Paris: Gallimard, 1971), pp. 31–8.

34. See, for example, Richard K. Ashley, 'The Poverty of Neorealism', in Keohane, *Neorealism and its Critics*, pp. 255–300; and, for a critical assessment from within the mainstream, Stanley Hoffmann, 'An American Social Science: International Relations', *Daedalus*, vol. 106, Summer 1977, pp. 41–59.

35. King, Keohane and Verba, *Designing Social Inquiry: Scientific Interference in Qualtiative Research* (Princeton, NJ: Princeton University Press, 1994), pp. 3–5. For a specific debate on this work, which underlines its central position in North American academe, see *American Political Science Review*, vol. 89, no. 2, June 1995, pp. 454–81.

36. Leszek Kolakowski, *The Alienation of Reason: A History of Positivist Thought* (New York: Doubleday, 1968), esp. pp. 1–10. For accounts of positivist scholarship within the disciplines of political science and IR see, respectively, David M. Ricci, *The Tragedy of Political Science: Politics, Scholarship and Democracy* (New Haven, Conn.: Yale University Press, 1984); and George, *Discourses*, esp. pp. 91–110.

37. King, Keohane and Verba, *Designing Social Inquiry*, pp. 6, 16.

38. Canguilhem in Foucault, *L'Ordre du Discours*, p. 36.

39. King, Keohane and Verba, *Designing Social Inquiry*, p. 6.

40. Ibid., p. 15.
41. Ibid., p. 18.
42. Ibid., p. 17.
43. Ibid., p. 7.
44. Foucault, *L'Ordre du Discours*, p. 37.
45. Sandra Harding, *The Science Question in Feminism* (Ithaca, NY: Cornell University Press, 1986), pp. 26–7.
46. Nietzsche, *The Gay Science*, pp. 121–2.
47. George Orwell, 'The Principles of Newspeak', Appendix to *Nineteen Eighty-Four* (Oxford: Clarendon Press, 1949/1984), p. 417.
48. Carol Cohn, 'Sex and Death in the Rational World of Defense Intellectuals', in L. R. Forcey (ed.), *Peace: Meanings, Politics, Strategies* (New York: Praeger, 1989), pp. 39–71.
49. Noam Chomsky, *Knowledge of Language: Its Nature, Origin, and Use* (New York: Praeger, 1986), pp. 276–87.
50. Robert G. Gilpin, 'The Richness of the Tradition of Political Realism', in Keohane, *Neorealism and its Critics*, p. 303.
51. Nietzsche, *The Gay Science*, p. 122.
52. Cohn, 'Sex and Death', p. 56.
53. Foucault, *Les Mots et les Choses* (Paris: Gallimard, 1966), p. 316.
54. Ludwig Wittgenstein, *Philosophische Untersuchungen*, in *Werkausgabe Band I* (Frankfurt: Suhrkamp, 1993), p. 250.
55. Theodor W. Adorno, *Jargon der Eigentlichkeit* (Frankfurt: Suhrkamp, 1964/1973), p. 416.
56. Mauthner and Valéry cited in Hans-Martin Gauger, 'Sprachkritik', in *Deutsche Akademie für Sprache und Dichtung*, Jahrbuch 1991, pp. 23–4.
57. Nietzsche, *On the Genealogy of Morals*, p. 80.
58. Theodor W. Adorno, *Negative Dialektik* (Frankfurt: Suhrkamp, 1966/1992), p. 153.
59. Ibid., p. 154.
60. Friedrich Nietzsche, *Götzen-Dämmerung* (Berlin: Walter de Gruyter, 1969/1889), p. 133. For a further discussion of freedom as a contested concept see William E. Connolly, *The Terms of Political Discourse* (Oxford: Martin Robertson, 1974/1983), pp. 140–78.
61. See, for example, Lisa Duggan, 'Making it Perfectly Queer', in *Socialist Review*, vol. 22, no. 1, 1992 pp. 11–31; and Steven Epstein, 'A Queer Encounter: Sociology and the Study of Sexuality', in *Sociological Theory*, vol. 12, no. 2, July 1994, pp. 188–202.
62. Les Murray, *Subhuman Redneck Poems* (Potts Point, NSW: Duffy & Snellgrove, 1996).
63. Hans J. Morgenthau, *Politics among Nations: The Struggle for Power and Peace* (New York: Alfred Knopf, 1949), p. 26.
64. Representative of this position is the work of the later Foucault. See in particular his 'The Subject and Power', in H. L. Dreyfus and P. Rabinow (eds), *Michel Foucault: Beyond Structuralism and Hermeneutics* (New York: Harvester Wheatsheaf, 1982), pp. 208–26. See also Barry Hindess, *Discourses of Power: From Hobbes to Foucault* (Oxford: Blackwell, 1996).
65. Mikhail Bakhtin, *Problems of Dostoevsky's Poetics*, tr. C. Emerson (Manchester: Manchester University Press), pp. 79–84, 181–6, 279–82, 292–3.

66. Jürgen Habermas, 'A Philosophico-Political Profile', in *New Left Review*, no. 151, May/June 1985, p. 94.

67. Christine Sylvester, 'Empathetic Cooperation: A Feminist Method for IR', in *Millennium*, vol. 23, no. 2, 1994, p. 317.

68. Adorno, *Negative Dialektik*, pp. 23–5, 156–8 and 'Der Essay als Form', in *Noten zur Literatur* (Frankfurt: Suhrkamp, 1958/1974), pp. 9–33.

69. Adorno, 'Der Essay als Form', pp. 19–20.

70. Adorno, *Negative Dialektik*, pp. 17–18.

71. Adorno, 'Der Essay als Form', pp. 24–5.

72. Nietzsche, *The Gay Science*, p. 343.

73. Gilpin, 'The Richness of the Tradition of Political Realism', p. 303.

74. Fred Halliday, *Rethinking International Relations* (Vancouver: UBC Press, 1994), p. 39.

75. Adorno, 'Der Essay als Form', pp. 22–5.

76. Adorno, *Minima Moralia: Reflexionen aus dem beschädigten Leben* (Frankfurt: Suhrkamp, 1951/1980), pp. 88–9. For discussions of the crucial importance that Adorno grants to the question of style see Gillian Rose, *The Melancholy Science: An Introduction to the Thought of Theodor W. Adorno* (London: Macmillan, 1978), pp. 11–26; and Terry Eagleton, *The Ideology of the Aesthetic* (Oxford: Basil Blackwell, 1990), pp. 341–65. For a feminist and postcolonial position that rejects clear writing styles for similar reasons see Trinh T. Minh-ha, *Women, Native, Other: Writing Postcoloniality and Feminism* (Bloomington: Indiana University Press, 1989), esp. pp. 15–20.

77. Terry Eagleton, *The Ideology of the Aesthetic* (Oxford: Basil Blackwell, 1990), p. 342.

78. King, Keohane and Verba, *Designing Social Inquiry*, p. 4.

79. Thomas Mann and Giorgio Colli, cited in Volker Gerhardt, 'Philosophie als Schicksal', postscript to Nietzsche's *Jenseits von Gut und Böse* (Stuttgart: Philipp Reclam, 1886/1988), p. 236. See also Bernhard Greiner, *Friedrich Nietzsche: Versuch und Versuchung in seinen Aphorismen* (München: Wilhelm Fink, 1972) and David B. Allison (ed.), *The New Nietzsche: Contemporary Styles of Interpretation* (Cambridge, Mass: MIT Press, 1985/1990).

80. Tom Stoppard, cited in *The New Yorker*, 17 April 1995, p. 111. For an application of dialogues to IR see James N. Rosenau (ed.), *Global Voices: Dialogues in International Relations* (Boulder, Colo: Westview Press, 1993).

81. Paul Valéry, 'Propos sur la Poésie', cited in Jean-Louis Joubert, *La Poésie* (Paris: Armand Colin, 1988), p. 53.

82. Ulrich Schödelbauer, 'Die Modernitätsfalle der Lyrik', in *Merkur*, no. 551, vol. 49, no. 2, Feb. 1995, p. 174.

83. Kristeva, *Recherches pour une sémanalyze* (Paris: Seuil, 1969), pp. 178–9, tr. L. S. Roudiez in the Introduction to Kristeva's *Revolution in Poetic Language* (New York: Columbia University Press, 1984), p. 2.

84. Jayne-Ann Igel, 'Der Zögling', in T. Elm, *Kristallisationen: Deutsche Gedichte der achtziger Jahre* (Stuttgart: Reclam, 1992), p. 158: 'war ich endültig gefangen, als ich ihre sprache lernte, meine / stimme ein vogellaut, der mich ihnen bewahrte; sie hielten / mich am hause gleich dem rebstock, dessen triebe sie be / schnitten, daß er die zimmer nicht verdunkele // und dicht bei der mauer des hauses spielte ich, unterm lichte / trocknender laken, die finger durchlöcherten den putz, nicht / missen mochte ich den leibhaftigen

klang meines namens, der / nach urin roch; die meinen namen in ihren munde führten, / hielten mich mit den zähnen fest am genick'

85. See, for example, Durs Grünbein, 'Zu Kieseln gehärtet: Über das lyrische Sprechen', in *Neue Zürcher Zeitung*, 30 Sept. 1995, p. 50; Jacques Derrida, 'Shibboleth for Paul Celan', tr. J. Wilner, in A. Fioretos (ed.), *Word Traces: Readings of Paul Celan* (Baltimore, Md: The Johns Hopkins University Press, 1994), pp. 3–72.

86. For instance, James Der Derian 'Fathers (and Sons), Mother Courage (and Her Children), and the Dog, the Cave, and the Beef', in Rosenau, *Global Voices*, pp. 83–96; Stephen Chan, 'A Story Beyond Telos: Redeeming the Shield of Achilles for a Realism of Rights in IR', in *Millennium*, vol. 28, no. 1, 1999, pp. 101–15; and Christine Sylvester, 'Riding the Hyphens of Feminism, Peace, and Place in Four-(or More) Part Cacophony', in *Alternatives*, vol. 18, no. 1, Winter 1993, pp. 109–18.

87. Peter Szondi, 'Durch die Enge geführt: Versuch über die Verständlichkeit des modernen Gedichts', in *Celan-Studien* (Frankfurt: Suhrkamp, 1972), p. 103.

88. Heidegger, 'Die Sprache im Gedicht', in *Unterwegs zur Sprache* (Stuttgart: Verlag Günter Neske, 1953/1959), p. 38.

89. Derek Walcott, *Collected Poems* (New York: The Noonday Press, 1986), p. 456.

90. Friedrich Nietzsche, *Thus Spoke Zarathustra*, tr. W. Kaufmann in *The Portable Nietzsche* (London: Penguin, 1954/1982), p. 205. See also his prefaces to *Daybreak*, pp. 1–5, and *On the Genealogy of Morals*, pp. 15–23.

91. David Campbell, *National Deconstruction: Violence, Identity and Justice in Bosnia* (Minneapolis: University of Minnesota Press, 1998), pp. 196–7.

92. Robert O. Keohane, 'International Relations Theory: Contributions of a Feminist Standpoint', in *Millennium*, vol. 18, no. 2, 1989, pp. 249–50.

93. Ibid, pp. 249–50. For a more detailed and excellent critique of this position see Cynthia Weber, 'Good Girls, Little Girls and Bad Girls: Male Paranoia in Robert Keohane's Critique of Feminist International Relations', in *Millennium*, vol. 23, no. 2, Summer 1994, pp. 337–49.

94. Halliday, *Rethinking International Relations*, pp. 39–41.

95. Max Horkheimer, *Traditionelle und kritische Theorie* (Frankfurt: Fischer Taschenbuch, 1992/1937), p. 249.

96. Nietzsche, *Thus Spoke Zarathustra*, pp. 128–30.

97. Ibid, pp. 280, 284.

98. Ibid, p. 284.

99. Ibid, p. 243.

100. King, Keohane and Verba, *Designing Social Inquiry*, p. 6.

101. Karl Popper, *Unended Quest: An Intellectual Autobiography* (La Salle, Ill.: Open Court, 1976), p. 19.

102. Jacques Derrida, *Eperons: Les Styles de Nietzsche* (Chicago, Ill.: University of Chicago Press, 1979), pp. 56–7.

Part II
Attempting to Form the Debate

4
Seven Types of Ambiguity in Western International Relations Theory and Painful Steps Towards Right Ethics

Stephen Chan

Since its inception, the discipline of international relations has struggled to establish the rigour of its methodological base in the academy, and it has struggled to establish whether and how it might have any moral place in the world. At the begining of the twenty-first century both struggles have reached a high point. Methodologically, the discipline has begun a transatlantic separation, with a US emphasis on neorealism and neoliberalism (both in its categorisations and its positivistic tendencies not a considerable departure from the interwar debate between realists and idealists), and a British concern not only for a historicised discipline, but for the intellectual history of the discipline itself. Steve Smith has written on ten self-images that international relations has held.[1] Simultaneously, there has been a growing concern on both sides of the Atlantic, in Australia, and in Mervy Frost's work from South Africa, with normative theory. This is meant to be both rigorous and emancipatory – although how it emancipates is not satisfactorily defined; in the postwar struggles, people may have needed ideology or religion, but seldom philosophy at the barricades. Nor is it clear how normative theory, drawn from enlightenment origins such as Hegel and Kant, or from postmodern figures such as Foucault, or from Habermasian critical theory, can establish norms for (let alone emancipate) those considerable parts of the globe where the Western enlightenment project never settled (such as China), which are premodern (such as the rural areas of much of Africa), and which have not so much a distinction between instrumental and ideal speech, but an ideal that one day it might be free to speak. What it articulates then will not be Hegelian, Kantian, Foucaultian or Habermasian.

Nevertheless, it has been said that international ethics is important enough to be a clear field of its own.[2] What, perhaps, is meant by such work is not that the work itself emancipates, but that it frees the worker, the scholar, to think about emancipation. If it takes a clear field to do this, it says much for the chains the discipline has spun with its own attempts at methodology. It says little about actual emancipation beyond the scholar, little about praxis – since, in the anglophonic discipline at least, on both sides of the Atlantic, the number of international relations scholars who have fed a dying child or cleaned a Kalashnikov can be counted on the fingers of one hand. At the beginning of the twenty-first century, there hangs over international relations, at least its normative wing, a dreadful ambivalence: to problematise freedom is to free nobody; to problematise in terms of Western schools of thought is not to understand everybody. A painful way beyond this ambivalence is the subject of this chapter. First, however, a word is in order on the mirage methodology has created. Within Western international relations, there are not ten self-images at all, but seven types of ambiguity.[3]

Ambiguities

One grand ambivalence and seven ambiguities might seem a stew rather than a discipline. In fact, international relations *is* a discipline precisely because it has with disciplined effort laid down various sedimental layers, and these stay in place while the cauldron heats and the liquid bubbles. The suspicion of layers has resulted in various descriptive labels – the three paradigms, the three great debates. One either historically succeeds another, as in the three great debates, or stands somewhat discrete from the others, as in the three paradigms. Each sedimental layer deals, in some way, with four of the seven ambiguities, and this reflects success upon the discipline. They are able to deal with:

1. To what extent international relations is a social science (a claim most rooted in the behaviouralism of *both* realism and pluralism in the 1960s and 1970s) and to what extent a humanity (in the historical conditionality of the English school and in current interests in philosophy);
2. To what extent international relations is a science in the pure academic sense of *Wissenschaft* or pure knowledge, and to what extent it is scientific in its applied, particularly predictive sense and policy sense;
3. To what extent international relations is a realism, that is, dealing with a brute and stark reality without the task of superimposing

values, and to what extent it provides a moral commentary to what is real, or even posits the sort of moral universe to which reality should aspire;

4. To what extent international relations should be positivistically based, in the realm of the senses and their sense of evidence, and to what extent it should admit to the fragmentation of knowledge, the unreliability of evidence, and that knowledge can only successfully (and momentarily) deconstruct the real.

These ambiguities have been dealt with by giving their various antagonisms *methodological* space. Each sediment may, therefore, contain various methodologies and these make statements and coexist. The coexistence provides the discipline with its equilibrium which is also, simultaneously, its politesse. Manners work best, however, when bedfellows are used to one another, know which part of the bed is theirs, know the rules of engagement in whatever troilism is being brewed (or stewed). There are three interrelated ambiguities, however, which have only tentative space and unsedimental space at that, within the discipline. These are:

5. To what extent knowledge can be truly epistemologically based, or whether ontologies construct multiple epistemologies;
6. To what extent multiple epistemologies and multiple ontologies are reflected in a West versus the rest divide, so that the discipline, in its global appreciation, is only partial rather than universal; but is nevertheless hegemonic, thereby aping that paradigmatic realism many in international relations hoped had sunk to the lowest sedimental level;
7. To what extent the discipline itself must be seen in terms of a structure–agency problematic, in which the structure is more multifaceted than before, because the agents are revolting, are bringing great cloves of garlic and clashing spices to all the layers of the English stew, and seeking to stir themselves into the sediments at the stew's bottom; while the response of the sediments is, at least in part, to turn into concrete. You can have too many methodologies but, above all, you should not have foreign methodologies – so here's stodge for you all!

The more global structure/agency problematic of which ambiguity 7 is only a small-scale academic type has only tentatively entered mainstream British international relations discourse. Recently, Vivienne Jabri has completed a new book which imports Anthony Giddens to international relations.[4] There has also been a somewhat fractured debate between Carlsnaes and Hollis and Smith on the one hand, and Hollis/Smith and Jabri/Chan on the other.[5] This debate spilled over into the areas of all three unsedimental ambiguities. More on that below; here it should be said that we are concerned with new and unsedimented ambiguities, and not the well-sedimented question related to levels of analysis. International relations set out to view the international system as its academic jurisdiction and, although it has concerns with states, non-state pluralism, and capital-bearing or capital-deprived classes, it remains largely and determinedly global and systemic in its sedimental base. The key word here, however is not 'level', but 'analysis'. The three ambiguities are not so much positing non-systemic levels as suggesting that the discipline has inadequate tools for analysis of ontologies, particularistic or alternatively universal epistemologies, and revolting agents who see themselves as champions of and contributors to a global structure alien to a Western-conceived structure. There are, in short, few or no methodologies to deal with these ambiguities. The politesse of coexisting extant methodologies is inadequate and, in fact, what existing sedimental layers in international relations and their coexisting methodologies do is to *describe* the state of a discipline whose universalistic theories are largely unrecognised by three-quarters of humanity, most of literate humanity, and most universities in the world. If recognised, then it is with heavy conditionalities.[6]

Culture

I have argued many times elsewhere that cultures are not given adequate space in international relations. I have argued that there are other ways of seeing;[7] and that if international relations wishes, in turn, to see how it and the world is being variously seen, then it must draw upon the methodologies of other disciplines more sympathetic than international relations to a multiplicity of claims for universalism. (Others have methodologically addressed the question of their own Western sedimentations.)[8] I do not wish to repeat all these arguments here. However, it may be well to reprint a point-by-point summary I made of how the processes of seeing, not seeing, and partial seeing on all sides are constructed. If we assume, momentarily, a system of states, let us start with the construction of states.

1. Differently in different states, and at different times, culture has been affiliated to nationalism, and nationalism to state, to give a differentiated identity to the rest of the world.

2. This is a dynamic and continuing process and occurs in various locations at the present moment.

3. Each process of identity and differentiation creates its own Other.

4. Epistemological processes reinforce the rational base of identity and differentiation and, either directly or by extension, call into question the 'truthfulness' of the Other.

5. In various situations, this critique of the Other, combined with a vindication of self, is represented by complex eschatological and soteriological systems.

6. Popular rhetoric of damnation and reward is founded on complex thought systems.

7. There is no such thing as a simple or 'fundamental' theological state, and no reduction possible that constructs a simple model of a revolutionary state.

8. All such states, however, are socialised to one degree or another into the international system.

9. They may consent to this for reasons of practical association, but not always or necessarily for purposive association.

10. In this process of socialisation, the question proposed by Western scholars has consistently been lopsided: 'How much of ours has been adopted by them?' rather than 'How much of theirs has been adopted by us?' The imbalance in global socialisation has been mistaken as an acceptable normative foundation in international relations.[9]

What is sought in this essay's work is how to rectify, academically at least, such imbalances. It is to construct a methodology to bring theirs into a more equal marriage with ours. This has implications of course for how, for instance, a universal sense of human rights might be constructed (as opposed to declared and, sometimes, hegemonically enforced); and how a praxis that at least understands some other's idea of freedom might be founded. Nothing is emanicipatory in an assumed or imposed world.

Postmodernity for starters

Although postmodernism has emphasised a plural, almost fragmented world, only a surprisingly small number of international relations postmodernists have made the point that the pluralisms of other cultural forces should be brought into the discipline.[10] Even fewer, having made the point, have proposed methodologies for this bringing in. There was certainly some attention to method by the hermeneuticists and dialo-gicians.[11] However, it is to Rorty in particular that we now turn, who said there is no universal skyhook for anything,[12] let alone international relations. Moreover, in his idea of the long scientific revolution, we might see a context for this present chapter in the sociology of interna-tional relations knowledge.[13] In the twenty-first century, we shall all, perhaps, be multiculturally founded normative theorists.

Until then, what is of interest here is not Rorty's celebration of differ-ence. That has been discussed elsewhere by many others, such as Nicho-las Higgins.[14] What is at stake, in a world of difference, where the universal moral community might not be possible, is the idea never-theless of moral communication. This is what Rorty means by 'universal discourse' and 'solidarity'.[15] What, however, does this solidarity seek to overcome? Here opinion is divided. Cornel West, a problematic student of Rorty, talks about fundamental (cultural and religious) 'cleavages and conflicts which are not so much incommensurable; they just clash'.[16] The clash, in academic terms, is between incommensurability and forms of commensurability that at least reduce or mediate clashes. Much of my writing to date has tended towards statements of imcommensurability but, here, I wish to discuss the mediation of clashes by means of a scholarship of solidarity. Such scholarship must not impose methodol-ogies or foundation philosophies: there *cannot* be a Kantian critical theory of Islam that makes sense in Mecca; not a Hegelian constitution of family, civil society and state in China that makes sense in rural China – outside of convenience, temptation and easy fit – just as there cannot be a Confucian constitution of family, civil society and state in Europe that makes sense in Budapest (although a Chinese scholar could make the same broad and generalised easy fit). Some years ago, I suggested that if it were possible to establish a *syncretic* scholarship of solidarity (there *can* be a mix, if ingenious, of *both* Hegel and Confucius), then the place to find its possibilities would be in liberation theology;[17] certainly for its accommodation of both peasant need, peasant ethic and Chris-tian ethic and praxis, but also because it is possible to combine a Christian liberation theology (which many Western scholars assume to be the only sort) with an Islamic liberation theology.

An Islamic liberation theology

Islam can also claim to be a totalising method and ethic. The work, therefore, of Hassan Hanafi, Professor of Philosophy at Cairo (and author of a thirteen-volume study of revolution) is invaluable. He sketches four methodologies by which Christian and Islamic thought might meet, but rejects them in favour of something without the aim of totalising thought or text. This is liberation theology which immediately prioritises praxis. 'Situations of oppression and poverty are visibly seen far away from the ambiguity of the text.' It is something which concerns the oppressed and poor and is a struggle in which the wretched of the earth participate. It seeks a new world order as much as a new theory, but seeks certainly a freedom from dogma. Hanafi cites suras from the Qur'an, in which the key words are 'betterment' and 'righteousness' which are counterpoised to 'mischief' and 'evil'.[18]

> Shall we treat those who believe and work deeds of righteousness the same as those who do mischief on Earth?
> Shall we treat those who guard against evil, the same as those who turn aside from the right? (38:28)

What this may be seen as seeking to establish are three things: first, a priority of praxis over theory – if the latter cannot serve the former it becomes a game of words and texts; second, it raises a conception of right as something opposed to evil; and, third, the cause of 'betterment' is both praxis and right – right and not evil.

Well-being as a measure of right

Although scholars such as Chris Brown have tentatively suggested a measure of a human right as that which is not a human evil, and that security from fear and need are the best guarantors of rights,[19] it is to the work of an economist that we now turn. Partha Dasgupta has applied forms of critical theory and political philosophy to development economics (it is not just international relations that has been infused with new life; the Martin Wights of several disciplines are contested now). Having said that, he has done so in an unusual way. With the same guiding principles as his sometime collaborator, Ken Binmore (who explicated Rawls, among others, through game theory[20]), Dasgupta seeks to show that the destitute of the third world, even when seemingly 'irrational' in their decisions, exercise highly rational as well as moral forms of utility in their thought.[21] The basic message is that, *provided* one unlocks the social and cultural conditionality of choice, the recognition of evil and the preference for betterment have universal resonance. Well-being is a universal value.

This view is not unlike the consequences of Rorty's statement: 'Differences...[are] unimportant when compared with similarities with respect to pain and humiliation.'[22] Rorty talks of cruelty in the same vein. What international relations has failed to do is to recognise pain and humiliation; it has not recognised evil because most of its practitioners, in upholstering an increasingly armchair discipline, have never confronted evil, cannot properly imagine it, and would perhaps be tempted to theorise it. Recognitions of the sort outlined here require not a theory, but a praxis of betterment. Once, in Paris, medieval scholars debated how many angels could dance on the head of a pin. Now, again in Paris, it might be time to dance ourselves in the painful steps of a praxis against evil. This would give the discipline its absent ethic and help resolve its ambiguities.

Intellectual foundations for a praxis

There are three steps in what might be best regarded as a research programme rather than a paradigm,[23] a research programme because the intellectual foundations for a praxis are difficult ones.

1. There is a *preliminary* emancipatory work by scholars in researching what is agreed, *from their different cultural foundations*, to be right or, at least, not evil; what is necessary for betterment and well-being in both moral and utilitarian terms.
2. There is a second step in understanding how each agreement might be *constructed* in terms of *differing knowledge*. There is a history *and* conditionality involved in how knowledges confronted modernity and internationalism, and what other cultures have sought to accept and reject from the West.
3. From such work, the idea of the international is delimited from its Western enclosure of the world so that there is (a) a differentiation between an international system and the international society (or societies) that underpins (or subverts) and it (b) a series of enclosures with doors seeking to lead onto a common courtyard of social *mix*, though not always homogeneity.

Since not much will come of the call for academics to handle rifles and starving babies, this will at least be a reminder of the world at large – which needs practice and praxis more than it needs theory. Certainly it needs more than theory alone to make the ontologies of the oppressed understandable, in terms as meaningful to them as us and to assist (and this is the harder part, beyond the research programme suggested above) the agency of those who struggle, and thereby reduce the centralising moral ambiguity of a discipline which speaks partially, but which has assumed and declared universally.

Notes

1. Steve Smith, 'The Self-Images of a Discipline: A Genealogy of International Relations Theory', in Ken Booth and Steve Smith (eds), *International Relations Theory Today* (Cambridge: Polity, 1995). Of course, the idea of a transatlantic divide is highly generalised, with conspicuous exceptions on both sides.
2. Chris Brown, 'International Ethics: Fad, Fantasy, or Field', *Paradigms*, vol. 8, no. 1 1994.
3. The term is, of course, lifted from English literary scholarship and the radical critic, William Empson.
4. Vivienne Jabri, *Discourses on Violence* (Manchester: Manchester University Press, 1996).
5. Walter Carlsnaes, 'The Agency–Structure Problem in Foreign Policy Analysis', *International Studies Quarterly*, vol. 36, September, 1992; Martin Hollis and Steve Smith, 'Two Stories about Structure and Agency', *Review of International Studies*, vol. 20, no. 3, 1994; Vivienne Jabri and Stephen Chan, 'The Ontologist Always Rings Twice: Two More Stories about Structure and Agency in Reply to Hollis and Smith', *Review of International Studies*, vol. 22, no. 1, 1996.
6. See the surveys in Stephen Chan, 'Beyond the North-West: Africa and the East', and A. J. R. Groom, 'The World Beyond: The European Dimension', in A. J. R. Groom and Margot Light (eds), *Contemporary International Relations: A Guide to Theory* (London: Pinter, 1994). In his review of this book, Steve Smith admitted: 'Many readers of the book will doubtless feel embarrassed, as I did, about knowing so little about what was being done outside a small geographical area', *Millennium*, vol. 24, no. 1, 1995, p. 154. They do not recognise us, just as we do not recognise them.
7. 'Cultural and Linguistic Reductionisms and a New Historical Sociology for International Relations', *Millennium*, vol. 22, no. 3, 1993.
8. 'Culture and Absent Epistemologies in International Relations', *Theoria*, 81/2, 1993.
9. From Chapter 11 of Stephen Chan and Andrew J. Williams (eds), *Renegade States: The Evolution of Revolutionary Foreign Policy* (Manchester: Manchester University Press, 1994).
10. A recent exception is Molly Cochran, 'Postmodernism, Ethics and International Political Theory', *Review of International Studies*, vol. 21, no. 3, 1995.
11. Without being slavishly Gadamerian, the 'Finnish School' of Osmo Aspunen shows how hermeneutical styles of investigation can bring the other into our understanding. See *inter alia*, Billy Mukamuri, *Making Sense of Social Forestry: A Political and Contextual Study of Forestry Practices in South Central Zimbabwe* (Tampere: Acta Universitatis Tamperensis, Ser. A Vol. 438, 1995); Mika Mervio, *Cultural Representation of the Japanese in International Relations and Politics* (Tampere: Acta Universitatis Tamperensis, Ser. A Vol. 448, 1995).

12. Richard Rorty, *Objectivity, Relativism and Truth* (Cambridge: Cambridge University Press, 1991), p. 13.
13. Richard Rorty, *Philosophy and the Mirror of Nature* (Oxford: Blackwell, 1980), ch. VII, 'On Kuhn's Scientific Revolutions'.
14. Nicholas Higgins, 'A Question of Style: The Politics and Ethics of Cultural Conversation in Rorty and Connolly', *Global Society*, vol. 1, no. 1, 1996.
15. Richard Rorty, *Contingency, Irony and Solidarity* (Cambridge: Cambridge University Press, 1989).
16. Interview with Cornel West, 'American Radicalism', *Radical Philosophy*, vol. 71, 1995, p. 35.
17. Stephen Chan, 'A Summer Polemic: Revolution, Rebellion and Romance. Some Notes Towards the Resacralisation of International Relations', *Paradigms*, vol. 7, no. 1, 1993, p. 98.
18. Hassan Hanafi, 'Cultures and Societies, Social Justice and Liberation Theology in Dialogue', in Tuomo Melasuo (ed.), *The Mediterranean Revisited* (Tampere: Tampere Peace Research Institute, 1994), pp. 79–81.
19. Chris Brown, 'Human Rights and the Limits of an Ethical Community', paper presented to the Conference on Human Rights, Human Wrongs, University of Wales at Aberystwyth, July 1995.
20. Ken Binmore, *Playing Fair* (Cambridge, Mass.: MIT Press, 1994).
21. Partha Dasgupta, *An Enquiry into Well-Being and Destitution* (Oxford: Clarendon, 1993).
22. Rorty, *Contingency, Irony and Solidarty*, p. 192.
23. See Michael Nicholson, *Imaginary Paradigms: A Case of Mistaken Identity* (Canterbury: Kent Papers in Politics and International Relations, 1992).

5
A Story Beyond Telos: Redeeming the Shield of Achilles for a Realism of Rights in IR

Stephen Chan

'Sing, oh Muse, sing for our time too.'

(The opening to Homer's *Odyssey*)

This chapter sets out to tell a story, and to do so in both an archaic and modern way, using primarily the characters and motifs of Homer's *Iliad*. In a way it is, therefore, an effort loosely in the style of Horkheimer and Adorno's use of Homer's *Odyssey*, and is meant to be an antidote to the more sterile formats of a formal IR. The point of the story is that, unlike Shapiro and Der Derian's view, a story does not have to embody a telos. The world has stories to tell, and it is the responsibility of IR scholars, not just to deconstruct them for their political animations, but to reinvent them as the basis of solidarities and the imagination implicit in successful dialogue.

The poet, Auden, said the shield of Achilles was terror-filled, made by the gods and emblazoned with scenes of death. No one was redeemed on the shield. The revolutionary French artist, David, painted the scene foretold on that shield: Achilles sacrificing twelve Trojan youths on the funeral pyre for his friend, Patroclus. At the edge of the centre, lying as a footnote to the carnage, and its heroic cause, the body of Hector is sprawled bound to Achilles' chariot. Although Achilles tries daily, dragging the body behind his chariot, he cannot tear Hector apart. The gods, having given him up to death, full of admiration for his happy fear and duty, preserved his body. Poor Hector: he clasped his infant son for the last time; the child cried because his father looked so fearsome in his horsehair plume and helmet. Then he stood at the gates, spear in hand, to await the onslaught of Achilles. Hector was fated. He could not free his subjectivity from the will of the gods.

Nor, however, could Achilles. It was said he had an early choice: obscure old age or a glorious short life of heroism, and he chose short-ness. But he lived the shortness in such a one-dimensional manner that he became almost the grand caricature of heroism. The only ambiguity about him has been read into his life from the present era's concern for sexuality: he dressed in a negligee before the war against Troy; he seemed to love his friend, Patroclus, a man who fell in combat to Hector, even more than his female bed-mate, Briseis. But, once he took a sword in hand, and particularly once he donned the Olympian armour, his character was as encased as his body.

What is this antiquity to us? Why tell this story?

Although international relations as an academic discipline has come, slowly, to talk of stories,[1] they are at most stories about stories. No one steps out of the scholarly format. The format has enveloped the profes-sion. I mean by this not a rarified or reified story, but a narrative, a tale, pure and proper – in which the lesson is found in the fantasy. Bertrand Russell included Byron in his *History of Western Philosophy*, precisely because his iambic fantasies were able to problematise freedom's behaviour in the face of both power and escape. In our own postwar era, Marguerite Duras is as much a philosopher as a novelist. And which of Sartre's works will we remember most? It's a catchy fashion. Julia Kristeva writes a novel acutely wishing to parallel Simone de Beauvoir. Bernard-Henri Levy even makes a bad film reminiscent of his bad novels. In its humourless, depersonalised way, IR imports into its format only the refereed essay and eschews roman-ticism and expressionism. It labours rationally to build the stone-by-stone wall of objective truth, upon epistemological foundations that are uni-form, and substitutes uniformity for a true universality.

How then will it import – since it is now a discipline of importations – the revival of interest in Walter Benjamin, with his self-interrogations in essays that are part story?[2] How does the *arrière-garde* import what was, decades ago, the *avant-garde*? How will it import the interest in Georges Bataille, whose stories, accompanied at least by a *recit*, articulated a pornographic imagination?[3] Now that we know who Pauline Reage really was, it is possible to construct and articulate *The Story of O* as an IR text about the normative possibilities of powerlessness, to have the exact antidote at last to realism.[4]

Let us pause here. Is this not merely a rhetoric, a false staking of ground? Has not someone like Michael Shapiro recently written that realist IR, with its state-centric concerns, is no more than a set of stories – as are those realisms of other states and cultures?[5] Moreover, are the flashing references to Benjamin and Bataille, for instance, meant even briefly to illuminate, or are they gratuitous? In short, is this story of Achilles being told as no more than a rhetoric and pyrotechnic? At best, aphoristic?

It means to be aphoristic, at least in part. This, too, is story-telling: not just metaphor as a methodology, but its condensation; a minimalism that existed in, for instance, Japanese poetry as well as Japanese interiors and gardens. However, it also existed as a means of writing Western philosophy. Both Nietzsche and his latter-day disciple, Cioran, have been deliberately aphoristic. Perhaps, for Nietzsche, it was a means of writing truth. 'Only that', he said, 'which has no history can be defined.'[6] Meaning had to begin without the luxury of predetermined reference points. Cioran, according to Susan Sontag, wanted to make denser Nietzsche's work, that is, he presented his own work as a series of proposals to problematise the world; and wrote as lyrically as possible, while demanding an almost aesthetic intuitive recognition of the arguments involved. 'Good taste', says Sontag, 'demands that the thinker furnish only pithy glimpses of intellectual and spiritual torment.'[7]

I do not mean to be so demanding. However, there is something to it. Entire periods of Chinese poetry saw writing as the careful presentation of only a few words. The *reader* furnished the connecting material, that is, the reader wrote the story. The interlocutor not only writes back, but writes to overwhelm a provocation. The present chapter is indeed a provocation. This is the methodology of aphorism. However, it is not only a provocation; not only aphoristic. It sets out to tell a story, but not as a traditional teller of stories. In short, even if other writers in IR now make use of stories – or stories of stories – they become narratives like essays. They are didactic *in the first instance*. To that extent, they may be fables. I am thinking here, above all, of *fantasies*. What emerges from a fantasy is its imaginative, even perverse, manipulation by others.

This is precisely the point of mentioning Bataille and Benjamin. Bataille was also, in some sense, a descendant of Nietzsche. He saw Nietzsche as a man who condemned himself to solitude. A man without predetermined reference points has to be, in an absolute sense, alone.[8] What Bataille did was less extreme than Nietzsche. However, he questioned all accepted references to and definitions of rationality, beauty and baseness. A follower of Hegel as well, he took on little of IR's communitarian and spiritual Hegel. Instead, like Icarus flying so high that the sun melted his wings, Hegel provided *too much enlightenment*, too much illumination. Blinded by the sun, Bataille feared that the base things of the earth could no longer be seen. Thus his concern with the writing of pornography: the profane that relieves the glare of the sacred. However, it is not as simple as that. Despite also writing undeveloped or undeveloped stories and discontinuities, it becomes clear that the continual anguish of eroticism, of love driving even basely forward, is what unites humanity. Everything else may as well be a blindness.[9]

Having said that, what this means for stories is simple. Stories do not have to be noble. They can be base, even pornographically so (hence the reference to *The Story of O*, above). Baseness, also, carries history forward. This is why an IR, derived from the Enlightenment, cannot easily incorporate a Bataille or, for that matter, a Walker Benjamin. Although his famous fragmentary essay/story, 'One-way Street', is almost his personal paradigm of discontinuities, not to mention the terrors of the universe, it is a brief fragment which I wish here to quote:

> the *concept of knowledge* marks an illusory point of intersection. Only in its multiplicity does the concept of knowledge stand up. Its unity cannot lie in its own sphere; it cannot be a summation, a judgement. If by 'unity' is meant a unity not just of knowings but also as knowledge, then there is no such thing as a unity of knowings.
>
> Truth rightly occupies the systematic place that has been so frequently usurped by the illusory aggregate of knowledge. Truth is the quintessence of knowings as a symbol. Yet it is not the aggregate of all truths. Truth expresses itself in a system or in its conceptual summary. Truths, however, can be expressed neither systematically nor conceptually – much less with acts of knowledge in judgement – but only in art.[10]

I am not proposing a totally expressionist IR, but certainly an artistic IR. This, then, is my point of departure from the Shapiros and Der Derians of the IR world – although I applaud what they have done. In a succinct and elegant 1993 essay, Der Derian argued, via Nietzsche, that the world was unsafe and perilous; truths were too; the domestication of truth, through the devices of onto-theologically-founded epistemic realisms, has been merely to hide fear. This is the foundation of realism and state-centric preoccupations with security. In this light, the arguments to sustain the 'knowledge' of security have been teleological, and *stories*.[11] Knowledge is, thus, a fable, and knowings are different, perhaps competitive, fables. Writing in 1989, Shapiro laid out the antecedents of his current wares:

Insofar as 'social reality' emerges in various writing genres, investigations of how the world is apprehended require inquiries into various pre-texts of apprehensions, for the meaning and value imposed on the world is structured not by one's immediate consciousness but by the various reality-making scripts one inherits or acquires from one's surrounding cultural/linguistic condition.[12]

His recommendation, so that we might recognise such textualised representations of meaning, is to 'politicize' the text and its textual practices. We shall not, therefore, be fooled.

Like Der Derian, he is concerned with technology's condensation of time – both cite Virilio here – and how technology now privileges the language of decision-making within state-centric and fabulist conditions, and how technology's speed and ability have begun to mystify extermination as something once called war.[13]

But my point is exactly, what are we to do with such recognitions of such representations? What do we do if we are not fooled by forms of telos? Is this all there is to stories – that we are not fooled, and that we can do nothing? This, itself, is a mysticism: that stories are merely the vehicles of a telos, of a representation. The points of departure are that stories are an *art*; that an artistic IR can go beyond not being fooled; that the stories of the world can tell truths; and that, without seeking any representation of the universal, certain common truths can lead to common actions and, indeed, a common set of international ethics. A fantasy follows – a magical realism – in which a myth is replayed, but becomes no longer a cradle myth of only the West. It touches base with other stories, some aphoristic, others less so. The reader constructs his or her own ethic, perhaps. He or she, reading the story, written as art, bordered by the suggestibility of a Benjamin-esque or Cioran-esque essay, will ask if he or she would, in truth, act this way – or recognise a common truth that people *should* act this way. This would be towards a solidarity.

This is merely a hope. We had better begin where we were before such problematic texts and their questions. If we go back to the first classics of the West, we are confronted by stirring adventures. Precisely because there is no evident need to deconstruct Achilles, or evident benefit, we eye the slaughter merely as an arcanum to which we have not been invited to find the key. However, whatever view Horkheimer and Adorno took of Achilles, they did not do the same with Odysseus. The man who, by guile, accomplished what Achilles, by force, could not – the fall of Troy – took ten years to return from the Trojan campaign.

Hounded by the gods, confronted in turn by disasters and temptations, stripped of all compatriots and property, he finally, by his own efforts, returned to his home in Ithaca. Horkeimer and Adorno argue he was the first person in the entire history of Western literature to claim his own subjectivity.[14] To use today's terms, his agency triumphed over the gods' structure. There could never be another Trojan war after Odysseus, because men and women were at once freed from divine manipulation.

This was a bold claim. It was not so late in other literatures. Although, in the Bible, the story of Job is one which expresses powerfully the limits and contingencies, if not the illusion, of subjectivity, there is no one else in the Old Testament who is able to live without God. However, in the which were stories precursors to the Bible, in Sumerian literature, Gilgamesh made a fair stab at subjectivity. Even within Homer's work, before Odysseus leaves Troy, there is one terror-inducing display of subjectivity. Horkheimer and Adorno missed it. Tippett, in his great opera, saw the tragedy, if not the uniqueness, of it. This was the reclamation of Hector's body from its abuse by Achilles. There is a painting of this too, and it cannot be looked upon without the most terrible sense of pity that one must go so far to compensate, even partly, the capriciousness of Heaven.

Ten years of war have passed. For ten years he has not stood outside his own city. One by one, he has seen his sons die on the battlements. His daughter is possessed by prophecies of doom. King Priam's favourite son is Hector. Hector's name means 'he who stands'. He stands now outside the city gates. He is going to take on Achilles in mortal combat. But Achilles is the son of a goddess. He wears the heavenly armour. His shield is a reiteration of all the doom prophesied within the dispirited walls. Even without armour and shield, three inches of his body is vulnerable. Hector is only a man, the son of a man and a woman. In the Hollywood film his own armour is steel-grey, but his sword-belt is inlaid with silver and sapphires. An apparition that shines like the sun is charging down upon him. He knows the city gates have shut behind him. He loses his nerve. He tries to run. Priam watches him pierced by the spear of Achilles, unable to outstrip his fate, a silver and sapphire butterfly pinned and writhing on the blood-red ground.

Then, for days after, Priam watches Achilles in his chariot, dragging the body of his son around and around the bolted, breathless walls of Troy. No army sallies forth. No soldier would obey the order. If Hector could not stand, the city is dead. It is only a matter of time. Resign yourself to fate. Everyone will soon be lashed to chariots and dragged from death to decay. Achilles looks up and laughs at the white hair of Priam.

This goes on and on. Each day the sun rises and Achilles tries again to mutilate the corpse.

It is still dark. The horizon holds a thin pink finger. Priam, by himself, appears at the open gate of Troy. It shuts behind him as it shut behind his son. The gods see what he is doing. They are amazed. And impressed. Impressed beyond fate. One of them comes down from the sky to guide him. He is going to the camp of Achilles. How will he bargain for the release of Hector's body?

He has crept in unseen. The sun is only now clearing the horizon. They are taking breakfast. The one with the very long hair, uncut since birth, is being fed fruit by a slave girl. One hand is open on the arm-rest. Still no one has seen him. He is kneeling. Achilles feels lips. He looks down. Priam looks up. 'Take pity on me, Lord Achilles, for I have kissed the hand of the man who killed my son.' He is a king, a very old king, he is a grieving old man. Where are his armies? Achilles cannot help himself. Even his nature recognises a nobility beyond what any man should rightly be asked to do, beyond what a man should ask himself to do. Achilles raises Priam to his feet. With grace, without second thought, gives the father his son.

Was this not subjectivity? The self recovered from the gods who also recovers its progeny? We can appreciate it now in a deconstructed classic. We will listen to the occasional bombastic note in the opera anew. We will not ever, ourselves, kiss the hand that murdered our children. Ours is a reflective life. We reflect on the deaths of children on television. They are far away. Perhaps, precisely because they are on television, like the Gulf War, their deaths never happen.[15] Slight pressure on the remote control. Four lines of a curved rectangle disappear into a dot.

To enlarge the dot, to read its message, is the claim of accomplishment by technology. To enlarge the dot, to bring it to life, like a spear passing through, like a silent dropping to one knee before someone terrible, this should be the mission of understanding and meaning of IR.

What Priam did was the consummation of a life practising grace and honour. The test was to do this within grief and in the face of humiliation and fear, against the backdrop of a decade's violence. This became a value we can emotionally recognise. We have never done it ourselves. Even intellectually, we can process the ingredients of our view of the act into an emotion. Let us now translate it back into an intellectual cognition.

But, first, a shorter, more contemporary story about child soldiers. We see these too on television. In a way it is a relief from the pictures of their brothers and sisters starving. They are being victimised but, at least, in that terrible hierarchy of victimhood, they are not wizened little corpses who are still, piteously, just alive, eyeing the sky for the UN food drop that now, if it comes, if it ever comes, will come too late.

As well as television, scholars have sat among them and analysed why they die. It is a scholarship of morbidity and may be accused of morbid voyeurism, but at least it was done face to face.[16]

Not too many interviews with the child soldiers. As if they had no story of their own to tell. Not even a single PhD thesis on the child army of Museveni who swept down from the Mountains of the Moon to take Uganda. Their parents had been killed by tyrannous regimes. The orphans regrouped in the mountains. The banana trees become scarcer. A few goat herds higher up. Snow now, and there, on the equator, the ruins of an antique colonial ski lift. Tracks from the columns of elephants who, without Hannibal, crossed the mountains into Zaire to escape the war. Who makes the child soldiers fight? The terrible officers of Museveni? Yes, but what makes the children let the officers make them fight? Are they, as children, without any subjectivity at all? For the body of his son, an old man, long ago, did something amazing. The children practise on an assault course. They dodge in and out of the pylons of the ski lift. They remember fathers and mothers. And each bullet in their AK 47s is already named.

We shift location, it is just a few years earlier. We are still almost contemporary to ourselves. The white settlers are holding out in Rhodesia. The rebels are massing on the Mozambican frontier. Nyasha told me this story after the war. On the University of Zambia campus, wearing a backless sundress, the healing scar of a bullet emerging still decorated her lower back like an abstract tattoo, a sort of butterfly. 'You know, we were 14, we knew history was upon us. To have our own tomorrow we too had to fight to seize it. You think youthful subjectivity is choosing which music to hear? One day, the whole class, without a word or a plan, at the same moment stood up at their desks. We just walked out and walked to the border, and took up arms.'

Is it with the comfort of critical theory that we, the television switched off, claim to emancipate the world, never standing up from our armchairs?

And, although there are no books on the Ugandan war, there are endless studies of the one in Rhodesia. What do they say for those in IR?

They say that peasants went to war with what we would call fantasy in their hearts. The gods were calling them out to fight. The land was saying, 'fight'. Magic was urging on the struggle.[17] As with Mao and the Red Army, peasant recruitment was via a syncretic mixture of simple Marxisms and appeals to the idea of justice, and the sacralisation of that idea of justice.

And when the new guerrilla soldiers began dying, for the technology and firepower of the Rhodesian army were immense, and the students who became guerrillas, in particular, were used as cannon-fodder while their officers learnt tactics, grief – pure and simple – became the undertow of the tide of rebellion.

What I have called the 'Finnish School of IR', led by Osmo Apunen, has tried to deal with sacrality and grief. His PhD student, Billy Makamuri, wrote elegantly of the components of syncretic belief and the interpretation of sacrality. He expressed Apunen's belief in both Pierce's and Gadamer's hermeneutics as a source of understanding.[18] However, there is a problem here. If we live in a society that by its medical technology can delay grief, by its entertainment can trivialise grief, and by its politics can exploit grief and turn the death of Diana into an institution, what is the grief of others in war and starvation to us? What is Hecuba to us?, asked the quintessential Lacanian prince Hamlet, overfull with cognitions and the deconstruction of despairs. What if we, in the academy, having no point of contact with grief, sought to understand the world that grieves by theorising grief? In the autobiography he completed days before his death, Feyerabend wrote:

> Having found a theory, the proud inventor often thinks he or she has found a shortcut to nature, society, human existence. A few words, a few formulas – and the secret is revealed. But try to apply the words or the formulas to some concrete event such as the sorrow following the loss of a friend, and the theoretician either will say that these are subjective particulars, not 'reality,' or will use ad hoc hypotheses, or will resort to so many shortcuts, approximations, and additional assumptions that we are no longer dealing with the theory itself but with a complex system of more concrete ideas.[19]

He continues that this also happens in physics. Why, then, attempt to recompose the recognition of an emotion, if indeed we might recognise it in the first place, into an intellectual cognition? It is to rescue the project of IR, bound into exactly the traps outlined, of course cheekily, by Feyerabend – leaving aside the question as to whether the project is worth rescuing in the first place.

The shaken nature of the world

If we were to apply a loose philosophical meaning of realism – that which may be taken or proven as demonstrably real – then we proceed *behind* the realism of IR, in which the 'real' world of states and interests was taken as given; it was the world as it seemed to have been found. Ever since, IR scholars, borrowing badly-translated Continental thought, have sought to deconstruct this 'real', but not to demonstrate or reconstruct an alternative realism. Recently, Patomäki has sought to develop a 'critical realism',[20] and constructivists have sought the methodologies that might, in a sophisticated way, help them negotiate the world as it is found.[21] Nothing, at least, is vulgar any more. The refinement of methodology, however, again sidesteps that original demonstration of reality. The world, as found, as *we* find it anyway, may not be what it seems. Even hermeneutically, we may interrogate or conduct dialogue with a chimera. How do we demonstrate reality in IR, and how, methodologically, might we do it with as few short cuts, approximations and assumptions as possible?

Inoguchi with others wrote that, from the point of view of the Vietnamese, realism might not be constructed with a notion of power centred, as it was in the 1960s, around nuclear weapons. Rather, from their experience, it would be centred around people's war.[22] The Eritreans, at close of the twentieth century, seem to have taken such a view very literally indeed. The prescient observation of Inoguchi, however, is partial. From the first Vietnamese novel to be published in the West about the war, we find a resignation before the war, a nostalgia for an event before it came, a pre-grief to enable the grief to come when, later, it would need to come, a sorrow.[23] The sorrow was utilitarian, constructed beforehand, the living co-attribute to fate and death. We might loosely call it something 'cultural', but that is not only general but bland – a categorisation, a pigeonhole. The thing about the sorrow of war was that it was very beautiful. The veteran's memory makes it abstract, and misses war like a lover misses love in an abstracted memory of it all, every specific moment of death or heartbreak safely merged into a mist. This comes to everybody *afterwards* but, in this case, it came both *before* and after. The real world to come is prefigured and, afterwards, refigured; and reality, that problematic basis to realism, is subjectivised, precomposed and recomposed. Is this to infuse the politics of the world with poetics? We shall now transpose some of this mistiness to IR's realism.

But first, what is being, basically, said here? That what is real is contingent upon realities. That realities are both political and poetic, have methods to deal with both foreboding and consequence and, thus, there can be no static or 'found' condition in realism. That subjectivity is not located in an event, but the psychological means of dealing with an event, before and after it occurs; and that, for IR's realism, what is missing in its applied, predictive mission is the ability to discern the prefiguring of experience.

What allows us to discern various prefigurings must lie, first, if within the bounds of realism and its concern with states, in an investigation of the syncretic foundations of state. A typology is given below. The problematique here, of course, is precisely that which has always haunted IR and was most elegantly articulated (then sidestepped) by Waltz.[24] How does the analysis or proposition of a subjective individual make the transition to the analysis or proposition of subjectivities on the part of states? There is no easy way to deal with this. An ingenious sidestep is to say that the first can be treated as a metaphor of the latter. More ponderously, we could repeat the well-worn dependencies of state upon nation, of nation upon culture, and of culture (if somewhat manufactured) upon people who can subscribe to it, or of culture (if more or less 'historical') upon people who can transpose it to a sense of the future. This sliding scale has been around since the French Revolution and is, of course, precisely the problematique within the so-called Cosmopolitan and Communitarian debate – the linkage between moral individual and either a moral universe or a moral society. The misgiving over an easy glide from one to the other is fully accepted here. We can only hope there will be days of reckoning far away from academic thought as democracy captures more states and the will, and beliefs, of peoples may be seen as congruent with those now said to be the beliefs of their states.

A typology of states

1. The world where historical motifs are generalised, if not reified, to underpin authoritarian regimes: countries like Mobutu's Zaire.[25]
2. The world where historical and philosophical 'stories' are generalised if not recreated, to underpin regimes that are to an extent authoritarian but, simultaneously, beneficent: countries like Kaunda's Zambia.[26]
3. The world of chauvinisms, accurate to an extent in themselves, but adapted to direct modern government and its policies: countries like Mao's China[27] or Lee's Singapore.[28]

4. The world of text-based normativities – which may be given inter-pretation on literal and exegetic grounds: various Islamic coun-tries.[29]
5. The world which is text-based but given interpretation on a sectarian, even minor sectarian, basis: countries like Libya with its almost com-prehensively unremarked Sanusi inheritance.[30]
6. The world which is text-based but given opportunistic interpretation for a clan or family purpose: countries like Saddam's Iraq.[31]
7. The world of successful revolution which has lost its text, perhaps in action and struggle transcended it, and has engendered its own pecu-liar idealism: countries like Eritrea.[32]
8. The world of successful revolution which long ago transcended or distorted its text and adopted an idealism that exercises an expun-ging cruelty towards the reality it encounters: Cambodia under the Khmer Rouge.[33]
9. That future volatile world of revolution in which texts collide and the syncretic belief systems, lately compounded to resist oppression, overthrow it and enter an international relations gormless before it: countries like a future Mexico under the Zapatistas.

With all of this, how can sense be made of a certain debate within the high social sciences of the end of the twentieth century? If, as Habermas and Giddens, a little differently, argue, the project of modernity is not dead; or if, as Baudrillard argues, the world has decomposed into its own postmodernity; or if large parts of the world, alternating children with-out food and children with guns, are premodern; where does that leave the types of state, above, who want to be partly or contingently modern, and who seek to establish for themselves the nature of those contingen-cies? The easy notion that, by intercourse with the modern world, they are inevitably socialised within it,[34] disregards the resistances to easy and complete socialisation. This is not, of course, to deny *some* socialisa-tion, but to affirm the one found fact we might easily accept in IR: there is not enough socialisation to avoid turbulence and conflict. Socialisa-tion has not conquered subjectivity. Nor, however, has subjectivity stepped outside all socialisation. Mullahs both wished for a World Cup football victory over the USA and could not control the advent of foot-ball as a liberalising device within Iran itself. A new term might here be useful and I wish to draw upon the work of a philosopher who, unlike many adopted (and adapted) into the IR canon, actually struggled and was persecuted for his work and beliefs. Jan Patocka was one of the three first spokespeople for Charter 77 in Czechoslovakia (Václav Havel and

Jiri Háyek were the others), and his philosophy grew out of his embattled life. He spoke of the world as 'shaken'.[35]

Christopher Logue's is, by far, the best poetic recasting of the story of Achilles and Hector.

> And when the armies met, they paused,
> And then they swayed, and then they moved
> Much like a forest making its way through a forest.[36]

How like Patocka's description of two armies locked in combat and seeming to merge

> Into a single body – it is a curious comparison. Only he will under-stand it who affirms both himself and the enemy, who lives both in the whole and in the parts. Such a one may then picture to himself a God allowing these colourful threads to slip through his fingers – with a smile on his face.[37]

Only Priam and Odysseus refuse any god this smiling luxury and divine birthright. Because, after all, why do men, women, children fight and die? Kill? It is for something believed so strongly there is no other choice. It is a belief or principle at its *best*. It may be for the image of a father or mother slain by somebody on the other side. Each has a personal vision and *version* of truth and justice. In this way, two great armies, two antagonist amorphous collections of roughly coinciding versions of truth, merge bloodily into one. The world is shaking. It is a shaken collection of high-value conflicts. No Achilles is less wrong than any Hector. But there is a sense of chivalry and compassion. Courtesies are exchanged alongside atrocities on the battlefield. And, after battle, Achilles *always* returns the body of Hector to Priam. Or rather, if there is a normative vision of the world, he does.

Patocka uses a Heraclitean word play. *Xunos* is commonality, impli-citly universal. But Heraclitus also uses, in this same sense, the word *polemos* (war) or *eris* (strife). Unity, in short, comes out of discord.

> *Polemos* is ... at the same time both that which engenders the city, and also the original insight which renders possible philosophy. *Polemos* is not the devastating passion of a savage invader, but that which creates unity. The unity which it founds runs deeper than any ephemeral sympathy or coalition of interests; adversaries encounter

one another in the shake-up of all received wisdom, and thereby create a new mode of human existence – perhaps the only one which, in the storm-tossed condition of the world, offers hope: the unity of the shaken, who are nevertheless fearless in the face of danger.[38]

For Patocka, this is a rising above the nihilism implicit in the Nietzschean tradition. To be truer to Zoroaster than Nietzsche, it is to say the world emerges from fire. According to Patocka's English commentator:

> Heraclitean wisdom . . . is accordingly a matter of the individual rising up above his or her own particular standpoint *within* the forcefield of these conflicts, to contemplate, and to affirm, the process as a whole; thereby helping to create a species of solidarity consciously grounded on the principle of 'unity in discord': a culture of mutual respect between those willing, if need be, to take significant risks, each for their personal vision of the truth, as these visions jostle and collide, both with one another and with the more thoughtless prejudices of the world.[39]

In this Trojan war of our own era, modernity surely lives on, but there is no longer a *project* of modernity. It is an ingredient among the shaken – perhaps the gin diluted by tonic, perhaps only the olive, an almost gratuitous aesthetic in the dry martini – but the project is to rise above mere modernity, mere anything, while dying for it anyway, and understanding why others, for other things, die. On the shield of Achilles, no one was redeemed until Achilles himself died. The solidarity of killers who are also victims is the solidarity of the shaken.

If it is in conflict that subjectivities recognise other subjectivities, this is a very different realism for IR. May this be slightly reworked to provide a foundation for a normative vision of IR? Below, I attempt this in a preliminary and outline way. It still owes to Patocka, and to Greece, but expresses some views very firmly my own.

It's a human right if you'll die for it

Just as IR cannot resolve its leap from individual to the state, and thereby contains a problematique between individual morality and the cosmic or civil structure of morality, so also philosophy as a discipline has long held a debate as to the parameters of private and public morality.[40] Bernard Williams's famous little piece on the public nature of the Greek sense of shame comes to mind.[41] In that conjunction that once encompassed Ernest Gellner, there remain still social anthropologists who are also philosophers. Peristiany and Pitt-Rivers were concerned with honour and shame and the strategies and transactions these values entailed. More recently, just before Peristiany's death, they published a collection to do with honour and grace.[42] Here shame and honour are antagonist values, and one pursues a public strategy to avoid one and claim the other. If they are, in a sense, dyadic in the public world, I believe a similar dyad can be constructed in the personal world, except that here the relationship is far more dialectical (and perhaps confused) than the usually starker public manifestations of shame and honour. Here I speak of grief and love, those qualities that animated Priam, even though he had to act shamefully to accomplish something honourable.

1. If we were to speak of honour, grace, self-sacrifice, grief and love, simultaneously Orphic and oriental values, Nietzschean and rightly Zoroastrian, these may be at least heuristic values by which, *both in public and private*, we might live our lives.
2. If we were then to speak of a historical process, which gives exactly a historical dimension to those values, we should be speaking of a process of their *sacralisation*.[43]
3. The contemporaneous process both of history and secured value combine into a pre-politics, that is, the moral space that makes at least a compassionate politics possible.
4. The recognition of a plurality of such moral spaces, with their different histories and sacralisations, is that interlude or moral recognition, *in which we make moral space for such plurality*, that is the precondition for an ethics in the way in which Levinas spoke.[44]
5. However, being thus ethical is stormy business. At least it is hard. The solidarity for all moral spaces is precisely that which is most susceptible to being shaken.
6. The key to being able to recognise moral space, whether hard or not, is to perceive those values for which people will sacrifice themselves, and if not themselves, then, like Priam at that moment at the feet and hand of Achilles, their honour.
7. Each such moment of sacrifice is the bedrock to value. Each is a moment of subjectivity in that it is the subject who dies or shames his or herself. The shared value is animated by a series of essential ontological acts of self-dissolution.

8. A free epistemology, therefore – or, at least, a free solidarity of epistemologies – allows and centralises such ontology. If there is emancipatory work in IR, it is towards this.
9. This overcomes the limiting work proposed by Chris Brown, when he
argued that, if we cannot agree on universal rights, we can locate
universal wrongs and at least avoid those.[45] Instead, we locate the
moments and values of sacrifice, the honour and grace involved, and
the love and grief they contain. These become the components that
make possible, not a universalism, but a solidarity, even if it is a
solidarity of the shaken. It is also a solidarity of subjectivities. What
is made possible is an investigation into the preconditioning recognitions for a hermeneutics of subjectivities. Compounded, shaken, not
stirred (at least not stirred with one methodology), will be the next
century's realism.

Hecuba on the beach

What is Hecuba to us? After the fall of Troy, the Trojan women are
gathered together on the beach. Troy burns in the background. Their
husbands are dead. They are about to be transported as a form of booty
to Greece. Helen is among them. Hecuba has just seen her husband,
Priam, killed. They are the merely looted. Any possibility of subjectivity
has also died. The lines given them by the Greek dramatist, Euripides,
express exactly this sense of loss. Two and a half thousand years later,
Shakespeare has Hamlet call Hecuba to mind when his will to act is
frozen by anxieties. He also cannot express his subjectivity.

On the beach, Hecuba looks balefully at the great wooden horse. It is
beautiful, just as Achilles, out of his armour, so her husband told her,
was beautiful. The architect of the horse, Odysseus, is setting out for his
home in Ithaca. Three thousand years later, there will be one of the
world's greatest universities in a town named after Ithaca. This is the
conceit of learning: it will recover knowledge from the gods. More
daring than Prometheus, learning will facilitate the greatest subjectivity,
the greatest freedom.

Odysseus does not yet know he will take ten years to reach Ithaca. He
probably went round Cyprus and Crete a few times, was possibly in
Samothrace (wasn't, years later, St Paul also shipwrecked there?), probably did a quick tour of the Cyclades, before passing under the mainland
of Greece to arrive at Ithaca on its western side. A small island. And
he achieved subjectivity along the way. But failed to recognise the
subjectivity of others. He fled the love of Calypso. Somewhat more

chivalrously, he acknowledged the unstated but implicit love of Nausicaa, the princess who rescued him from shipwreck, but left her with only his polite words.

Yet he achieved the subjectivity Horkheimer and Adorno celebrated. Let not our adoption/adaptation of Horkheimer and Adorno take this at face value; or assume our own historicised subjectivity has a face value that is universal.

Here, in Robert Fagles's elegantly colloquial new translation, is Odysseus at the table of Nausicaa's father.

> I'm nothing like the immortal gods who rule the skies,
> either in build or breeding. I'm just a mortal man.
> Whom do you know most saddled down with sorrow?
> They are the ones I'd equal, grief for grief.
> And I could tell a tale of still more hardship,
> all I've suffered, thanks to the gods' will.
> But despite my misery, let me finish dinner.
> The belly's a shameless dog, there's nothing worse.
> Always insisting, pressing, it never lets us forget –
> destroyed as I am, my heart racked with sadness,
> sick with anguish, still it keeps demanding,
> 'Eat, drink!' It blots out the memory
> of my pain, commanding, 'Fill me up!'[46]

Such a subjectivity. Is this the end-of-century, end-of-millennium IR, an academic profession able at last to gorge itself on respectability, facilitated by the wines and sweetmeats of its philosophical importations?

The subjectivity of Priam was more austere, able to subject itself to others willingly. He redeemed Troy. Forever after, the imagination of sympathy has lain with the Trojans; the man, Hector, attempting to stand before the demi-god, Achilles. And with Priam. Flames on the horizon, as her slave-ship pulled away from Troy, Hecuba constructed for her future exile's memory the image of Priam.

Notes

1. See, for example, Hidemi Suganami, 'Stories of War Origins: A Narrative Theory of the Causes of War', *Review of International Studies*, vol. 23, no. 4, 1997.
2. See especially 'One-Way Street', in Walter Benjamin, *Selected Writings, Vol. 1, 1913–1926* (Cambridge, Mass.: Belknap Press, 1996).
3. Still a defining note on Bataille's work: Susan Sontag, *Styles of Radical Will* (New York: Farrar Straus & Giroux, 1969), ch. 2.

4. Against all odds (and bets), the female *littérateur* Dominique Aury in 1994 confessed to having been Pauline Réage, author of the 'pornographic' *Histoire d'O* (in English: *Story of O* (London: Olympia, 1970)), in which the antithesis of power, completely self-conscious submission, provided at least an ironic commentary on power and, perhaps, established a possibility of powerful self-realisation through powerlessness.

5. Michael J. Shapiro, *Violent Cartographies: Mapping Cultures of War* (Minneapolis: University of Minnesota Press, 1997).

6. Cited in Krishan Kumar, *Utopia and Anti-Utopia in Modern Times* (Oxford: Basil Blackwell, 1987), p. 32.

7. Susan Sontag, *Styles of Radical Will*, p. 81.

8. Georges Bataille, *On Nietzsche* (New York: Paragon Press, 1992).

9. Georges Bataille, *The Tears of Eros* (San Francisco: City Lights, 1989).

10. Walter Benjamin, 'Truth and Truths/Knowledge and Elements of Knowledge', in *Selected Writings*, pp. 278–9.

11. James Der Derian, 'The Value of Security: Hobbes, Marx, Nietzsche and Baudrillard', in David Campbell and Michael Dillon (eds), *The Political Subject of Violence* (Manchester: Manchester University Press, 1993), pp. 99–104.

12. Michael J. Shapiro, 'Textualizing Global Politics', in James Der Derian and Michael J. Shapiro (eds), *International/Intertextual Relations* (Lexington, Md: Lexington Books, 1989), p. 11.

13. James Der Derian, 'Virtual Security: Technical Oversight, Stimulated Foresight and Political Blindspots in the Infosphere', in Stephen Chan and Jarrod Wiener (eds), *Twentieth Century International History* (London: I. B. Tauris, 1998).

14. Max Horkheimer and Theodor Adorno, *Dialectic of Enlightenment* (New York: Herder & Herder, 1972). David Held gives a summary in *Introduction to Critical Theory* (Cambridge: Polity Press, 1990) in his Appendix; and Stephen Chan offers a revisionist account in 'Listing (and Lisping) Typologies Towards an Unchained Medley: Against the Gentrification of Discourse in I.R.', in Vivienne Jabri and Eleonore O'Gorman (eds), *Women, Culture and International Relations* (Boulder, colo: Lynne Rienner, 1999).

15. A reference to Baudrillard's comment of course. Jean Baudrillard, 'The Reality Gulf', *The Guardian*, 11 January 1991.

16. See Alexander de Waal, *Famine that Kills* (Oxford: Clarendon Press, 1989).

17. For example, Terrence Ranger, *Peasant Consciousness and Guerrilla War in Zimbabwe* (London: James Currey, 1985); and David Lan, *Guns and Rain: Guerrillas and Spirit Mediums in Zimbabwe* (London: James Currey, 1985).

18. Billy Mukamuri, *Making Sense of Social Forestry* (Tampere: Acta Universitatis Tamperensis Vol. 438, 1995), esp. ch. 2.

19. Paul Feyerabend, *Killing Time* (Chicago, Ill.: University of Chicago Press, 1995), pp. 93–4.

20. Heikki Patomäki, 'How to Tell Better Stories of World Politics', *European Journal of International Relations*, vol. 2, no. 1, 1996.

21. For example, John Ruggie, *Constructing the World Polity* (London: Routledge, 1998).

22. Hayward R. Alker Jr, Thomas J. Biersteker and Takashi Inoguchi, 'From Imperial Power Balancing to People's War', in James Der Derian and Michael Shapiro (eds), *International/Intertextual Relations*.

23. Bao Ninh, *The Sorrow of War* (London: Secker & Warburg, 1994).
24. Kenneth N. Waltz, *Man, the State and War* (New York: Columbia University Press, 1954).
25. The literature on Mobutu is very unsatisfactory. For a typology in which he loosely fits, see Robert H. Jackson and Carl G. Rosberg, *Personal Rule in Black Africa: Prince, Autocrat, Prophet, Tyrant* (Berkeley: University of California Press, 1982).
26. For a deconstruction of Kuanda's 'historically-derived' philosophy, see Stephen Chan, *Kaunda and Southern Africa: Image and Reality in Foreign Policy* (London: I. B. Tauris, 1992), esp. ch. 5.
27. W. J. F. Jenner, *The Tyranny of History* (London: Allen Lane, 1992).
28. A very balanced view is Christopher Tremewan's 'Singapore in the Asian Human Rights Debate', in Rorden Wilkinson (ed.), *Culture, Ethnicity and Human Rights* (Auckland: New Zealand Institute of International Affairs, 1997).
29. An excellent but largely unremarked collection is the special *Islam and Politics* issue of *Third World Quarterly*, vol. 10, no. 2, 1988. For a brief though illuminating note on Islamic scriptural method, see Hugh Goddard, *Christians and Muslims* (Richmond: Curzon Press, 1995), pp. 40–4. For an example of this in action, see Faruq Sherif, *A Guide to the Contents of the Qur'an* (London: Ithaca Press, 1985).
30. For a most sensitive treatment, see John Davis, *Libyan Politics: Tribe and Revolution – An Account of the Zuwaya and their Government* (London: I. B. Tauris, 1987), esp. chs 4 and 5.
31. As with Mobutu, the literature on Saddam is deeply unsatisfactory, but see the fascinating if incidental thoughts in Daniel Brumberg, 'Islamic Fundamentalism, Democracy, and the Gulf War', in James Piscatori (ed.), *Islamic Fundamentalisms and the Gulf Crisis* (Chicago, Ill: American Academy of Arts and Sciences, 1991), especially his remark on p. 195, in which Saddam is depicted as a 'situational fundamentalist'.
32. Whether the idealism lasts or not, it was the decisive final animation of the struggle. For its views of women, see Amrit Wilson, *The Challenge Road* (London: Earthscan, 1991); for the account of a (literal) fellow traveller, see Thomas Keneally, *Towards Asmara* (London: Hodder & Stoughton, 1989).
33. This is going to be the hard one and I'm sorry I have no satisfactory literature to cite. The interesting anecdote, however, of international naivety on this issue is that, one day in the middle of the UN electoral preparations for Cambodia, the UN director of elections rang Professor A. J. R. Groom and myself at Kent to ask if we might chair a Burtonian problem-solving workshop with the Khmer Rouge. There are limits to the enigma of possibility.
34. For example, Ronald Dore, 'Unity and Diversity in Contemporary World Culture', in Hedley Bull and Adam Watson (eds), *The Expansion of International Society* (Oxford: Clarendon Press, 1985).
35. Not yet in English. The French edition used here is *Essais hérétiques sur la philosophie de l'historie* (Lagrasse: Editions Verdier, 1981). I have trusted Andrew Shanks's translations more than mine, from his *Civil Society, Civil Religion* (Oxford: Blackwell, 1995), see esp. ch. 3.
36. Christopher Logue, *The Husbands* (London: Faber & Faber, 1994), p. 51.
37. Shanks, *Civil Society, Civil Religion*, p. 125.

38. Ibid., p. 123.
39. Ibid.
40. For example, Stuart Hampshire, T. M. Scanlon, Bernard Williams, Thomas Nagel and Ronald Dworkin, *Public and Private Morality* (Cambridge: Cambridge University Press, 1978).
41. Bernard Williams, *Shame and Necessity* (Berkeley: University of California Press, 1993).
42. J. G. Peristiany and Julian Pitt-Rivers (eds), *Honor and Grace in Anthropology* (Cambridge: Cambridge University Press, 1992).
43. Here, I draw above all on the work of Micea Eliade, *The Myth of the Eternal Return* (London: Arkana, 1989); and *The Sacred and the Profane* (Orlando, Fla: Harcourt Brace Jovanovich, 1959).
44. For an actually lucid condensation of his own views, see Levinas's interview by Richard Kearney, *States of Mind* (Manchester: Manchester Press, 1995), pp. 179–99.
45. Chris Brown 'Universal Human Rights: A Critique', *The International Journal of Human Rights*, vol. 1, no. 2, 1994, pp. 41–65.
46. Homer, *The Odyssey*, tr. Robert Fagles (New York: Viking, 1996), p. 186.

6
Stories of Priam and Job, the Slaughter of Their Families, and Twenty Theses on the Suggestiveness of Good for the Person of IR*

Stephen Chan

There is in IR a concern for truth, justice and good. These, however, tend to be argued as abstract principles or, at least, as abstracted ones, removed from any 'real' world. IR has become, as many sought, a tributary of a German ideal philosophy. There is not, however, much expressed concern for the true *person*, the good man or woman. If, however, we imagined a rigorous praxis, so that the person of IR became also a person of truth, of justice and of good, what sort of person would that be? In what way may such a person be imagined? This essay offers suggestive answers to these questions.

Prologue

In what way do we imagine? In the etymological sense, an act of imagining is what you do with images. The interpretation of an image, its rendering into language, must first take place in metaphor. In literature, and in the epistemologies of several languages, metaphor can act as a logical device: it advances argument. Even in texts used, tentatively or with interpretation, in IR, this use of metaphor is well-established. Nietzsche and Walter Benjamin, for example, cannot be disassociated from metaphor. Even Hegel's spirit of history was essentially metaphorical. Here, the metaphor does not even need to be interpreted. History is a given. In one of his prefaces, Hegel explained it merely by constructing another metaphor, saying the spirit of history was something like God's Holy Spirit; and this Holy Spirit is, of course, also both a metaphor and a given. It has enough substance, at least, for philosophies and theologies to be constructed upon it.

I do not propose, in this essay, to be so ambitious. However, what I wish to do is to use metaphor, not as a reality or a given in itself, but as an analogy to what we might recognise as a given. This will be an argument by analogies.

Second, I wish to be aphoristic – as were Nietzsche and a string of both European and oriental authors – but, in keeping with the requisite cautions of academia, I shall be presenting *elaborated* aphorisms. This is as well, since an aphorism succeeds by means of condensing a metaphor. The metaphor must be unpacked before it can be given interpretation.

Third, I wish to tell stories, and these stories, with their metaphorical structures, are populated by those who are analogous to the sorts of persons we, in IR, should seek to be, or not to be. Again, to refer to Nietzsche, the Greeks succeeded in *being* Greeks, without uncertainties, overcoming the problem of authority, by a self-view that rested on nothing *but their own actions*. The stories of Greek tragedy helped the realisation of this self-view and the recognition of action.

Finally, the stories in this essay are both occidental and oriental – those occidental being derived from the Greek – and the intention is to widen the reference points of IR beyond the eighteenth-century West.

A note on metaphor

Valerie Shepherd, citing Lakoff and Johnson, suggests that we accept metaphors as truth-bearing if they satisfy one or both of two conditions. The first is that they contain an 'imaginative rationality', and we are able to accept that rationality on the basis of our ontological experience of that rationality's relationship to truth. The second is that the truth in the metaphor is substantiated, or decreed, by persons or institutions in authority.[1]

I would like to add a third condition. Here, I am mindful of Altaf Gauhar's translations from the Qur'an, which he accomplished before founding the journal *Third World Quarterly* in London. He begins his translations with the enigmatic note: 'These translations were undertaken at a time when the only book to which I had access was the Qur'an.'[2] He does not tell his readers that this was because he was a political prisoner in Pakistan – having been incarcerated for taking a stand on behalf of justice; trying to live as a just man. Translating the

Qur'an, however, is a problematic exercise: what is to be taken literally, and what metaphorically, has long divided Islam, and Gauhar laments the ascendancy of the literalists.

> Translating the Qur'an is not a literary exercise.
> If it is impossible to translate the lyrical word
> how can one convey the meaning of the divine
> word in mundane language? In translating the
> verses of the Quran one strains to understand
> them. The quality of the translation is determined
> by the quality of one's understanding – and
> understanding is reflected in one's conduct. The
> Qur'an can be translated into action alone.[3]

In short, one's lived actions become metaphors of God's words. We are mystically imagined by God into righteousness. So, the third condition is a spiritual one. We behave because we cannot imagine Any Other Imagination of another behaviour. If by a circular route, Gauhar came to recognise the metaphors in the Qur'an, they were true because they were linked with his being true.

Twenty theses

1. Friendship is a truer base for communitarianism than citizenship

To make such a statement, one is moving away from Hegel's civil society as a model for IR. Mervyn Frost's global civil society cannot exist without the assumption of a global citizen, settled within global norms.[4] There has been a discernible move, in IR, to widen its conceptual referents, and recent work on Levinas and Buber is a case in point.[5] A philo-theological discourse is augmenting a simply philosophical one. In this chapter, the point of departure was indeed anticipated by Levinas, but articulated by his student, Derrida, in his meditation on Levinas's death.[6] The *Politics of Friendship* echoes many of Levinas's concerns to do with the public and private spheres, and how an ethical life might encompass the two. Derrida's book, however, is indeed a meditation – as opposed to a formal argument – and its informality is manifest in its rush towards a sudden conclusion, where friendship becomes the condition for human happiness and progress. In the different informal way, outlined above, this chapter seeks to present an argument for IR, and also echoes Levinas's concerns, but seeks to do so apart from Levinas proper, and apart from Derrida.

For a start, there is Jan Patocka's dramatic image of two armies clashing and, in the mêlée, they seem to merge 'into a single body'.[7] Patocka argues that they merge in more than the physical sense. Each soldier fights, and is prepared to die, for significant values. Few people kill for no reason at all. In a value-tossed world, where enemies clash, this is the 'solidarity of the shaken'. This would seem a barren environment for friendship, but it is in exactly such a place within the wars of international relations that a start should be made in searching for it; and it is here that various chivalries towards one's opponents may be noted. In the last significant battle of the twenty-year war of liberation waged by the Maoris in New Zealand, in the late 1800s, a doomed Maori garrison is grimly holding out against European shelling. Without artillery of their own and, by now, also out of ammunition, the male and female warriors are firing wooden bullets, carved off their splintered pallisades. Their war of liberation is doomed – as are they. However, they find the time, courage and – they would have said – good manners, to crawl out into no man's land to rescue wounded European soldiers, and return them to their own ranks. And they decline honourable terms of surrender. Rather die.

The New Zealand political philosopher, Andrew Sharp, musing on the Maori–European political divide a hundred years later, suggested that, in the face of competing and irreconcilable systems and concepts of justice, what the world may at least hope for is the commonality of kindness.[8] What I am proposing, in this chapter, is a kindness in the face of death – and this is true friendship; and that the person of friendship embodies a higher normative value for IR than the myth of the global citizen.

2. Friendship is a moral stand made in public, but celebrates a private good

Here, I wish to use the metaphor of the *junzi*, the Confucian gentleman, and his use of *ren* – which, literally, means 'two persons'. Although *ren* is commonly translated as 'compassion', this is because no single word in English conveys the discourse embedded in *ren*. The 'two persons' are the public person and the private one. The public one follows a set of ethical rules and, indeed, does so within a complex *li*, ritualised propriety. The private person, however, *must* also be ethical out of inalienable inner necessity or moral imperative. *Li* is an outer manifestation of an inner compulsion (thus casting light on the preoccupation with what might otherwise seem like ritual alone).[9] However, the inner or private worth is *defined* by *li*, although *li*, by itself, cannot articulate the self beyond such definition. It is the defined *and* intrinsic self who has no choice but to be moral.

Thus, the *junzi*, although demonstrably righteous, honest and knowledgeable, still has a core value not fully manifest in the rituals; and the core value is special in that there is no Confucian hierarchy to enforce it or mandate it. There is no question of authority. It is the inner human benevolence that is here more important than any divine sanction or command. It is a private good, celebrated as well as defined within the practice of public morality and its rituals.[10]

3. Happiness is the accomplishment of a public virtue

Now, if all this seems rather, or even too subtle, there is a Western equivalent. Here, we are speaking of Aristotle and, in particular, Aristotle's writings on the pursuit of happiness. It is now well-accepted that, by 'happiness', Aristotle is speaking of a rewarding life of living and doing well, of doing good. It is, in fact, a *rewarded* life, since happiness is a 'complete good' that is 'self-sufficient', in the sense that the fulfilled life is able to stand apart from those unfulfilled and 'incontinent'.[11]

Robert Arrington compares this position to his own account of Kant: 'For Kant, it is strict adherence to duty for duty's sake that should constitute the motive for all human action.'[12] It is as if, by a combination of this Kant and an agreed Aristotle, we have a sort of Western Confucianism. The difference between Kant and Aristotle, however, according to Arrington, is that Aristotle has no emphasis on duty.[13] It is a *natural* human good to seek happiness, and this is best done by cultivated people within the public sphere of politics. It is in this arena that good may be done to others and the doer be regarded as good and become happy. The natural and the public merge. Moreover, beyond politics, the most virtuous and best way to live, leading to most goodness or happiness, is to live a life of study and thought.[14]

However, to live, either in politics or theory, one must have a modicum of 'external goods' – like good birth, even good looks – 'since we cannot or cannot easily, do fine actions if we lack the resources'.[15] Since one cannot give oneself over, entirely, to the pursuit of resources – since wealth is not a good in itself and cannot in itself promote happiness – it would seem happiness – and good – are contingent on provisioning. Aristotle overcomes the problem of authority: he suggests a natural order of things; but, even in the absence of an external hierarchy, he accepts the need for 'external goods'. A good or happy life is, thus, doubly rewarded – both as a completed good in its own right, and as a provisioned life in the first instant. There is implied here a sort of duty: to use provision in the natural urge to good, so there is a double contingency to happiness. It is, first, contingent on 'external goods' and, second, contingent on the 'external goods' being used in a good way. Good is thus not only natural but, as will be seen later, necessitous. The Greeks, again as noted later, had a view of external necessity but, next, we begin to turn to the intimacy of a necessitous self and its relationship to the public good.

4.   But happiness is only completed in the private heart

There is a Biblical completion of all this, in the admonitions that one may sin in one's heart without ever sinning in public; and that one should love one's neighbours as oneself. The equality given to public and private here, and the equality to self and other, is terrifying. Not only that, but this equality is replicated in major religions: everyone is One Heart in branches of Buddhism; Krishna reminds Arjuna that he is able to see into the hearts of all people. The terror of this is precisely the animation of twentieth-century psychoanalysis, including the pioneering work of Freud (and not just Freud, since his Vienna has been seen as a striking series of public architectures to a brooding interiority of spirit).[16]

Here, given the end of the twentieth century, we might look briefly at the interpreter of Freud, Lacan (bearing in mind that a satisfactory rendition of Lacan is almost as problematic as a satisfactory rendition of Freud). The Lacan I present here is terrifying by the simplicity, or fundamentalist nature, of his analysis. It is not so much that we are all caught up in *la faute* – what, in English, we have translated as 'transgression' – but that our lives are subsumed within the implication of a perpetual transgression – locked somewhere between, according to Lacan's seminar, Freud's early sense of transgression that pointed towards the necessary death of the father, and his own dying sense to do with the ultimate transgression, the instinct towards death itself, and death's dialectic with life.[17]

In the state between, we have a desire for good, and a desirous need for *jouissance* (Marseilles slang for the joy of 'jerking off'), and Lacan's seminar locates a meditation on *jouissance* (of course) with the work of de Sade. It is the condition of *jouissance* – in which transgression is joyful and foreboding, with or *without* God's authority or condemnation, but has nevertheless its own peculiar ethic, but which is, in its combination or combined perversity, terrifying – that renders Aristotle's living and doing good impossible. For a start, we cannot live in good if we are within *jouissance*. Nor can we seek to avoid *jouissance*, since we cannot otherwise complete our own dialectic. However, since we know just how terrifying is our own *jouissance*, how can we do good to any other, since that person will have his or her own terrifying *jouissance*? Lacan says, notwithstanding the death of God and the vanished law, that there is this 'unfathomable aggressivity' which repels us all from crossing a frontier into good.[18] Thus, the admonition to love one's neighbour as oneself is, for Lacan, the most terrifying of admonitions.

In this sense, no one can be happy, since no one can be 'good'. If one *could* be good, however, and thus happy, this happiness needs to be completed in the good heart. Lacan says that, since this is impossible, there is a non-Aristotelian process, and this is through a law of evil, rather than a law of good (although he later ends his seminar by ridiculing such categories[19]). Under this law of evil, my doing good allows me to have a shelter from my own *jouissance*. 'I shelter behind my fellow man.'[20] My perversity is not present in my act. However, this act is not the full truth of *why* I act. In this rendition, therefore, the wish to do good must be at the expense of being true to oneself.

5.   Happiness thus comes from the accomplishment of good and the inner recognition of good, and this is a greater condition than 'truth'

Now one should, of course, recognise when Lacan is striving for effect and performance. A subtle 'jerking off' enters his own seminar. Nevertheless, he establishes that any notion of an intrinsic goodness within a self and any impulse towards the doing of good must be contingent (since we cannot be continent). Since, however, there is a dialectic even between death and life, and since even writers like de Beauvoir wrote at length on the ethical impulse still found within de Sade, what we might say, at this stage, is merely that we have lost any temptation towards one-dimensionality when we address the good person from the perspectives of Confucius and Aristotle. This is not to say there cannot or should not be goodness within good people. One suspects Lacan was setting up an entire apparatus simply to have a go at Kant, whose universal mirror of humanity and the justice of the cosmos would be at least speckled if his humanity was seen as not possibly being as harmonious as the (distantly) observed cosmos.[21] Good is problematic, therefore, but may be contingently accomplished. One of those contingencies is to do with a sacrifice of truthfulness – except that, contra Lacan, we might say that, in fact, borrowing Patocka, we all recognise each other's contingencies anyway, and the solidarity of the shaken may be, at least, a solidarity of the *jouissants*. For now, the doing of good, in a more mundane expression of it, has been seen as more important than the preoccupation with truth in IR.

For instance, Beverley Neufeld has commented on IR's search for truth and asked why in the terms of the *good* of gender equality, IR has not spent as much time in seeking to do good.[22] Her question has some resonance: in South Africa, a Truth and Reconciliation Commission was established *after* the good of constitutional equality was accomplished. Speaking Truth to Power,[23] at best, can only be a *part* of political struggle and, sometimes, as in Patocka's image of two armies merging in the clash, truths can be in conflict and impossible to disentangle. Moreover, even a just cause must sometimes be dressed in lies. It was good, for instance, to overcome Naziism – but the Allied cause proceeded under its own propaganda. As for Naziism, it had – in a sense – a greater arsenal of eighteenth-century truth at its command and interpretation than the Allies ever did: in thought, Nietzsche; in letters, Goethe; in music, Wagner. In a continuing sense, the postwar project of critical theory has not been to establish truth as such, but, first, to reclaim it, second, to cleanse it and, third, to restate it in a way that is beyond the interpretation of tyrants. Nietzsche is *ours*, once again. However, the critical project has halted, even in Europe, not a single determined atrocity, gulag, or ethnic cleansing; and, speaking of gulags, the Soviets had, they claimed, the most scientific truth on their side and, for years, the best of the Western intellectuals believed them.

In this sense, at least, the public atrocities and private turmoils of the twentieth century form their own symmetry. Good is contingent both publicly and privately. To be happy within good is rare, so that happiness sits within a struggle towards the accomplishment of good. Each particle of accomplished good is, in de Beauvoir's words, spoken within the universe of contingency, an accomplished 'interim mercy' and, thus, a momentary redemption, a glimpse of the happy condition.

6.   Both public shame and intimate necessity propel one to accomplish good

The contingency of good, however, is not only due to the internality of our *jouissance*, but the externalisation of the *jouissance* of others: of wickedness being expressed, even if that expression is inadvertent, a manifestation in fact of unhappiness. It is here that Bernard Williams's mediation on the relationship between public and private morality in ancient Greece is the beginning of an illumination of how good was actually conceived in Athens – the injunctions of Aristotle notwith-standing – and how it was practised.

Before considering Williams, however, a brief digression might be in order to view how the ancient ideas of good survived in Greek commu-nities until the twentieth century. Writing of the *sophron*, the commu-nity mediator, whose wisdom and sense of fairness are regarded as a community resource, Peristiany wrote that his role in contemporary Greek Cypriot villages 'consists in steering a course that allows an actor to gain his ends without losing his reputation'.[24] The idea of reputation is that it is also, if not a community resource, on display within the community.

Although I have written earlier on the story of Achilles,[25] I have commented less on his opponent, Hector. Achilles was able to defy Agamemnon and, consequently, jeopardise the entire Greek project and the lives of thousands of warriors. The recognition, by these very warriors, of his sense of personal honour was enough to save him, or his reputation, from shame. Homer constructed him, however, as a force of nature. Achilles counterpoints every other human actor in the *Iliad*. Hector, by contrast, is princely but human. 'Born to a princely status he is a model of courageous and honourable virtue, qualities he has learned by responding to *aidos*, a sense of shame, which makes him sensitive to the judgement of others ... [unlike Achilles] Hector attempts to tread his way with care, balancing the claims of different obligations and responsibilities', all of which are publicly recognised and evalu-ated.[26]

How one might tread, very publicly, as a politician must, was the subject of one of Bernard Williams's famous short essays where he, almost playfully, suggests that (given a number of propositions which he depicts as widely held by the public) 'the hope of finding politicians of honourable character, except in minor roles and in favourable cir-cumstances [is] very slim'.[27] Here a direct link between private character and public behaviour is drawn, and one offers judgement on the other. In ancient Greece, however, a different means of judgement was in play; and this was where public morality was precisely political.

The title of Williams's book, *Shame and Necessity*, is also precise. In the Greek world, it was a necessity to avoid shame. To draw a generalised Chinese parallel, Greeks also could not lose face. How might this, how-ever, be of importance to IR? It is important because of its normative alternative to critical, especially Kantian, notions of what is moral and just. As in world cultures that did not experience a European Enlight-enment, so also in key instances of European culture itself before the

Enlightenment. 'There must be options for ethical thought and experience that the Kantian construction conceals. There are; in exploring them it is helpful to bear in mind how Kantian associations constantly work to short-circuit our understanding of them.'[28] It is here that Williams interposes the concept of shame. There is no need here to launch a disquisition on shame. The Greek word for it, *aidos*, means, literally, covering up and, by derivation, covering up one's private parts. The *Iliad*, and the other Greek classics are redolent of heroic actions and immense virtues undertaken to avoid shame. Hector did not *have* to face Achilles: the city gates had safely shut in Achilles' face. He went out to face him, and to face death, to avoid any possibility of shame.

Now all of this is capable of an immense reductionism: that the Greeks had only a normative schema rendered possible in public; that, if it was pre-Kantian, it could at least be viewed as proto-communitarian; that Aristotle, far from being original, merely glossed elegantly an extant condition; that the rules of the Greek public sphere allowed the concealment of private *jouissance*; and that Lacan was right, and Williams offers the same exception[29] – only Antigone advanced to the precursor of an Enlightenment that then took 2200 years to catch up with her.

I wish to take up only one of these: that *aidos* did not function alone. Rather, to function at all, particularly in persons of heroism and virtue, it needed to be counterpointed with *nemesis*, meaning here an indignation if one is exposed, particularly if unfairly, to shame. Williams quotes Redfield, who came up with the contemporary discursive vocabulary, that *aidos* and *nemesis* are 'a reflexive pair'.[30] This indignation can be applied to an indignation on one's own behalf, or *on behalf of others*. There is, to borrow freely from Lacan's vocabulary, the heroic concern for the public consequences of someone else's *jouissance*; a concern, in short, for someone else's intimacy. The bedrock to this is not only a reflexivity in Redfield's terms, but an understanding of how one's own public behaviour is counterpointed with a knowledge of one's own intimate thoughts and one's own intimate knowledge of oneself and one's faults, contradictions, and imaginations of transgressions; and those of others. This is instantly psychoanalytical material, and a communitarian bond of immense complexity. No instant depictions of civil society here, and no easy deconstruction of the reflexive underlay to Aristotle's *polis*.

7.   Tragedy is, therefore, the failure of necessity, and the hegemony only of shame

The Greek tragedies, particularly of Euripides, can be read also as reflexive expressionism; although this expressionism is established within the ritualised conventions of Greek theatre. On the one hand, there is literalness: a divide between heaven and earth, the gods and humanity; simultaneously, heaven and earth are the components of an enactment of reflexivity, in which (to continue Lacan's terms) the privacy of human *jouissance* is precisely relocated to heaven. The gods represent that public space where an otherwise private caprice could be displayed and probed. Thus, the gods may be malicious as well as capricious – these not being one-dimensional qualities, but deliberate counterpoints to the struggle towards a public community of morals on earth. To this extent, there is an element of idealism in the Greek tragedies: that the intimate impulse to good, the necessity to display an Aristotelian good in public, is natural. It is a supervening or alternative nature that, tragically, may enforce a hegemony of shame.

This may be read, as I suggested, within a dramatic expressionism, and the play and the theatre separate into characters the private dialogue of reflexivity – but also give reflexivity its *emotional* as well as intellectual dimension. The impossibility of any public exploration of *jouissance*, except through the rituals and conventions of theatre, meant of course rich material for followers-after Freud, such as Lacan, and his interrogation of Antigone is a case in point.

In a sense, Lacan's complaint against Kant, cited earlier, may be satisfied by the depiction of the Greek tragic universe as a more fully embodied Kantianism, that is, there are, at the proposed apex of the moral universe, natural laws of *both* good and bad, or right and wrong, and not just a *Recht* alone. In Greek tragedy, itself an interrogation and interpretation of myth, this dualism is given personification (and, of course, this has to be, otherwise there are no characters in a play), but the personification, therefore, goes *beyond* even reflexivity, and enters action: it establishes an interactive universe with multiple dialogues and multiples of consequences. The true nature of causality, therefore, a persistent enquiry of Greek philosophy, is reflected also in Greek theatre.

What Lacan is *implying* in his seminar, when his Freudianism becomes a journey towards a death that, nevertheless, only appears as a death precisely because it is in a dialectical relationship with life, is that *jouissance* is also a participant in a dialectical relationship with that which is not *jouissance*. In short, even *jouissance* has embedded within it the condition of an ethics beyond itself.

This does, however, tend to render Lacan's reading of *Antigone* rather flat.[31] He makes of her almost a prototypical Kantian, observing the natural laws of the universe against the mere strictures of the state. I wish to publish, at a later point, a full analysis of Lacan's *Antigone*, and argue that she deconstructs the entire rest of his seminar. For, although she reproaches heaven for its caprice, there is no caprice within her own self. She is merely pure. Nothing necessitous within her impels her towards tragedy.

8.   It is necessitous to have good fortune in order to satisfy the intimacy of necesity itself

The problem of seeking, at this time, to analyse Greek mythology and tragedy – perhaps even philosophy – is to take its literal dimension far too seriously. Its *metaphorical* use, as I have tried to suggest, of heaven and earth in both a dialogic and physically interacting relationship, is to personify, give body to, and then interrogate a certain intimate interiority.

The celebrated work of Martha Nussbaum can also be reread with metaphorical relocation in mind. Although she somewhat cogently announces the difficulties of Aristotle's declared intention to offer a philosophy within *phainomena*[32] (a phenomenology, in this case what appears as real, that is, an ethics within realism), she then seeks to save *phainomena* by including within it common *belief* as to what was real.[33]

I think here she identifies, but does not always carry through, a significant flaw in Aristotle's work – and this should be a warning to all within IR now condensing proto-Aristotelianisms for their own work – that 'what is commonly believed to be real' readily becomes 'what is commonly *wished* should be real'; and she instances Aristotle's own thinking on the question of luck or fortune. Here, the word for luck is *eudaimonia*, which Nussabaum does not translate as such,[34] thus acknowledging a debate as to its meaning. For it is this same word that Aristotle uses for 'happiness', or at least what most contemporary scholars have translated as 'happiness' (although Nussbaum does, in an extensive footnote, almost wryly note that, given our Kantian heritage, it was perhaps inevitable we should take *eudaimonia* to mean, or at least imply, a happy *state*, whereas its place within Aristotle is more to do with a happy *activity*, and this is, as discussed above, an activity towards the good).[35]

Having said that, a *literal* translation of *eudaimonia* is, of course, 'good demon', and this is where the idea of luck is found. Within one word, both happiness and luckiness are at least implicit, as is a dialectical relationship between the two.

There was also a huge contemporary debate on these two components of the one word. Aristotle is against luck. However, as Nussbaum succinctly indicates, Aristotle proposes no *argument*, in any scientific sense, against luck. It is, he suggests, simply socially better not to believe in luck.[36] His *wish* is against luck. His wish is for the good, whether as an activity or an achieved state of happiness.

It is here that Nussbaum launches her celebrated disquisition on Priam, the righteous, good-bearing father of Hector – Hector who was himself as humanly good as humanly possible – and Priam, the good ruler of the *polis* of Troy, Troy the good city. Yet Troy was ransacked by the Greeks, Hector was slain by Achilles, and Priam was himself killed (after seeing his sons killed), and his wife dragged off to slavery. He was good but, obviously, not happy. Although Aristotle's response is to argue that the good person will *usually* be happy; here, as Nussbaum points out, in a *slight* concession to luck, Aristotle steps outside the view held by Plato and Kant that good, in its essential sense at least, can never be harmed.[37]

I do not wish, here, to enter this debate beyond a certain point. It *is* entered, however, to reinforce my earlier point about the need for 'external goods', in Aristotle's (again) own admission, to facilitate the good life itself. To those external goods, such as money, good birth and good looks, might now be added good luck: the good demon who might stand against the bad demons, the caprices and maliciousnesses of heaven.

Or, if we are to reread Nussbaum herself, substituting metaphor for the Greek world as we literally find it in Greek writing and Greek tragedy, we might say that the unpredictability of heavenly luck could be better rerepresented as the unpredictability of a *jouissance* – whether dramatically relocated to heaven or located within our most intimate selves. After all, whether afflicted by heaven literally, or afflicted by the abolition of his *wish* that good would lead to happiness, Priam is going to have extended moments of interiority in which he will question himself pure and simple (or impure and rather complex). Whether his internal dialectic will then mirror that of heaven, or heaven's is a mirror of his, his interiority is here inescapable.

It is a wonder, in fact, that the aspiration to goodness, under these conditions, did not drive Priam mad. Given the possibilities of madness, it is a wonder Lacan did not accord pride of place, in his seminar, to the Socratic exchanges of the *Phaedrus*, rather than to *Antigone*. Socrates here almost seems to celebrate madness, including madness as a precondition of philosophising. All this takes place of course, as in all Plato's renditions of Socrates, within a dialogue. This is a weird dialogue. Much of it is about the beauty of speech and how to make speech more beautiful. It is within this debate that, simultaneously, madness can be the source of the highest goods (including happiness), and can be the foundation of Plato's work in the *Republic*, counterposing intellectual purity, and elevating it over madness and the appetites. There is a real debate here and, because it is explicit (though not well-known), it illuminates the possibility of implicit debate within Aristotle. Of interest to this essay also is Nussbaum's comment:

> But what is most striking, Plato here shows himself (as elsewhere in the later dialogues) ready to judge questions about the best life from the point of view of the interests, needs and limits of the being in question. The best life of a human being is found not by abstracting from the peculiarities of our complex nature, but by exploring that nature and the way of life that it constitutes. Unlike the life of the ascending person of the *Symposium*, this best human life is unstable, always prey to conflict.[38]

Not only is it prey to conflict, it is prey to immense conditionalities as to what we can take to be true. Thus, Socrates makes an early speech in the *Phaedrus*, citing the poem of Stesichorus on the saga of Helen and Troy.

> This story isn't true.
> You did not embark on the well-benched ships.
> You did not come to the citadel of Troy.[39]

Every truth can be recentred. Instability and conflict may be augmented by recentation and repudiation, by repentances. A life may be like a painting that has been painted over (literally called a 'repentance' by the Renaissance painters who did it); a story retold. It is necessitous to have good fortune to be sane or mad enough to recognise the intimacy of ourselves and the intimacy of necessity. The capriciousness of heaven, or the capriciousness of our interior selves, may be such that the enactment of good is so contingent that our normative value can be a rhetoric standing aloof from a struggle and have no realisable meaning.

'This story isn't true.' We have explored the Greeks enough for now. It is time to branch out to other, and Other, stories.

9. The struggle to be happy and satisfied is against the capriciousness of the universe

Around 400–300 BC, an amazing 'global' intellectual development occurred. It was the height of Greek thought, of course. It was also (although this must be said approximately) the time when Hinduism began its own 'classical' phase, turning away from an emphasis on a universal cosmology to how one should live in *this* world, and with what concomitant duties and styles of living. It was when the Buddhist religion, moving away from its Hindu origins began claiming appreciable converts, and when the Emperor Asoka wrote the first proto-Buddhist ethics and edicts for public behaviour, stressing that *dhamma* resides in what one *does*, rather than what one believes. In Judaic history, it was the time of the final consolidations of the scriptural canon that became officialised in the new Jewish state, founded after Babylonian exile. Within this movement, the last revisions and additions were made to the Book of Job. This is the only *theological* book of the Old Testament, in that it contians the only debate on the personal nature and personal consequences of moral belief. The final additions, of course, suggest the official triumph of God; and its poetic language can only be rivalled by the Song of Solomon. However, before the scribes officialised and aestheticised the virtue of God, the nature of human virtue was given a thorough examination both by a 'bad' demon and by God's own latitude and complicity in the torture of Job.

Now, despite its beauty, this is not Greek tragedy, and lacks the dimension of metaphor. It was meant to be read literally. God really does help and even cause the torture of Job. Moreover, it is not really even successful literature. Job is tortured as the result of a heavenly bet, and this caprice does not sit nicely upon the creator of Leviathan, to which His virtue has transmuted Him by the end of the book. Indeed, the book's beginning, with Satan visiting God's court in heaven, bears all the hallmarks of an unrefined folkloric origin. What is compelling is the old central portion of the book, deliberately written as a theological dialogue. In this, Job *cannot* be happy, even though he was internationally famed for his goodness. God has pointed His finger against him, and that is that. His family is destroyed, his possessions removed, his health dissolved. He does not even have the respite of Camus's Sisyphus, who could meditate upon happiness while walking down the hill to his eternal rock. Job's friends attempt to convince him that he should simply curse God and allow himself to die, rather than cling so piteously to life.

But Job will not curse God. His stubbornness is heroic, and the later interpolation of the character of Elihu is precisely to castigate the heroism of his refusal. For the scribes would have picked up that, in refusing to curse the heaven that had afflicted him, Job was demonstrating something heaven did not: Job had a will to propriety, to goodness, that was so necessitous within himself – and he had nothing left outside himself – that not even a pact between Satan and God could destroy it. The heroism was all he had by way of his *own terms* for living and, since he could *do* no more, *being* good by refusing to speak ill.

But he could never, under such circumstances, be happy. Later, God restores to him his lost chattels, and gives him a new wife and family (as if they had also been chattels, amenable simply to being replaced). Was Job made happy again? What if he remembered, lovingly, those he had lost? I should think Job was never truly happy again. In the Book of Job, a distinction is made between good and happiness, and it is good – by itself, not leading to any other condition – that is a first-order value.

10. The true test of friendship is to struggle for others who are shamed

God's test of Job was to shame him in the face of the world. Job's friends, who came first to comfort him, proved to be not full friends. He had been so shamed, it was better to die. Even more, however, they were not full friends because they denied him his last right to his own sense of necessity: his necessity, in the face of heaven's caprice, still to be good. To struggle on behalf of those who might be lost to luck, to heaven's favour, is the true sign of friendship. Who, however, in the Book of Job, could remonstrate with God? There is no equivalent of Prometheus in that book.

11. Friendship that stands in the face of shame is the ultimate public good, and should be seen as a hyper-good

Prometheus showed friendship to the *world* of humanity. Am I returning, at last, to the propositions at the essay's beginning? Yes; and returning also momentarily (although there will be one last return) to Nussbaum. In one of her long, explanatory footnotes, she discourses on *philia*, or 'friendship';[40] only *philia* goes well beyond friendship. It requires that two people should be linked by 'affectionate feeling', in Nussbaum's language, but she also hints that there is something far more significantly intimate here, and it is this which is to be explored in the remainder of the essay. In the meantime, the *widest possible* significant intimacy, hinted by Nussbaum, is illustrated by the story of Prometheus, stealing fire from the gods for the sake of the warmth and progress of humanity, and being, even more than Job, condemned to a living death (or the repeated pains of dying) for his transgression. He did this for a *philia* which, even under daily torture for millennia, he never recanted.

There is a parallel here in the Sanskrit word, *Vishwabandhuttwa*, which means 'the entire world' and 'friendship'. Here, friendship is not containable: it is both an intimacy and a public good. Taking the long way round, it is what Levinas would have wanted Derrida to understand. To use the words of the Hegelian philosopher, Charles Taylor, this friendship can be classified a 'hyper-good', that single good chosen above all others,[41] because simply, at the end of the day, as I shall seek to explain, it encompasses and contextualises all others.

12.   In this sense, friendship becomes brotherhood and sisterhood

Here, clearly, we are going beyond the 'friendship' of Aristotle where, in some readings, a good man might merely sustain, perhaps further cultivate, his goodness by having 'good' friends.[42] The friends merely reinforce one's own self. Here, we are talking of a greater affective relationship – one beyond the implicit self-love of Aristotle. This is what the (largely forgotten) Nobel Prize winner, Pearl Buck, meant in renaming the Chinese classic *The Water Margin*. She entitled her translation *All Men are Brothers*, and at a stroke, depicted the communitarian *and* proto-socialist essence of a novel from the feudal thirteenth century. Made famous in the West by the Japanese television series in the 1970s, and simultaneously deconstructed by Bert Kwouk's (Kato in *The Pink Panther*) amazingly racially stereotyped voice-over, the ethic of the original novel was never captured. That novel, however, recounted how 108 heroes, from generals and judges to buffoons and fishermen, found themselves hounded into an equality based on friendship for one another, and a great enough friendship for the world at large to risk death for the amelioration of poverty and the war against corruption. They were the true civil society the state had bypassed. There is nothing in our communitarianism that was not prefigured in *The Water Margin*, 500 years before Hegel. (Trust the West to discover this classic only as a parody of itself.)

The Water Margin has largely a male cast. This did not prevent the Chinese Red Army, recruited by a deliberate recourse to *The Water Margin*, from having, for only the second time in Chinese history, fighting cadres of women soldiers. Nor did its soteriological message, that heaven may endorse those who struggle for the freedom of their own good, fail to be incorporated into the syncretic Christianity of the nineteenth-century Tai Ping uprising, which preached the equality of women, and which fielded an army of one million men and women in its last doomed campaign against the Manchu dynasty. Having said that, the formal and deliberate enunciation of women, as a category in their own right, awaited the advent of feminism, although, even here, within IR, the enunciation of an *international* womanhood, encompassing third world women on *their* own terms of sisterhood as well as ours, did not really happen, however imperfectly, until Christine Sylvester;[43] and Sylvester would not have entered her conclusions with conviction without having first conducted fieldwork among Zimbabwean women.[44] A world cannot be declared from a library. For IR, the world can only be appropriated by a deliberate embrace of friendship.

13.   Although the category of friendship may only be artificially differentiated from brother and sisterhood

Both Pearl Buck and Christine Sylvester are using the terms 'brother' and 'sister' metaphorically. They imply a friendship stronger than the English word 'friendship' can satisfactorily express. They imply a *philia*, a friendship with an affectivity. Sylvester implies an *emotional* bond with her 'sisters', as well as the intellectual recognition that, because of years of subjugation, a solidarity exists. She is in *philia* with those whom she is also in solidarity. She is, as far as the English can express it, without the almost English concomitant of *eros*, in love with her sisters.

This is the *agape* love of the New Testament and of Christology. Differentiated from *eros*, it is, in effect, a love of humanity. This is commonly enough understood, though not always commonly remembered. Because of it, however, the different translations of a particular passage, to do with *agape*, are compelling: 'Greater love hath no man but that he lay down his life for his brother'; 'Greater love has no man but that he die in the place of his fellow man'; 'Greater love does not exist but that a person dies in the place of their friend'.

14.   All recipients of good become friends

The implication of this *mélange* of meanings, all related to one original word, speaks of not only the limitations of accomplishing a universal normative theory only in English, but also, more importantly in the context of this essay, the universality of friendship. To die in the place of one's friends, or at least alongside them: there is the stirring story of E. P. Thompson's brother, a young major, parachuted in to help the Yugoslav partisans, and captured only a short time later. 'By what right do you, an Englishman, come here to make war against us?', asked his prosecutor. He replied in terms of both justice and friendship and, according to his brother, his dignity and lightness galvanised his condemned 'friends' in the final hours before they were all shot. Yet he had only known them that very day. What is suggested here is that the impulse should be to do good *generally*; and all those to whom good is done automatically become brothers, sisters, friends. Friendship is also, thus, an activity, not a state.

15.   And one becomes responsible for the good of others and that others, in turn, do good

What, then, is the consequence of Beverley Neufeld's question, if applied not to IR in general, but to the praxological person of IR? It is an obligation to be 'friendly' to the world, and to make 'friends' by doing good. The condition of 'doing' good, however, is not necessarily an easy action. Her and my complaint has, at its base, merely the proposition that IR's concern with telling the 'truth' is not enough. I should take a step further and say that speaking the truth from a library is even more an insufficiency. All this risk-free truth-speaking is, in any case, a calumny against the original critical project of Horkheimer and Adorno, with its immediate memory of Auschwitz. It was meant to be against the risk of this happening again; but it was not the truth-bearing theorists who were most noticeable in the fight against a genealogy of gulags and killing fields where, alone among contemporary genealogies, nothing seems, essentially, to change.

In any case, the English separation of 'truth' and 'good' might seem to some, in riskier parts of the world, a convenient safety mechanism: the good is avoided for the sake of truth. In Farsi, however, the term *Hagh* can mean 'good', or 'truth', or 'God', simultaneously or interchangeably. Each resonates with the others, so that the good is also truthful and holy.

The stringency of the Mahayanan Buddhist *Bodhisattva* is an example rarely contemplated by IR. (A *Bodhisattva* is usually translated as a 'saint', but this is imperfect. This person is rather the *imperfect* embodiment of exemplary goodness: imperfect precisely because embodied; humans are not that good at goodness so that, in the following passage, we have both stringency and a barely concealed lamentation at all the suffering that exemplary goodness implies.)

A Bodhisattva resolves: I take upon myself the burden of all suffering. I am resolved to do so, I will endure it. I do not turn or run away, do not tremble, am not terrified, nor afraid, do not turn back or despond.

And why? At all costs I must bear the burdens of all beings, in that I do not follow my own inclinations. I have made the vow to save all beings. All beings I must set free. The whole world of living beings I must rescue, from the terrors of birth, of old age, of sickness, of death and rebirth, of all kinds of moral offence, of all states of woe, of the whole cycle of birth-and-death, of the jungle of false views, of the loss of wholesome dharmas, of the concomitants of ignorance – from all these terrors I must rescue all beings ... I walk so that the kingdom of unsurpassed cognition is built up for all beings. My endeavours do not merely aim at my own deliverance. For with the help of the boat of the thought of all-knowledge, I must rescue all these beings from the stream of Samsara, which is so difficult to cross, I must pull them back from the great precipice, I must free them from all calamities, I must ferry them across the stream of Samsara. I myself must grapple with the whole mass of suffering of all beings. To the limit of my endurance I will experience in all the states of woe, found in any world system, all the abodes of suffering. And I must not cheat all beings out of my store of merit. I am resolved to abide in each single state of woe for numberless aeons; and so I will help all beings to freedom, in all the states of woe that may be found in any world system whatsoever.

And why? Because it is surely better that I alone should be in pain than that all these beings should fall into the states of woe. There I must give myself away as a pawn through which the whole world is redeemed from the terrors of the hells, of animal birth, of the world of Yama, and with this my own body I must experience, for the sake of all beings, the whole mass of all painful feelings. And on behalf of all beings I give surety for all beings, and in doing so I speak truthfully, am trustworthy, and do not go back on my word. I must not abandon all beings.

(From the Vajradhvaja Sutra)

We note here that the truth is only a part of the *Bodhisattva's* goodness (*and* endurance), and this is manifestly a good accomplished *in* the world, not from a library of the 'international'; and the juxtaposition of doing good and the endurance the doing of good requires constitute a reflexivity, itself constituted the hard way.

16.   This establishes a relationship of intimacy beyond one heart

If, however, we cannot be 'saints', are we at least able to take risks? Achilles knew he risked death if he went to avenge Patroclus; not death at the hands of Hector – he would walk through Hector – but death in a cosmic schema of balances where, in a brief window, he could choose between fates. His was not a simple revenge tale, therefore, but a commentary on necessity. He *had* to fight Hector and, as Nussbaum eloquently argues, the Greek understood both his original withdrawal from the war and his return. Although they understood this in terms of honour – the insult of Agammenon which caused Achilles to withdraw was not as great as the insult of Hector who killed Patroclus – the public dishonour at the hands of Agammenon was not as great as his intensely private sorrow, *married to* the public death of his finest friend.

However, although Nussbaum does not say this explicitly, there is something deeper here. Dressed in the armour of Achilles, Patroclus alarms the entire Trojan army. Only the intervention of Apollo saves the city and Hector, in administering a *coup de grâce* to Patroclus, laughingly reminds him that he is not, after all, Achilles. But then Hector steals the armour to wear himself, and *he* is definitely not Achilles. So that, when Achilles and Hector face each other at last, they are *both* wearing Achilles' armour. This is the apex of Hector's private insult to Achilles, for, in wearing this armour, and being mistaken for Achilles, Patroclus symbolised the *philia* between the two men. Not only is there no *philia* between Hector and Achilles, Hector has slain the object of *philia* and, by donning the armour himself, desecrated *philia*. This connection is explained at once by Nussbaum's commentary on a part of Aristotle not usually uncovered in IR.

> The strong emotions of respect and esteem that are part of the Aristotelian *philia* generate a desire to be more *like* the other person. This principle works powerfully in society, where shared public models of excellence play an important motivating role. But Aristotle clearly believes that the intimacy of personal *philia*, with its strong feelings and its history of shared living, has a motivational power through emulation that could not be replaced by a more general social modelling. His point is similar to one made by Phaedrus in the *Symposium*'s first speech, when he argued that an army composed of lovers would excel all others in excellence because of the strength and aspiration that can be generated by the presence of a uniquely loved person.[45]

The horror of war, therefore, returning to Jan Patocka's image of the clash and merger of two rival armies, is that arrays of *philia* could be massed on both sides; and, beyond the point of taking Aristotle literally, perhaps share a larger *philia* somewhere between personal love and public citizenship. For what do we fight and die, if not for only personal reasons alone? There is a *philia* which is, as I have suggested, for a greater good and which is Promethean.

17.   And is an eternal value

In so far as mythodologies and legends locate *philia* between partners, only in the Sumerian epic of Gilgamesh and Enkidu does *philia* overcome death. Although this epic is best represented in contemporary arts by Martinu's rather unjustly neglected 1958 opera, *The Epic of Gilgamesh*, in which Martinu seeks to portray the king as Everyman – seeking not just eternal life but a love that can defeat death – it is well to remember that this is humanity's oldest written story. Gilamesh defeats all mortal opponents and repudiates all the bargains of lesser conditions of love, and finds that only the strongest love defeats death itself.

By way of contrast, but also affirmation, civilisations that did not spread from Mesopotamia to the Mediterranean, such as the oriental civilisations, would maintain the illusion of death itself, but the eternality of a love that long ago transcended personification.

18.   Its eternality also dissolves the divisions in normative debate

Although IR theorists have often, though casually, wondered aloud about the trinitarian history of their discipline – three paradigms, three great debates – its fundamental methodological device (and limitation) resides precisely in its attempt to pose, then oppose dualisms, whether expressed as dialectical, dyadic, or dialogical. The ease with which this is slipped into (at least partially) explains the reductionisms of normative debate into set-piece Kantian and Hegelian formulas. The entire aim of a multicultural or even pluri-gendered critical theory would be to overcome a ready recourse to dualisms and polarities.

Speaking of the pluri-gendered, I should, in passing, comment on the determination of *categories*, into which the world must fit, and the determination of gender, in the first instant, by physical characteristics and sexual practice. Were Achilles and Patroclus, Gilgamesh and Enkidu lovers then? Well, yes they were, but not with the sense of homosexuality and the sexual orientations and consummation of love. You see how it works. The first question is, 'are they male or female?' The second question is, 'are they homosexual or heterosexual?' Nothing against either, and nothing to do with the current debate as to whether ancient Greek homosexuality allowed orgasm within or without penetration.[46] After all, in Hindu tantric sex this question could not arise. Curiously, in nineteenth-century Europe, in some literary and artistic circles, a condition and practice of 'urning' was entered – there is a giant canvas in the Musée d'Orsay, by Jean Delville, celebrating this among the students of Plato – in which what we might now take for an unconsummated compromise, a frustration, was depicted as an ideal. It was an effort to establish a deliberate equidistance between the homoeroticism possible in friendship (and implicit, if not explicit, in Greek art) and the physicalities of a realised homosexuality. This equidistance was a realisation in itself, a perpetual tantric state.

   This is by way of a rather cheeky and playful parallel. Does it *have* to be cosmopolitan or communitarian? Although people like Molly Cochran seek to overcome the divide,[47] the question is: should there be a divide in the first place? The effort to become 'more *like* the other person' is both a commentary on individualism and on community, and empathy becomes the precondition to the possibility of theory. I suggest a greater intimacy within IR.

19.   Risking death is the greatest good and the greatest intimacy

Another reiterative recitation of heroism near the essay's end. Not yet. There is finally a comment on Lacan. Although Lacan recognised and worked within Freud's later sense of life being in a dialectic with death, he was, in the end, too bound by Freud to declare an escapee's still reflective observation. Just as Achilles remained, despite his symbolism of *philia*, a force of nature, rather than a person: Auden's great poem on 'The Shield of Achilles' depicts all the terrible scenes that were to come from Achilles' choice of fate. Once he donned the armour and picked up the shield, his fate was sealed. But, in that moment of surveying the armour, in that small delay before assembling it on his body, in that last second before picking up his shield, he could still have changed his mind. Looking at the shield and the prophecy of carnage, Auden seemed to say, should have given him a moment's reflexivity. The heroic life, therefore, must be a reflective life in order to be personal, human, and capable of a *philia* beyond one person.

   What, then, is this risking of life for others, even for strangers, if not something only for saints? It is precisely because we are not saints that it is heroic. The overcoming of *jouissance* is heroic and, if not its overcoming, its placement – even though a core of ourselves – as a second-order value, in the face of a sacrifice based on empathy, friendship, *philia*; and *good* is something that leads the always dying self towards a happy accommodation with itself. Risking death does put life into perspective not otherwise possible: it charges a narrow reflexivity with something quite unable to be expressed only in the logics of writing. It is the self-centredness of *jouissance* that is overcome, but provides an intimate self-knowledge greater than mere *jouissance*. It is worth going on, Lacan concludes, if only to approach a limit, the momentary crossing of which leads to beauty and art. But this can be done through *philia*'s full rendition and this is, finally, human and not art. Death, I should say, feels more often human than artistic, for the person doing it.

20.   Heroism is thus the only emancipatory work

In the postwar years, nothing has been emancipated by critical theory. Its application in any praxis has also not been conspicuously successful. It has infused contemporary discourse, but *only in association* with other discourses, proto-discourses, politics and opportunisms has it been invoked as an actor in the politics of the international. What should IR, in the face of this lack of success, do?

At the end to all this, I declare a return to a form of structuralism; not economic structuralism, but the sort pioneered by Levi-Strauss, where he articulated the crystalline nature of myth's logic, and how it is *this* logic – available *only* in myths – that is the foundation to any studies of the universal. It is, he says, the precise model that articulates the point between whatever a reality is, and our components of thought that seek to understand that reality.[48] In this essay, I have concentrated upon certain Greek myths to suggest how this is possible even for a Western IR, although I have made the point of other cultures having their own myths many times over, and the need for a historical socio-anthropology of IR.

Second, even though this seems contradictory to my first point, I declare an emancipation of Kenneth Waltz's first image: an emphasis on 'man', rather than the state, or the international system[49] (although Waltz's rather antique use of the term 'behavioural sciences' had better be revised in keeping at least with the French psycho-linguists and psychoanalysts). Individuals as components of myth is, in fact, the assumption behind the methodology of Nussbaum and other contemporary classical thinkers.

Third, since the study of the individual involves his and her contradictions and neuroses, I declare the advent of psychoanalysis as the tool that fills the critical void of how the *person*, with his or her personal problematiques, or mere problems, fills the world in IR. Lacan and Derrida will be seen within IR much more than hitherto.

Fourth, since we have now approached the *person* of IR, and we are seeking the *good* person of IR, what is needed within IR's normative contemplations is something almost ritualistically programmatic and practical – not merely ideal and a reification of Enlightenment debate. It should still be born of discourse and reflexivity, but should be more like the work of Hans Kung, ostensibly within theology, but evident in a huge range of discursive and ethical writings and of sympathetic comparative theologies, *and* in alternative political actions to do with the convening of both political and scholarly figures from all parts of the world (Rorty included among others[50]). The question here is, basically, not just what IR *thinks*, but what it must *do*; and, here, the question of a necessitous *good* becomes, at last, unavoidable; a good that stretches notions of citizenship towards the widest friendship and the idea of sacrifice for *philia*.

Fifth, I declare a heroism, at the very least as a metaphor for IR; but heroism is a possible condition of daily action. Those priests who first discoursed on a liberation theology, in discourses every bit as complex as IR's, and then picked up rifles to enter the jungles, defying both their states *and* their church, to do a higher good for a higher truth, are still the finest example of the contemporary genre. And what is the betting that Sub-Commandante Marcos of the Zapatistas was not once an academician – even now unable to resist postmodern puns at his own expense, but resisting an army, now beyond conceits and discourse, launching revolution as a tellable story.[51]

In this essay, I have told stories, advanced theses that can be read or, in being read with the elaborative narrative, can be supported, interrogated, deconstructed, made problematic – but, in the end, they have, hopefully, established a position. Metaphorical narrative can be reflexive within itself. This will be, I hope, the beginning of a new wide-ranging but moral classicism for IR, in which the image of good is paramount, and the search for authorities from one era and one half-continent only is lost. Otherwise, how long before IR becomes ashamed of itself?[52]

Notes

1. Valerie Shepherd, *Literature about Language* (London: Routledge, 1994), pp. 65–7.
2. Altaf Gauhar, *Translations from the Quaran* (London: Islamic Information Services, 1977), p. 1.
3. Ibid., p. v.
4. Mervyn Frost, *Towards a Normative Theory of International Relations* (Cambridge: Cambridge University Press, 1986).
5. For example, Charles Rustin, 'Buber and Levinas: Meliorism vs Humanism in International Political Theory', paper delivered to the ECPR Third Pan-European Standing Group for International Relations, Vienna 1998. See also Rustin's PhD thesis for Hebrew University on Buber and International Society, 1999.

6. Jacques Derrida, *Politics of Friendship* tr. George Collins (London: Verso, 1997).

7. French and German as well as Czech editions of his work exist. See Jan Patocka, *Essais hérétiques sur la philosophie de l'histoire* (Lagrasse: Editions Verdier, 1981). His champion in English is Andrew Shanks, *Civil Society, Civil Religion* (Oxford: Blackwell, 1995), especially in Chapter 3. For his first use in IR, see also Stephen Chan, 'A Story Beyond Telos: Redeeming The Shield of Achilles for a Realism of Rights in IR', *Millennium*, vol. 28, no. 1, 1999, esp. pp. 110–12.

8. Andrew Sharp, *Justice and the Maori* (Auckland: Oxford University Press, 1990).

9. See Mircea Eliade, *A History of Religious Ideas*, Vol. 2 (Chicago, Ill.: University of Chicago Press, 1982), pp. 22–5.

10. Chan Hoiman and Ambrose Y. C. King, 'Religion', in Robert E. Gamer (ed.), *Understanding Contemporary China* (Boulder, Colo: Lynne Rienner, 1999), p. 329.

11. The direct quotes from Aristotle are taken from the translation by Terrence Irwin and Gail Fine: *Aristotle Selections* (Indianapolis: Hackett, 1995). *Nicomachean Ethics*, Book I, Chapter 7; Irwin and Fine, p. 355.

12. Robert L. Arrington, *Western Ethics* (Oxford: Blackwell, 1998), p. 68.

13. Ibid.

14. *Nicomachean Ethics*, Book X, Chapter 7; Irwin and Fine, pp. 440–2.

15. Arrington, *Western Ethics*, p. 71.

16. See Allan Janik and Stephen Toulmin, *Wittgenstein's Vienna* (New York: Touchstone, 1973).

17. Jacques Lacan, *The Ethics of Psychoanalysis 1959–1960: The Seminar of Jacques Lacan*, ed. Jacques-Alain Miller and tr. Dennis Porter (London: Routledge, 1992), p. 2.

18. Ibid., p. 186.

19. Ibid., p. 325.

20. Ibid., p. 190.

21. Ibid., p. 189.

22. Beverley Neufeld, 'Feminism and the Concept of Community in International Relations', in Stephen Chan and Jarrod Wiener (eds), *Twentieth Century International History*, (London: I. B. Tauris, 1999).

23. The term was directly imported to IR by Steve Smith, 'Power and Truth: A Reply to William Wallace', *Review of International Studies*, vol. 23, no. 4, 1997, p. 511.

24. J. G. Peristiany, 'The *Sophron* – a Secular Saint? Wisdom and the Wise in a Cypriot Community', in J. G. Peristiany and Julian Pitt-Rivers (eds), *Honor and Grace in Anthropology* (Cambridge: Cambridge University Press, 1992), p. 122.

25. As have others; Bernard Knox points out, fascinated, that Achilles maintained his sense of personal honour, even in Hades. See his Introduction to Homer, *The Odysey*, tr. Robert Fagles (New York: Viking, 1996), pp. 37–41, esp. pp. 40–1.

26. J. K. Campbell, 'The Greek Hero', in Peristiany and Pitt-Rivers, *Honor and Grace in Anthropology*, p. 131.

27. Stuart Hampshire, T. M. Scanlon, Bernard Williams, Thomas Nagel and Ronald Dworkin, *Public and Private Morality* (Cambridge: Cambridge University Press, 1978), p. 71.
28. Bernard Williams, *Shame and Necessity,* (Berkeley: University of California Press, 1994), p. 77.
29. Ibid.
30. Ibid., p. 80.
31. Lacan, *The Ethics of Psychoanalysis,* see chs XIX–XXI.
32. Martha C. Nussbaum, *The Fragility of Goodness: Luck and Ethics in Greek Tragedy and Philosophy* (Cambridge: Cambridge University Press, 1995), p. 240.
33. Ibid., p. 243.
34. Ibid., see p. 318.
35. Ibid., p. 6.
36. Ibid., p. 320.
37. Ibid., pp. 328–9.
38. Ibid., p. 221.
39. Cited ibid., p. 202.
40. Ibid., p. 328.
41. Charles Taylor, *Philosophical Papers,* Vol. 2 (Cambridge: Cambridge University Press, 1985), pp. 15–57. For an effort to apply this to IR, see Stephen Chan, 'Aspirations and Absent Methodologies in Universalism: Towards a Multicultural Normative Theory', in Jan-Stefan Fritz and Maria Lensu (eds), *Value Pluralism, Normative Theory and International Relations* (London: Macmillan, 1999).
42. Aristotle, *Nicomachean Ethics,* Book IX, Chapter 9; Irwin and Fine, p. 430. Although cf. my text related to my n. 45, following, for a more radical reading of this passage.
43. Christine Sylvester, *Feminist Theory and International Relations in a Postmodern Era* (Cambridge: Cambridge University Press, 1994).
44. Christine Sylvester, *Zimbabwe: The Political Economy of Contradictory Development* (Boulder, Colo: Westview, 1991); and 'Simultaneous Revolutions: The Zimbabwean Case', *Journal of Southern African Studies,* vol. 16, no. 3, 1990.
45. Nussbaum, *The Fragility of Goodness,* p. 363.
46. For a summary of the current debate as to what was and what was not Greek homosexuality, involving the work of the scholars Nikos Vrissimtzis and Kenneth Dover, and the most recent book by Martha Nussbaum, see Ben Rogers, 'Deviance, if you like', *The Guardian,* 26 August 1999.
47. Molly Cochran wrote a small series of articles. For her first word on how cosmopolitanism was at least implicit in a Hegelian framework, see 'The New World Order and International Political Theory', *Paradigms,* vol. 8, no. 1, 1994, esp. p. 120.
48. Claude Levi-Strauss, *Structural Anthropology* (New York: Basic Books, 1963), esp. ch. XI.
49. Kenneth N. Waltz, *Man, the State and War* (New York: Columbia University Press, 1954).
50. See Hans Kung and Helmut Schmidt (eds), *A Global Ethic and Global Responsibilities* (London: SCM Press, 1998). For commentaries on this work, see Stephen Chan, 'Rorty as Shadow Warrior: Hans Kung and a Global Ethic',

Review of International Studies, vol. 25, no. 3, 1999, and Caesar V. Mavratsas, 'Blueprint for a Universal Morality', *Global Dialogue*, vol. 1, no. 1, 1999.

51. See Nicholas Higgins, 'Mexico's Mayan Conflict: The Zapatista Uprising and the Poetics of Cultural Resistance', *Alternatives*, vol. 25, 2000.

52. Some of the thoughts behind this essay were catalysed by my colleague at Nottingham Trent, Chris Farrands, in his graduate school seminar paper, *Touching Friendship Beyond Friendship*. Ranka Primorac questioned me throughout its writing, and she was the recipient of a 58-page letter that first explored these ideas of transgression and *jouissance*.

Part III

The Inclination of Middle Eastern Civilisation

7

Can a Declined Civilisation be Reconstructed? Islamic 'Civilisation' or 'Civilised' Islam?

Mehdi Mozaffari

Introduction and assumptions

The question of the possibility of reconstructing a declined civilisation is important, especially in the current world-time where globalisation, the clash of civilisations and dialogue between civilisations figure high on the world agenda. But there is no clear-cut answer as to whether a recon-struction is possible. Much depends on what we mean by *civilisation*, *decline* and *revival*, and also on our understanding of *reconstruction*. Civ-ilisation is often defined in vague and ambiguous terms: 'The inevitable destiny of a culture',[1] 'The kind of culture found in cities',[2] 'Civilizations are invisible, just as constitutions',[3] and so on. In reality, these kinds of definitions say nothing tangible and workable about civilisations. Fer-nand Braudel provides us with a better one when he defines civilisation as 'both moral and material values'.[4] Immanuel Wallerstein, who is also sceptical about the various definitions of civilisation, makes a distinction between 'historical system' on the one hand and 'civilisation' on the other. In his view civilisation refers 'to a contemporary claim about the past in terms of its use in the present to justify heritage, separateness, rights'.[5] Wallerstein's definition refers only to the cultural dimension of civilisation, leaving aside its material (political, economic and military) component. We know that civilisation is broader than culture and histor-ical systems considered separately; we also know that civilisation is not merely about the claimed heritage of the past. Civilisation may also be a question of present time and the future. Therefore, the inclusion of historical system or material dimension into the cultural body and mem-ory seems indispensable, at least if we are to have a workable concept.

I intend to propose a workable and empirically verifiable concept which arises from the assumption that the great civilisations consist of two inseparable parts. The first part is an explicit world vision which can be a set of cultural systems, an ideology or a religion, most often the latter. The second part is represented by a coherent political, military and economic system usually concretised as an empire or a historical system. I call civilisation 'a junction between a world vision and a historical system'. In other words, when a specific world vision is realised through a historical system, this fusion is called civilisation. Only the historical system is an empirical reality. The world vision alone is an ahistorical, diffuse and elastic concept. When a historical system is realised without being based on a comprehensive world vision, the formation gives rise to tribes, empires, states and other forms of political entites, but not civilisations. Similarly, when a world vision stands without a body, a physical shape, it is merely an ideology, a culture or a religion.

Many civilisations declined and ultimately died without having experienced a renewal. A few survived or lived longer than others because of their skill, their cumulative character, and especially their flexibility and capability to adapt before anything else. No civilisation is eternal, civilisations are forever changing. In a world-time of low-intensity communications, different civilisations can live separately, side by side, conserving their specific identity. In a world-time of high and intensive communications, however, the civilisational differences tend to diminish. If intercivilisational relations are intensified, the capacity to preserve civilisational particularities tends to become strongly diminished, depending upon the degree, intensity and durability of communication. A kind of fusion between different civilisations is theoretically plausible. No civilisation can be the same and be renewed at the same time. They influence each other culturally and devour each other ferociously. Despite the importance of the external clashes and conflicts that civilisations face, the real causes of decline and extinction are generally internal. The decline is a *longue durée* phenomenon which stretches over many successive centuries; yet the adherents of a declined civilisation have difficulties in realising and admitting the decline in time. When the decline is admitted and internalised, it is often too late for renewal. Renewal does not mean reproduction. Renewal means, roughly, the exchange of the old currency for the new one, while there is still time. In a sense, renewal means *sauver les meubles* while the damaged house is still standing. Reconstruction must be distinguished from reproduction. A house damaged by earthquake cannot be reproduced in the same way, in the same place and with the same materials if the owner of the house wants to avoid new damage. The house must be reconstructed, not reproduced. Furthermore, while reproduction evokes a fixed and static mentality – the mentality of prisoners of the past which is nostalgic towards the good memories – reconstruction calls for invention and requires innovation. The former is oriented towards the past, the latter towards the future. Civilisations do not reproduce themselves. They produce other civilisations.

The pivotal question dealt with in this article is: can a declined civilisation reemerge as a new civilisation? This is a crucial and general question which is not necessarily associated with a specific civilisation. At some point in time, all civilisations face questions about their capabilities for survival. This rule is also valid for a dominant and powerful civilisation. In reality, the essence of Samuel Huntington's highly polemical book is more about reflections on how to avoid the decline of Western civilisation than about clashes between civilisations.[6] This article deals with Islamic civilisation. In this connection I will first raise the questions of *decline* and *revival* in general terms. Taking my point of departure in civilisations like the Greek and Roman, the different theories about decline and revival will be discussed, before I deal, later on, with the theories that specifically concern themselves with the decline of Islamic civilisation.

Theoretical considerations: *decline* and *revival*

In the course of history, thinkers from different disciplines such as theology, history, politics, philosophy and sociology have studied the phenomenon of decline. To some authors, the study of decline is of more interest than the study of the law which governs progress.[7] Already in the Book of Genesis and in Mesopotamian creation stories, the fall of man almost coincides with the making of the world.[8] In the classical period, authors like Ibn Khaldun (1332–1406), Machiavelli (1469–1527), Giambattista Vico (1668–1744) and Montesquieu (1689–1755) were among those who studied this phenomenon. Contemporary authors who deal with the study of decay include Spengler, Quigley, Toynbee, Braudel and, more recently, Samuel Huntington. Despite all the brilliant works in this field, however, a coherent and general theory of decline does not really exist. There are assumptions and there are specific analyses of specific civilisations, for example, the decline of the Roman Empire by Montesquieu, or the decline of Islamic – Arabic empires by Ibn Khaldun, or perhaps even the decline of Western civilisation as presented by Spengler and Huntington. If one were to try to conceptualise these authors' approaches to the problem of decline, I think it is possible to identify three different approaches: the biological – cyclical, the conjunctural and the structural. The first one sees civilisations being similar to human biological life: birth, youth, adulthood, old age and finally death. It is almost within the same perspective that, for example, Quigley sees civilisations as moving through seven stages: (1) mixture, (2) gestation, (3) expansion, (4) age of conflict, (5) universal empire, (6) decay and (7) invasion.[9] Seen from a cyclical point of view, the renewal of civilisation is contradictory to the natural rhythm of biological evolution. Once a civilisation has passed through the golden age and decay, its subsequent extinction is inevitable. Arnold Toynbee shared this vision of Quigley's, although with an important difference. Toynbee believed that a challenged civilisation, that is, one facing decay, is still able to survive (or renew itself), depending on its various capabilities. The conjunctural approach emphasises the impact of external wars on the disintegration of empires and civilisations, while the structuralists look for elements related to the construction (body and spirit) of a civilisation. Elements such as economics, internal crises and fatigue, social breakdown, and important transformations in the fields of commerce, infrastructure and communications are considered structural changes. For instance, Toynbee explains the fall of Greek civilisation by a combination of internal and external factors.[10] On the other hand, concerning the fall of the Roman Empire, he focuses on the role played by economic factors.[11] For Montesquieu, what initially caused the fall of the Roman Empire were the internal divisions within the metropolis Roma. The grandeur of Rome was another decisive factor for its fall.[12]

In dealing with the rise and fall of Islamic empires and dynasties Ibn Khaldun observes that their decline originates in two major factors. The first is the weakness and disappearance of *'asabiyya*[13] because civilization (*Umrân*), like the establishment of a new dynasty,

> needs group feeling through which its power and domination can materialize, and the desert attitude is characteristic of group feeling. Now, if a dynasty at the beginning of its rule is a Bedouin one, the ruler possesses austerity and the desert attitude . . . Then, when his power is firmly established, he comes to claim all the glory for himself.[14]

The second cause of the fall is injustice, 'which brings about the ruin of civilization'.[15]

Concerning the Western civilisation of our time, Huntington foresees the risk of the extinction of current Western civilisation through increased multiculturalism and multi-ethnicity. The third danger is independent of the West and stems from outside powers,[16] perhaps the New Barbarians represented by China and the Muslim world together against the West.

In reviewing the main approaches to the phenomenon of decline we saw that the authors had different opinions about the causes of decline; nevertheless, all were in agreement on the character of decline as a negative state which causes considerable damage to the structure of a civilisation, attacking its nerves and defence system, jeopardising it in parts and causing, finally, its death and extinction. Consequently, the decline of a civilisation can be defined as 'the rupture between the world vision and the historical system, whatever the cause(s)'.

On the subject of revival, there exists among authors an almost consensual opinion. There does not appear to be any notable author, old or contemporary, who has argued explicitly against the possibility of the revival of a civilisation. Even partisans of the cyclical thesis (for example, Toynbee) do not reject the possibility of recovery. The main difference among the authors merely concerns whether history has a *sense*. Those who do not believe that human history has a sense in itself believe in a sporadic correction of a declined civilisation and its eventual renewal. I label this approach 'corrective–renewable'. The approach of those who believe that history has a sense in itself I label 'progressive–cumulative'.

Toynbee, who belongs to the first category, believes in permanent movement, challenge and response:[17]

> The optimum challenge must be the one which not only stimulates the challenged partly to achieve a single response, but also stimulates him to acquire a momentum that carries him on a step further... To convert the movement into a repetitive, movement rhythm, there must be an *élan*.[18]

For Ibn Khaldun the recovery of a declined civilisation depends on: (1) the potential of the enlightened individual in an era of decline; and (2) the revival of *'asabiyya* under the aegis of a new world order.[19] It is in almost the same spirit that Brook Adams argues that the revival of an exhausted civilisation can only be realised 'with fresh energetic material by infusion of barbarian blood'.[20] On the other hand, an author like Melko thinks that 'in a period of culmination civilizations, like lesser

systems, face three alternatives: they either disintegrate, ossify or recon-
stitute themselves and develop further'.[21] Once the encounter between
a declined civilisation and a fresh and strong one is realised, the fre-
quent intrusion of alien civilisations makes it difficult to determine
whether recovery has taken place or whether the disintegrating civilisation has simply been replaced by another.[22]

Samuel Huntington, despite, and maybe because of, his alarmist attitude towards the destiny of Western civilisation, does not reject the
possibility of renewal. In his view, the gradual and irregular decline of
the West might continue for perhaps a century to come. Or 'the West
could go through a period of revival, reverse its declining influence in
world affairs, and reconfirm its position as the leader whom other
civilizations follow and imitate'.[23]

The alternative approach to the cyclical one is the progressive–cumulative, and it is based on the rejection of the cyclical theory and on a
belief in the cumulative character of human experiences. Against the
cyclical theory it argues that:

> A truly cyclical history is conceivable only if we posit the possibility
> that a given civilization can vanish entirely without leaving any
> imprint on those that follow. This, in fact, occurred prior to the
> invention of modern natural science. Modern natural science, how-
> ever, is so powerful, both for good and for evil, that it is very doubtful
> whether it can ever be forgotten or 'un-invented' under conditions
> other than a physical annihilation of the human race. And if the grip
> of a progressive modern natural science is irreversible, then a direc-
> tional history and all of the other variegated economic, social, and
> political consequences that flow from it are also not reversible in any
> fundamental sense.[24]

To Kant, one of the founding fathers of the progressive–cumulative
thesis, the story is 'one of the successive destruction of civilisations, but
each overthrow preserved something from the earlier period and
thereby prepared the way for a higher level of life'.[25] In this way, the
Roman state swallowed up the Greek and the Romans influenced the
barbarians, who in turn destroyed Rome, and so on down to our times.
More explicitly, Hegel (another founding father) explains the goal of
history by saying that 'the History of the world is none other than the
progress of consciousness of Freedom'. From his point of view progress
has been made in the following sense: 'The Eastern nations knew that
one is free; the Greek and Roman world only that *some* are free; while *we*

know that all men absolutely (man as *man*) are free'.[26] The idea of progress and the cumulative character of history has brought some contemporary authors to declare clearly and definitively that:

> Today there exists on Earth one civilization, a single global civilization... The single global civilization is the lineal descendant of, or rather I should say the current manifestation of, a civilization that emerged about 1500 BC in the Near East when Egyptian and Mesopotamian civilizations collided and fused. This new fusional entity has since then expanded over the entire planet and absorbed, on unequal terms, all other previously independent civilizations.[27]

In summary, the above shows that decline is a natural state for a civilisation; that the recovery of a declined civilisation is possible under certain conditions; and that there are substantial differences among authors on the issue of the sporadic or cumulative character of history.

Empirical considerations: rise and fall of Islamic civilisation

In its origin Islam was a successor civilisation of the second category, according to Toynbee's classification.[28] It is notable that Muhammad, the Prophet of Islam, explicitly claimed to be the true successor of the Abrahamian monotheist tradition, in which Islam – as a religion – is but a 'modern' and reviewed version of Judaism and Christianity. That is to say that, at its very heart, the religion of Islam renewed itself by borrowing from ancient Eastern and Mediterranean civilisations.[29] However, when Muhammad moved into Yathrib, an anonymous city north of Mecca, he established his government, elaborated a constitution and changed the name of Yathrib to 'Medina'; it was already clear that he was looking for something greater than merely founding one new state among others. The choice of 'Medina', which means city and from which the term civilisation (*tamaddun*) is derived, was a good indicator of the real intentions of the New Apostolate. Another significant indication was the multi-ethnic character of his disciples; Arabians were in a clear majority, but there were decisive numbers of Parsians (*Salman Pârsi*) and Ethiopians (*Balâl Habashi*). Muhammad aimed to achieve a universal religion through a universal message. After the Formative Age, which was dominated by Arabs who were animated by the will to create an Empire, 'Muslim civilization began only when Islamic schools spread throughout the *Umma* or community of the faithful, from the Atlantic to the Pamirrs. Once again, old wine was poured into new bottles.'[30] This was the beginning of the Axial Age.

During the Axial Age Islam became both integrative and dynamic. It was integrative in the sense that it easily integrated within itself not only different races, ethnicities and territories, but also – and especially – all the cultural, philosophical and scientific baggage that the new arrivals brought with them. It was also dynamic in the sense that it was able to absorb these alien ideas and concepts, because it had sufficient capacity to transpose them into an Islamic vocabulary and express them in Islamic terminology. The Islamic civilisation reached its zenith at the beginning of the ninth century AD, especially under the caliphate of Al-Ma'mûn (813–33), the founder of Bayt al-Hikma (Academia). From this epoch and until the thirteenth century Islamic civilisation became increasingly cosmopolitan, even secular. It functioned in a way which meant that 'the creative minority – philosophers and scientists in particular – viewed religion as a conventional matrix of social norms and communal behavior'.[31] In the time of the great philosopher and politologue Al-Fârâbi (827–950):

> Philosophers saluted the banner of religion in deference to political and social responsibility. The regnant political philosophy, inspired by Al-Fârâbi, held religion to be symbolic representations of the truth. The true and the good were determined autonomously, not on religious grounds, and these criteria became the measure and standard for religion. Philosophy was viewed as independent of, not as ancillary to, faith and theology.[32]

In this period, Muslims were prepared to discuss religious issues with others on a fair basis, without threats of retribution.[33] In fact, during this period, 'most Arabic-writing Faylasûfs (Philosophers) were either Christian, Jews, or Muslims; they all acknowledged the pagan Greek sages, especially Plato and Aristotle'.[34] Kraemer attributes the open-minded character of Islamic civilisation during the Axial Age to the emergence of an affluent and influential middle class which, having both the desire and the means to acquire knowledge and social status, contributed to the cultivation and diffusion of ancient culture.[35]

In the evolution of Islamic civilisation and its flourishing, one thing which is of tremendous importance also explains the gap that currently separates Islamic thinking from Western thinking. Referring once again to Kraemer, who has done excellent work on this subject,[36] we may say that Aristotelian thought dominated Muslims' 'logical investigations, their work in natural philosophy, and their reflections on ethics. But this tendency does not betoken a hardbound commitment to a specific philosophical system. Their political thought was fundamentally Platonic, and a blend of Aristotelianism and Neoplatonism pervaded their metaphysical speculation'.[37]

The question is now: How and under what circumstances did this brilliant, cosmopolitan, tolerant, integrative and dynamic civilisation decline? And when did the decay of Islamic civilisation begin? All authors agree that Islam created a civilisation. They also agree that the Islamic civilisation reached an apex between the ninth and the second half of the tenth century and continued for approximately three centuries. Fernand Braudel even gives two specific dates: one for the beginning and the other for the end of Islamic civilisation. To him the golden age began in 813, the year of Al-Ma'mûn's caliphate, and ended with the death of Averroës, the Cordoba physician and commentator on the works of Aristotle, in Marrakesh in 1198.[38] Braudel thus rightly included the Andalusian epoch – at least partially – in the golden age of Islam.[39] Whatever the exact period of the Islamic golden age, we must understand the causes of its decay. This question has generated various responses. For the sake of clarification I shall classify them as: (1) philosophical–intellectual, (2) geo-strategic, (3) technological–scientific, and (4) the 'Unification of the Worlds' theory.

Philosophical – intellectual explanation

The adherents of this thesis offer two major reasons for the decay of Islam. The first lies in the question of the quality and intellectual aspiration of Islamic philosophy. Muslims were well-versed in both Plato and Aristotle. While Aristotelian thought dominated their logical investigations and their reflections on ethics, their political thought was fundamentally Platonic.[40] Moreover, their approach to philosophy was more literal and textual than critical. The knowledge was used for the purpose of refinement and urbanity (*adab/âdâb*), rather than in a commitment to a specific philosophical system. Braudel attributes this fact to the force exercised by religion on philosophers. He says, 'As admirers of Aristotle, the Arab philosophers were forced into an interminable debate between prophetic revelation, that of the Koran, and a human philosophical explanation'.[41] Second, the general stagnation of Islamic civilisation was due to the uprising of a powerful Islamic dogmatism in the twelfth century which aimed at eradicating philosophy as a discipline incompatible with the religion of Islam. This movement was headed by theologians such as Al-Ghazâli (1058–1111)[42] and Ibn

Taymiyya (1263–1328). The rise of dogmatism put an end to the tolerant, integrative, cosmopolitan and dynamic character which was dominant during the golden age.

Geo-strategic explanation

According to this explanation, decay set in when power was taken over by soldier slaves (*Seljuqs*) in almost all the Muslim territories. Parallel to this there was a dramatic occurrence which had long and substantial consequences: after the twelfth century Islam 'lost the control of the sea'.[43] When Islam conquered the Mediterranean Sea around the end of the seventh century it was a fatal blow to the Byzantine empire and divided the unity of the European *Mare Nostrum*,[44] establishing, even until now, a *barrage liquide*, in Henri Pirenne's phrase. When Islam lost control of the Mediterranean, it became closed to Islam, which found itself permanently handicapped, unable to expand and ill-equipped for ordinary daily life.[45] The loss of the sea was not limited to the Mediterranean; the loss became, in time, worldwide. According to Toynbee the epoch of rupture began in 1498, when Frankish ships arrived in India; water-gypsies who did not even captivate the attention of Babur, the Emperor of India. Nevertheless, the oceanic voyages of discovery made by West European mariners were epoch-making historical events.[46] From this time on, Islam became merely a territorial power deprived of those modern means of communication which were the necessary and efficient instruments for political, economic and cultural power.

Technological–scientific explanation

The Galilean and subsequently the Copernican revolutions fundamentally changed the human view of the world and of humanity itself. These revolutions transformed the mentalities of human beings and led to the Renaissance and the birth of European civilisation. The point is that the Islamic civilisation remained untouched and uninformed. It continued in its traditional way, which at that time amounted to stagnation and further disintegration. The technological rationality which emerged was characterised by three elements: the progressive conquest of all areas of knowledge by mathematics; the application of scientific knowledge through associated technology; and the appearance of an impersonal bureaucracy.[47] None of these elements were present in the Islamic world. Furthermore, the technological revolution requires a secular scientific rationalism. Islam, after having experienced a dose of rationality,[48] secularity and cosmopolitan culture for three or four centuries (ninth to thirteenth), actually returned to dogmatism and a revival of theological sciences (*fiqh* and *kalâm*).[49] In short, the technological backwardness of Islamic civilisation at that time was enhanced by a gradual intellectual and mental backwardness. And this was the cause of its decline.

Unification of the world

This explanation may be described as a combination of the various elements that caused the decline of Islamic civilisation. In other words, the loss of sea power, the return to dogmatism and technological backwardness meant that the Islamic civilisation lost the ability to be dynamic and integrative. To this we may add the changes in orientation caused by these encounters. The revolutionary Western invention was the substitution of the ocean for the steppes as the principal medium of world communication.[50] The world became unified and divided at the same time: unified by the new Western communications web and divided by the end of encounters between non-Western civilisations. Shayegan gives a fine illustration of the depth of the new gap. He writes:

> The decline of these Asian civilizations brought their mutual cross-fertilizations to an end. The era of the great translations leading to fruitful encounters between India and China, Iran and India, China and Japan, came to an end. These great civilizations turned away from each other and towards the West. They withdrew from history, entered a phase of expectation, stopped renewing themselves and lived increasingly on their accumulated fat. They were like rich aristocratic families overtaken by events, ruined by a shift in economic reality, who keep up appearances for a time by selling off their inheritance bit by bit: jewelry, paintings, carpets, silver, everything, until the bitter day comes when there is nothing left.[51]

The unification of the world happened not only through the introduction of modern communications and transportation facilities. The most substantial change occurred in the field of the economy. 'For the first time in human history, an instance of a world-economy survived its "fragility" and consolidates itself as a capitalist system.'[52] Without going into further discussions about the rise of capitalism, it should be mentioned that this was a qualitative change in world history which had (and still has) a huge impact on all civilisations, including the Islamic civilisation.

Continuing its decline, the Islamic civilisation completely lost the impulses and the will which had characterised it during the golden age. The decline has been so striking that some authors have asked whether a Muslim civilisation still exists.[53] As we shall see later on, having doubts about the existence of such a civilisation is not the province only of Western authors; Muslims themselves (even Fundamentalists) are asking the same question. What about the Ottoman Empire which was Islamic and existed for several centuries, becoming extinct as recently as 1923? It is true that the Ottoman Empire was Islamic, but in name rather than in essence. In reality, the Ottoman Empire was culturally an almost inert construction which contributed little to the development of Islamic civilisation. The Ottoman Empire was merely a historical system without a world vision.

Until now, I have dealt only with explanations provided by non-Muslim authors. This is because, with the expection of Ibn Khaldun, there were few Muslim thinkers in the medieval period, which corresponds to the beginning of the Islamic decline, who were interested in studying the decay of Islamic civilisation. In fact, Muslims only became conscious of their own stagnation and fall after the Napoleonic invasion of Egypt in 1798. It was during the French occupation of Egypt that Muslims became aware of their own backwardness in social, political, technological and intellectual terms. With an extraordinary precision and accuracy Al-Jabarti described the story of this encounter.[54] This event had huge repercussions on Muslim awareness which started in the nineteenth century and continued in the twentieth. By observing the progress of Europe, thinkers and leaders such as Al-Afghani (d. 1897), Abduh (d. 1905), Tahtawi (d. 1873) and many others tried to reform Islam and the Muslim way of life. The important thing is that from this period on, all Muslims admitted to the decline of Islam and the need for reform. As a leading Muslim thinker of the twentieth century described it: 'During the last century, we became aware that, we, Muslims, we need a deep and correct reform in our religious approach. We need to revive Islam by returning to the limpid source from which we got lost during fourteen centuries.'[55] This citation illustrates a genuine Muslim discourse which sums up the essence of all the various discourses (Reformist and Fundamentalist under their different etiquettes) from the nineteenth century until now. The genuine discourse attests to the progress of the West and the backwardness of Muslims, as though they were two incontestable facts, but the solution that is proposed is not the logical result or consequence of the observed facts. Instead of looking forward, trying to join the idea and the path of

progress, it proposes regression and looks backwards by rhetorical statements such as 'returning to the limpid source from which we got lost
during fourteen centuries'.

In short, all Muslims have acknowled the decline of Islamic civilisation and internalised this fact, while at the same time they avoid drawing the necessary conclusions in accordance with the already observed,
admitted fact.

Speculative considerations: how to reconstruct?

While Muslims agree that Islamic civilisation has declined, they are,
however, significantly divided on the ways in which it might be reconstructed. Is reconstruction possible? Is there any empirical evidence? At
the beginning of this chapter I argued that reconstruction differs from
reproduction in the sense that the former does not aim to reproduce
something identical. On the contrary, reproduction, in a way, aims for
reincarnation. One is photography; the other is painting. Reproduction
is mechanical and reconstruction is intellectual. The process of reconstruction takes place in two stages. In the first stage, civilisation, which
is subject to revision and renewal, must be deconstructed. Without
deconstruction, the concept of civilisation will remain vague and
a historic. The deconstruction model that I propose, is founded on
specifying the elements of a civilisation, which, in a condensed form,
consist of two elements, a world vision and a historical system. Having
acknowledged this, we have to initiate the second phase, the reconstruction stage. Civilisations are generally long-lived, extending over many
centuries. When we talk about the reconstruction of a specific civilisation, we do not mean that the target civilisation should be reconstructed
over its entire long life. We have a selected moment, as well as selected
values, ideas, concepts, organising principles and so on, all related to the
specific civilisation. In this way the Islamic civilisation, which is the
subject of this study, does not necessarily mean fourteen centuries; it
means precisely the three or four centuries during which the Islamic
world vision and its historical system were unified, thus constituting
one integrated system. The advantage of such a method is its empirical
verifiability: we know when and in which specific periods the junction
occurred. In this connection the best, and perhaps unique, example of a
successful reconstruction of a declined civilisation is the Renaissance, an
experience of which we have historical proof. The Renaissance was a
reconstruction of the heritage of Greece and Rome. Athena represented
the main source of inspiration, the *Idea* and the *Spirit*, while Rome stood

for the *Body,* an organising power based on law and prosperity. Besides these two basic elements from which European civilisation sprang, Christianity was added as an *ad hoc* element, and, finally, rising capitalism completed the construction. The Renaissance model shows the ways and the mechanisms needed in order to carry out a successful reconstruction.

After the above discussion we must consider the possibilities, the opportunities and the views of Muslims themselves on the subject of an Islamic revival.

Three highways

Different authors present different classifications of Muslim attitudes towards the revival of Islam. Fred Halliday has identified four distinct responses or themes from within an Islamic discourse. 'The approaches they adopt are classifiable as: *assimilation, appropriation, particularism, confrontation;* to which may be added a fifth approach, present within Islamic societies and the non-Muslim world and falling outside an Islamic discourse. This fifth could be described as the *incompatibility* thesis.'[56] Already in 1948, long before the rise of Islamic fundamentalism and the Islamic revolution in Iran, Toynbee made a broader and, in a sense, prophetic classification of Muslims by dividing them into Zealots[57] and Herodians.[58] Leading Muslim figures have their own classification. Personalities such as Sayyed Qub (d. 1966), Al-Mawdudi (d. 1979), Shariati (d. 1977), Khomeini (d. 1989), Sorush[59] and Khatami make the same classification, although with small variations. They all divide Muslims into three categories: the Traditionalists–Conservatives, the True-Revolutionaries and the Corrupts (for example the Shah of Iran, President Sadat or the Saudi royal family). The views of each of these groups on the problems of revival are of course different. For the sake of clarity, I divide Muslim approaches on the renewal of Islam into three paths or three highways:[60] *Reproductivism, Communalism* and *Universalism.*

Reproductivism is animated by an *ideé fixe* and is an attempt to reincarnate an ossified body. What is to be reincarnated is the Medina model of the time of Muhammad himself (*Madinat ul-Nabî*),[61] and to some extent the period immediately following the death of Muhammad (632 AD), the epoch of the Rightful Caliphs (632–61). This approach has the advantage of being clear and precise. It refers to a specific time and space within which an explicit world vision did create an historical system. All these elements are empirically verifiable. The time is limited from 622 until 632 or 661. The space is geographically in Medina and other parts of the Arabian peninsula. The world vision is represented by the Message embodied in the Koran and the historical system is illustrated by the government of Muhammad and his four immediate successors. The Medina with its fixed set of values (unchanged for ever) is perceived as the Perfect City, the sublime form of human organisation and the unique valid model for humankind. What is important is that the Medina model is seen as neither a point of departure nor a single source of inspiration. It is, indeed, the arrival and the final point, the Harbour, not the Voyage. Consequently, the task of Muslims, today as at any time in history, consists of recreating the Medina model as closely as possible to the original version. Leaders and thinkers like Khomeini, Sayyed Qub, Mawdudi and many others who share this view do not, however, reject science and technology. In this respect, it is interesting to see how Ayatollah Khomeini admits to the advantages of new technology and what he has in mind concerning Western civilisation. In his *Political Testament*, he writes:

> If the illustrations (*mazâhir*) of civilization mean innovations, inventions and advanced industry, Islam nor any other monotheist religion is opposed to these things. But if civilization and modernization (*tajaddud*) means, as the professional intellectuals put it, freedom in all things illicit – prostitution, even homosexuality and such things – these things are in contradiction with all heavenly religious as they are in contradiction to scientific experts and rationalists.[62]

Mawdudi, another advocate of reproduction, explains the reason why Muslims may use modern science without qualms. It is because 'the modern science was not based on any particular philosophical perspective, nor did it promote a set of values or require an attitude from Muslims that could interfere with their faith'.[63] Muslims accept that there are some techniques which 'can be exchanged and diffused fairly easily in isolation'. What they reject is 'a certain scientific vision of the world in conjunction with a certain perception of reality'; they reject any new set of values, any way of thinking which might disturb the immutable set of Koranic values.[64] Hasan al-Turâbi, the influential Sudanese Islamic fundamentalist leader, is also representative of this tendency. To him, revival requires a 'total revival in all aspects', and is thus not understood to mean modernisation along Western lines. Revival is seen as a means towards the establishment of a new society where *shari'a* is applied. Furthermore, Turâbi today claims what was being claimed by Al-Ghazâli in the eleventh–twelfth centuries: renewing the fundamentals of religion.[65] Turâbi's argument is circular indeed: we have to revive Islam in all aspects for the purpose of returning to *shari'a*. These claimed values are static because the reproductivists do not recognise the autonomy and authority of human beings. On this question a scholar criticising precisely the fundamentalist approach writes that, in Islam, man 'is everything because he is the jewel of creation, distinct from the other created beings in that he incarnates the divine Logos; but he is nothing, because he is not a founding authority'.[66] Another important characteristic of this approach is found in their belief in the absolute supremacy of Islamic civilisation over all others, past as well as future. They believe in the existence of a single civilisation, which is of course Islamic, all others being either corrupt or unjust, all belonging to *Jâhiliyya* (ignorance). Consequently, now that Western civilisation is dominant, Muslims must opt for an antagonistic attitude *vis-à-vis* the West as they did in the formative period of Islam towards Persia, the Byzantine empire and other civilisations and empires. They could also 'wait for the West to destroy itself and then take the West's place in the world leadership'. This confrontation mentality ignores the reality that 'if the West destroys itself, either physically or morally, it will hardly perish alone'.[67]

Communalism refers to an agglomerate of various Muslim thinkers who have not yet formulated a coherent discourse; they are thus all aware of the weakness and inaccuracy of the reproductivist thesis and try to conciliate various aspects of Islam with some aspects of modernity. They may be called 'half and half': half zealot and half herodian; half traditionalist and half modernist, half democrat and half theocrat. Despite various differences among them, they all agree on the primacy of religious (Islamic) political rule. Their main reference model remains Medina;[68] 'the limpid source', though not as an immutable model,

> not in order to return and stay in the past which is pure regression, but for the discovery of the essence of our identity and its refinement in the mentalities and habits...as well as for the rational criticism of the past in order to find the proper support for today...and for a future more splendid than the past.[69]

They make a distinction between religion and ideology, arguing for a further distinction between Islam, which is eternal and unchaging on the one side, and human understanding of Islam which is changing, on the other (Shariati and Sorush). They believe in a religious society which makes the government religious; such a society remains an open one, where criticism is permitted and nobody is above criticism.

The above view was shared by such people as Afghani and Abduh in the nineteenth century, and by Shariati, Bazargan,[70] Arkoun,[71] Hasan Hanafi,[72] Sorush and Khatami in the twentieth century. From their point of view Medina remains the primordial source, but not an immutable one. They are in favour of a new interpretation of Islam in which reason must play a key role. In a sense they represent the *New Mu'tazila* of Islam. Some (Arkoun, Hanafai, Bazargan) are more rationalist than others. It seems that their favoured historical reference to Islamic civilisation is essentially the epoch of Al-Ma'mûn when Islam was tolerant, rational, cosmopolitan and powerful. This group is fully aware of the fall of Islamic civilisation, but they believe that a new one can/must be reconstructed. Because even if the glory (historical system) of Islam belongs to the past, the religion (world vision) is still alive, and 'religion is broader than a single civilization'. They accept 'the positive aspects of Western civilization', rejecting only 'Western vision on freedom and on human beings which is wrong, narrow and uni-dimensional'.[73] The fact that they do not reject Western civilization *in toto* as do the reproductionists, and that they pay respect to reason (though not an autonomous one), means that they implicity accept the multiplicity of civilisations too, civilisations which may enter into dialogue with each other. It is in this spirit that the Organisation of the Islamic Conference (OIC), which embraces all Muslim countries and is presently chaired (1997–2000) by Iran, recently launched the idea of organising a world dialogue among civilisations. To prepare for such dialogue a symposium was scheduled for February 1999 on inter-Islamic dialogue. According to the General Secretary of the OIC, the goal of this symposium was to achieve a 'unified Islamic strategy to guide the dialogue with other civilisations'.[74] Such statements and such ideas from this group sound positive and also have the appearance of being the appropriate solution for reconstructing Islamic civilisation. The problem resides in the ambivalence and also in the contradictory character of this kind of reconstructive project. It is not clear which part of the past is likely to be included in the reconstructed civilisation and which part is to be rejected. Nor is it clear how much of Western civilisation is likely to be integrated into the new one. Is the partial integration of Western civilisation to be limited to the technological rationality or might it also extend to the scientific mentality, the critical spirit, the idea of freedom and genuine human rights? How can individual freedom be combined with a religious government? Democracy, theocracy or theo-democracy? How can a monotheistic conscience developed in an agrarianistic social context and a pre-da Gama world vision be transformed into a prosperous and powerful civilisation in modern times? The most significant element of the Islamic heritage is currently religion and religious conscience. Is it possible, or even likely, to create – in our time – a new civilisation on the basis of the same religion or religion in general? These questions need answers or at least clarification, which is still lacking in communalism. That is to say, some communalists (for example, Khatami) do provide clarifications; these consist of the rejection of principles such as freedom which constitutes a pillar of Western civilisation. It is therefore no exaggeration to assert that they represent a communitarian thesis which will, at best, lead to the rise of a neo-Shar'î communalist revival.

Universalism. From this point of view, the reconstruction of a declined civilisation is directly conditioned by the world-time within which the new civilisation shall emerge. In the old world, living civilisations were in touch with each other, though not as closely as was to be the case. In such a world, a particular civilisation could renew itself after having gone through a period of weakness and decay.

One reason for the existence of this possibility was that the cumulative process consisting of perpetual learning and the accumulation of experiences proceeded almost internally, within the local universe of each civilisation. This also made it possible for various civilisations to live in separate spaces and side by side simultaneously. In our time, under the pressure of the world system represented essentially by what Braudel called the world economy, combined with increasing tendencies towards globalisation, makes the very existence of different civilisations, (each preserving its own set of values, world vision, specific moral and political organising principles), operating with their own parochial economic system (world economy) is hardly plausible. How can different civilisations continue to live together in a world which is administered by globalised capitalism, an increasingly standardised civilisation and standard human rights? In such a world, different cultures can easily live together and enrich each other. But there cannot be more than one civilisation as I have defined it. Furthermore, if we recognise that 'the need, even the urgency, for "universal references" has never been so strong as in our time',[75] we have no alternative but to admit to the existence of such references. Where may we look for the universal references in our day? For some it might be the internet. More seriously, perhaps, it seems obvious that the vast majority of these references are to be found in Western civilisation. Here a distinction should be made between Western civilisation and Westernisation. The two concepts are often mixed up, creating further confusion and misunderstanding, which has been used to manipulate people and justify authoritarian political regimes in Muslim countries. The distinction is that the former refers to a set of values and concepts which are embodied in a world vision, materialised in the form of a specific historical system that is generally called Western civilisation. Ideas like belief in progress, freedom, equality, justice, democracy, secularism, criticism and dialogue are representative of this civilisation. These are the basic concepts that operate in the West. That is not to neglect the ugly side of the West as evidenced by colonialism, domination, exploitation and war. The point is that the ugly side is not the whole story of the West, and it would be incorrect to reduce the West to only its non-civilised image. Furthermore, these elements are far from specific to the West; all empires and civilisation have been expansionist, have made war and have committed crimes, including successive Islamic empires (for example Ummayads, Abbasids, Ottomans). However, none of them was based on the trilogy of *Liberté, Egalité, Fraternité*, and all other related ideas; nor did any of them create an economic system (capitalism) which is applicable worldwide for better and for worse. Westernisation (modernisation in Huntington's jargon) is a mimic and mechanical adoption of some superficial and trival aspects of the way of life in Western societies; for example, the consumption of imported articles for the sole purpose of emphasising the consumers' distance from the indigenous environment. This is a kind of alienation, a plague.[76] It is also one of the main reasons why, in Muslim societies, the West is often perceived as trivial, morally decadent, luxurious, dominant and arrogant – all at the same time. In this imagery Westerners are caricatured as a bunch of immoral exploiters who, by stealing Muslims' natural resources, expend their time in leisure, drinking alcohol and practising free and bizarre sex.

Faced with Westernisation, Muslim universalists deny this reductionist and superficial picture of Western civilisation. They do not consider Western civilisation to belong only to the West. As Toynbee puts it: 'The West is not just the West's own parochial concern but is *their* past history too.'[77] They see a West with a basic set of values which, if not universal, is certainly 'universalizable';[78] it is a civilisation with the potential of being universal, because its basic set of values is broader than those of all other existing civilisations, taken separately.

The reconstruction project of Muslim universalists lies in: considering the existing Western civilisation as the necessary basis for a universal civilisation; the qualitative transformation of Muslims into actors and contributors to universality, instead of challenging it and ultimately having to submit to it; the preservation of cultural identities and the identities of Muslims. How may these things be brought about? The first step consists of a mental migration from a parochial and communitarian mentality, which looks backward, to one looking forward by joining a broader value system consisting of gender equality, religious equality, tolerant culture, social justice and so on, leaving aside the permanent suspicion of the West and rejecting the belief in a mysterious international plot against Islam and Muslims. These are figments of the imagination and result in unnecessary frustration and baseless cultural and political suppression. In the globalisation process that the world is going through, not only Islam is challenged; globalisation challenges every religion, ideology and culture, including Western ones.

On the other hand, we have to recognise that Islam represents a rich and high culture. Islam has a message for humanity. The concept of *Umma*, the Islamic notion of brotherhood, the recognition of differences between peoples, and certain principles concerning human moral and physical integrity are just a few of the many positive aspects of Islam which could be transmitted to the universal civilisation. What is needed is a reinterpretation of these concepts. *Umma* (community) is easily universalisable. In a period where everything is becoming global, where peoples are becoming citizens of the global village, and share the same destiny and face similar problems (environment, health, internet, CNN, disaster, and so an), they are in reality members of the same community: the *Umma*. So, the 'Umma of Islam' (*Umma al-Islâmiyya*) may be extended to the 'Umma of Humankind' (*Umma al-Insâniyya*). Moreover, Islam is alien to racism, preaching universality and equality among human beings; in reality these elements constitute the powerful pillars of Islam's strength, and they are highly qualified to contribute to the improvement of Western civilisation. Islam's particular focus on justice (*'adâla*) could also bring new blood to a civilisation which is suffering from a lack of justice. The virtue of compassion (*sabr*) and the quality of solidarity (*ta'âwûn*) are necessary for the correction of the dominant capitalist system. The list of components that Islam could contribute is long. Elements such as these must be saved and used as materials in a reconstruction. Considering the world power system of today, it is undeniable that 'something of the leadership . . . for all mankind is likely to come from the West. But moral vision cannot be left to the West alone. Muslims must face their share of the tasks. There is much in their heritage itself that should help them find the relevance of that heritage to Modern mankind'.[79] What is also necessary is a 'heroic act, maybe; Promethean audacity, perhaps; rebellion against established truths, undoubtedly'.[80] The problem is that these Herodians, who are called to audacity and rebellion, are in an absolute minority in Muslim societies. The Muslim thinkers and intellectuals who truly believe in a universal civilisation, with Islamic contribution and participation, are generally quite cautious when expressing their ideas. They have no wish to provoke sometimes violent reactions and they are sensitive to allegations labeling them as 'white man's niggers'. In general, they try to attract public attention to their ideas through the translation of classical works by thinkers such as John Locke, Jean-Jacques Rousseau, Voltaire and Hobbes and contemporary authors such as Karl Popper, Bertrand Russell and Jürgen Habermas. Nevertheless, taking the current situation in Iran as an example, it is astonishing that, in recent times, some groups composed especially of young men and women have emerged from the very heart of a fundamentalist culture and regime. One of these groups, among the most active and open-minded, is composed of people associated with the newspaper *Jâmi'a* (Society). In the issue of 1 July 1998 of this newspaper, one could read the following lines:

> In the matter of History and Civilization, we [Muslims, Iranians?] are playing the role of radical critic. Criticizing [Western civilization] is, of course, much easier than participating in its improvement.

Such a statement sounds normal in a democratic–pluralist society, pedestrian, even banal. But when we consider that this is published in today's Tehran, where Western civilisation is still perceived as 'satanic', the statement acquires a different dimension.

On 27 July 1998 *Jâmi'a* ceased publication in accordance with an order from a jurisdictional trial.

Conclusion: Islamic 'civilisation' or 'civilised' Islam?

In this chapter, I proposed a definition of civilisation which is workable in the sense that it is empirically verifiable. If we accept that civilisation is a junction between a world vision and a historical system, the decline can be define as a rupture in the junction. The revival is thus characterised by attempts to reconnect the defective junction. The reconnecting process cannot be mechanical, because it will take place under circumstances other than those under which the junction (civilisation) was initially fabricated. I called these circumstances 'world-time'. Therefore, the junction must necessarily obey new imperatives which are independent of the declined civilisation. This means that a revision of both world vision and historical system is required. That is why there is no question of the reproduction of a civilisation. There is no historical–empirical evidence supporting reproduction. But there is at least one example of the possibility of reconstruction: the Renaissance. Unless we completely deny the close lines of affinity between the European and Graeco-Roman civilisations, we must admit that European civilisation was, in its origins, a revived and reconstructed version of the Greek and Roman civilisations. Therefore, the reconstruction ultimately entails the creation of a new civilisation on the basis of old materials, with new ones added in a quite different world-time. The lifetime of the new civilisation depends on its ability in the permanent challenge and response process. Since the Renaissance, European civilisation has known many ups and downs, but it has also demonstrated that it was able to make the necessary corrections and improvements in time, while moving towards a broader and more general set of values. That is the reason for allocating a universal, or at least, a universalisable character to this civilisation.

Millions of Muslims dream of the revival of Islam. They then discover and acknowledge the decline of Islamic civilisation as described above. Since the nineteenth century the Muslims' dream has assumed different forms. The real struggle is taking place between those who believe that the reconstruction of Islamic civilisation can only be realised through new patterns, patterns which are not necessarily identical to the disconnected Islamic civilisation that exists today. Ideas and projects that call for the reproduction of the original model have little chance of fulfilment. As has been argued, the success of a reconstruction depends primarily on connecting with reality, meaning world-time. There are an overwhelming number of indications that the world is moving towards a broader construction, rather than a pure and narrow religious construction. The new waves of religious awakenings are, in fact, reactions to universality, at least to globalisation, rather than independent factors. I have argued that Islam as a civilisation is unlikely to be reproduced. At the same time, however, Islam is in possession of an inestimable set of values and visions which are highly likely to be incorporated into the new world system. The notions of *Umma* (justice) and also ' *asabiyya* are needed for the improvement of civilisation. Robert Cox provides us with a redefinition of *'asabiyya* by putting it in a world system context: *'asabiyya* as a supra-intersubjectivity, a new global Mahdi that may assume the form of a collectivity rather than an individual. This 'supra-subjectivity would have to embody principles of coexistence without necessarily reconciling differences in goals. It would have to allow for a degree of harmonization of trajectories of different macro-societies.'[81]

In this respect, it is important to mention that Islam is not the only civilisation or religion which is called upon to join what we might call the universal civilisation. Before Islam, there were Christianity and Judaism. This thesis has met with resistance and scepticism. Some authors argue that 'Islam is very different. In its fundamentalist form, at least, it makes impious demands: it wants to rule everything, to manage society, to regiment minds.'[82] Shayegan in his criticism refers – as he himself admits – to a fundamentalist interpretation of Islam rather than a genuine one. It is true that the rigid monotheist character of Islam represents an obstacle to a multi-religious civilisation. Nevertheless, we should not forget that Islam is, in its monotheist character, almost a copy of Judaism. Since Judaism became a component of Western civilisation, there is, at least theoretically, no valid reason why Islam should not do the same. It is possible that 'eventually Islam like Christianity already in some circles, will prove to have its most creative thrust by way of the great *secular* literature in which its challenge has been embedded, and will move among its heirs like a secret leaven long after they have forgotten they were once Muslims.'[83] However, in the end, the Muslims themselves must find their own way. But the situation can hardly be better described than when Braudel said that 'every religion, indeed, has its emergency exits. Islam may delay or oppose changes; but it can also be influenced and outflanked.'[84]

Islam, in its existing shape, constitutes an absolutely disconnected and disintegrated construction. What is needed is to connect Islam with the world-time. The idea of a new Islamic civilisation as a parochial and autonomous entity, possessing its own world vision, a specific historical system and a world economy, seems to be a matter of imagination rather than reality. The true way (*Sirât al-Mustaqîm*) is perhaps to join this *Spanish omelette* which is the world civilisation. The door seems to be open to a 'civilised' Islam; as a guest and as an owner, at the same time.

Notes

1. Samuel P. Huntington, *The Clash of Civilizations and the Remaking of the World Order* (New York: Simon & Schuster, 1996), p. 42.

2. P. Bagby, *Culture and History* (London: Longman, 1958), pp. 162–3.
3. Arnold Toynbee, *A Study of History* (London: Oxford University Press, 1995), p. 46.
4. Fernand Braudel, *A History of Civilizations* (Harmondsworth: Penguin Books, 1995), p. 5.
5. Immanuel Wallerstein, *Geopolitics and Geoculture* (Cambridge: Cambridge University Press, 1992), p. 235.
6. See Huntington, *The Clash of Civilizations*, ch.12.
7. Douglas Jerrold, 'The Lies about the West', in Manfred P. Fleischer (ed.), *The Decline of the West?* (New York: Holt, Rinehart & Winston, 1970).
8. In his short and insightful review of the evolution of studies on decline, Fleischer writes that 'During the Renaissance, the decline theory swung back to the secular side. Petrarch (1304–1374) called the period of pre-Christian Rome *antiqua*... the age of Constantine, *nova*, and his own time *tenebrae*.' (See Fleischer, *The Decline of the West?*.)
9. Carrol Quigley, *Globalization: Social Theory and Social Culture* (New York: Macmillan, 1961), pp. 146ff.
10. The configuration of Hellenic civilisation's social history after its 'breakdown' – the leading minority in society comes to depend more and more on force, and less and less on attraction; civilisation's religious history in the same phase – the internal proletariat creates a higher religion, Christianity, then draws its inspiration from one of the non-Hellenic civilisations; the role played by 'the external proletariat' (the barbarians) – the barbarians conquered the Hellenic universal state militarily and established successor-states on its domain. (See Toynbee, *A Study of History*, p. 56.)
11. The importance of the part played by economic factors in determining whether a universal state is to collapse or survive can be gauged by comparing the respective fortunes of the Roman Empire in its different regions. The western provinces, in which the empire collapsed in the fifth century, were relatively backward economically; the central and eastern provinces, in which, in the same century, the empire survived, were the principal seats of the Hellenic world's industry and trade. Their relative economic strength more than counterbalanced the relative unfavourableness of their strategic position; the centre and the east were more directly exposed than the west was to assaults from the Eurasian nomads of the Great Western bay of the steppe, and from the Sasanian power in Iran and Iraq. (See Toynbee, *A Study of History*, p. 63.)
12. 'Pendant que Rome conquérait l'univers, il y avait, dans ses murailles, une guerre cachée; c'étaient des feux comme ceux de ces volcans qui sortent sitôt que quelque matière vient en augmenter la fermentation.' Charles-Louis de Montesquieu, 'Considérations sur les Causes de la Grandeur des Romains et de leur Décadence', in Oeuvres Complètes (Paris: Gallimard, 1951), Tome II, p. 111: 'Ce fut uniquement la grandeur de la république qui fut le mal, et qui changea en guerres civiles les tumultes populaires. Il fallait bien qu'il y eût à Rome des divisions; et ces guerriers si fiers, si audacieux, si terribles au dehors, ne pouvaient pas être bien modérés au dedans' (ibid., p. 119).
13. According to Rosenthal's translation, *'asabiyya* means 'group feeling'. Robert Cox gives it an elaborated sense, defining it as 'the form of intersubjectivity that pertains to the founding of a state. It is the creative component in this

critical phase of human development; and in this respect *'asabiyya* has (for a westerner) some relationship to Machiavelli's *virtù*.' Robert W. Cox with Timothy J. Sinclair, *Approaches to World Order* (Cambridge: Cambridge University Press, 1966), p. 163.

14. Abdelrahaman Ibn Khaldun, *The Muqaddimah*, tr. Franz Rosenthal, 3 vols (London: Routledge & Kegan Paul, 1968), Vol. II, p. 101.

15. Ibid., vol. II, p. 103. In a more extensive sense, Ibn Khaldun explains that 'injustice should not be understood to imply only the confiscation of money or other property from the owners, without compensation and without cause. It is commonly understood in that way, but it is something more general than that' (ibid., vol. II, p. 106). 'When people no longer do business in order to make a living, and when they cease all gainful activity, the business of civilization slumps, and everything decays' (ibid., vol. II, p. 104).

16. See Huntington, *The Clash of Civilizations*, p. 302.

17. A civilisation which has been challenged is called to provide an adequate response. Its survival is dependent on the success of the response. He puts it in the following way: 'Civilizations, I believe, come to birth and proceed to grow by successfully responding to successive challenges. They break down and go to pieces if and when a challenge confronts them which they fail to meet.' Arnold Toynbee, *Civilization on Trial* (New York: Oxford University Press, 1948), p. 56.

18. See Toynbee, *A Study of History*, p. 137.

19. See Cox with Sinclair, *Approaches to World Order*, p. 164.

20. Brook Adams, 'The Law of Civilization and Decay', in Manfred P. Fleischer (ed.), *The Decline of the West?* (New York: Holt, Rinehart & Winston, 1970), pp. 57–61.

21. Matthew Melko, 'The Nature of Civilization', in Stephen K. Sanderson (ed.), *Civilizations and World Systems: Studying World-Historical Change* (Walnut Creek, Calif.: Altamira Press, 1995), p. 42.

22. Ibid., p. 44.

23. See Huntington, *The Clash of Civilizations*, p. 302.

24. Francis Fukuyama, *The End of History and the Last Man* (London: Hamish Hamilton, 1992), p. 88.

25. Quoted ibid., p. 59.

26. Quoted ibid., p. 60.

27. David Wilkinson, 'Central Civilization', in Stephen K. Sanderson (ed.), *Civilizations and World Systems: Studying World-Historical Change* (Walnut Creek, Calif.: Altamira Press, 1995), p. 46.

28. Toynbee believes that a civilisation may emerge through (1) the *spontaneous mutation* of some pre-civilisational society, (2) *stimulation* of a pre-civilisational society into changing into a civilisation by the influence of some civilisation that is already in existence or (3) *distintegration* of one or more civilisations of an older generation and the transformation of some of their elements into a new configuration (see Toynbee, *A Study of History*, p. 85).

29. See Braudel, *A History of Civilizations*, p. 73, and Sayyed Ali Khamenei (Supreme Leader of Iran), 'Today the World needs the True Islam', in *Ettela'at*, 9 July 1998.

30. See Braudel, *A History of Civilizations*, p. 73.

31. Joel L. Kraemer, *Humanism in the Renaissance of Islam* (Leiden: E. J. Brill, 1986), p. 14.
32. Ibid., p. 15.
33. Ibid., p. 29.
34. Marshall G. S. Hodgson, *The Venture of Islam*, Vol. I (Chicago, ILL.: University of Chicago Press, 1974), p. 430.
35. See Kraemer, *Humanism*, p. 4.
36. In my recent book, I arrived at the same conclusion as had many before me: that the Islamic political philosophy was based on Plato while the Western one is based on Aristotle. See Mehdi Mozaffari, *Fatwa: Violence and Discourtesy* (Oxford: Aarhus University Press, 1998) (Sura IV).
37. See Kraemer, *Humanism*, p. 6.
38. See Braudel, *A History of Civilizations*, p. 73.
39. On the Andalusian epoch, see Juan Vernet, *La cultura hispanoàrab en Orient y Occidente* (Spain, 1978) and Salma Khadra Yayyusi (ed.), *The Legacy of Muslim Spain* (Leiden: E. J. Brill, 1994). The Andalusian experience accomplished at least two main objectives: first, it created a cosmopolitan forum for different scholars of different disciplines; second, and as a result of the first, came the transfer of Hellenistic knowledge to medieval Europe. (See Mehdi Mozaffari, *Fatwa*, pp. 172–3).
40. See Kraemer, *Humanism*, p. 6.
41. See Braudel, *A History of Civilizations*, p. 83.
42. On Ghazâli, see particularly Henri Laoust, *La Politique de Ghazâli* (Paris: Paul Gauthner, 1970).
43. See Braudel, *A History of Civilizations*, p. 87.
44. In a sense this event did contribute to the rise of European civilisation which would progressively dominate the world. As Henri Pirenne puts it: 'L'Occident est embouteillé et forcé de vivre sur lui-même, en vase clos. Pour la première fois depuis toujours, l'axe de la vie historique est repoussé de la Méditerranée vers le Nord. La décadence où tombe à la suite de cela le royaume mérovingien fait apparaître une nouvelle dynastie, originaire des régions germaniques du nord, les Carolingiennes.' Henri Pirenne, *Mahomet et Charlemagne* (Paris: Club du Meilleur Livre, 1939), p. 187.
45. See Braudel, *A History of Civilizations*, p. 87.
46. See Toynbee, *Civilization on Trial*, p. 62.
47. Dariush Shayegan, *Cultural Schizophrenia: Islamic Societies Confronting the West* (Syracuse: The Syracuse University Press, 1997), p. 85.
48. In Islam, rationality at the beginning of the golden age was especially formulated and defended by *Mu'tazila*. See Richard C. Martin *et al.* (eds), *Defenders of Reason in Islam* (Oxford: Oneworld, 1997), and Joseph Van Ess, *Une lecture à rebours de l'histoire du Mu'tazilisme* (Paris: Gauthner, 1984).
49. It is astonishing that Al-Ghazâli, the most prominent figure of dogmatism, daubed his monumental work '*Revivification/Ihyâ*' which is a clear indication of the dominant trend of his time. In fact, the Revivification was a Dogmatic Renaissance: a rupture with philosophy and Hellenism and a return to theology.
50. See Toynbee, *Civilization on Trial*, p. 70.
51. See Shayegan, *Cultural Schizophrenia*, p. 44.
52. See Wallerstein, *Geopolitics and Geoculture*, p. 223.

53. See Braudel, *A History of Civilizations*, p. 111.
54. See Al-Jabarti's *Chronicle of the French Occupation*, tr. Shmuel Moreh (Princeton, NJ: Markus Wiener Publishing, 1995).
55. Ali Shariati, *Tamaddun va Tajaddud/Civilization and Modernization* (Speech – 10 Dey 1352/31 December 1973), pp. 2–3.
56. Fred Halliday, *Islam and the Myth of Confrontation* (London: I. B. Tauris, 1995), pp. 135–6.
57. 'The "Zealot" is a man who takes refuge from the unknown in the familiar. When he joins battle with a stranger who practises superior tactics and employs formidable newfangled weapons and finds himself getting the worst of the encounter, he responds by practising his own traditional art of war with abnormally scrupulous exactitudes.' Toynbee, *Civilization on Trial*, p. 188. The North African Sanusis and the Central Arabian Wahhabis (Saudi Arabia) are used as examples.
58. 'The "Herodian" is the man who acts on the principle that the most effective way to guard against the danger of the unknown is to master its secret. When he finds himself in the predicament of being confronted by a more highly skilled and better armed opponent, he responds by discarding his traditional art of war and learning to fight his enemy with the enemy's own tactics and own weapons.' (Ibid., pp. 193–4). As an example of an Herodian he names Mustafa Atatürk.
59. Abdul Karim Sorush (alias Hossein Dabbagh) studied pharmacology in Iran and history and the philosophy of science in England. After the revolution of 1979, he became one of the most influential ideologues of the Islamic Revolution and was a member of the Committee of the Cultural Revolution until 1987 when he resigned from the Committee. Sorush is the author of many books and articles such as *Religion is Broader than Ideology* (1993), and *Theoretical Contraction and Expansion of the Shari'a* (1990) (both in Persian). For a short review of his ideas, see Valla Vakili, *Debating Religion and Politics in Iran: The Political Thought of Abdolkarim Soroush* (New York: Council of Foreign Relations, 1996).
60. 'Muslims' here are both Muslim believers and those who are merely cultural or secular Muslims.
61. On the government of Medina under Muhammad, see (among others): Mehdi Mozaffari, *Authority in Islam* (New York: Sharpe, 1987), ch. 2.
62. Ayatollah Khomeini, 'Political Testament', in *Sahifay-e Nur* (*Light's Scriptures*) (Tehran: Sorush, 1990), p. 178.
63. Seyyed Vali Reza Nasr, *Mawadi and the Making of Islamic Revivalism* (New York: Oxford University Press, 1996), p. 53.
64. On this point, Mawdudi declares that 'We aspire for Islamic renaissance on the basis of the Qur'an. To use the Qur'anic spirit and Islamic tenets are immutable, but the application of this spirit in the realm of practical life must always vary with the change of conditions and increase of knowledge' (ibid., p. 51).
65. As'ad Abu Khalil, 'Revival and Renewal', in John L. Esposito (ed.), *The Oxford Encyclopedia of the Modern Islamic World*, Vol. 3 (Oxford: Oxford University Press, 1995), p. 435.
66. See Shayegan, *Cultural Schizophrenia*, p. 34.
67. See Hodgson, *The Venture of Islam*, Vol. III, p. 430.

68. Khatami's statement on Medina is insightful. He says that 'The civil society we have in mind has its origin, from a historical and theoretical point of view, in *Madinat ul-Nabî'*, which 'remains as our eternal moral abode'. See Sayyed Mohammad Khatami (President of the Islamic Republic of Iran), Statement to the Eighth Session of the Islamic Summit Conference (Tehran, 9 December 1997). *Bîm-é Mowj (Fear of the Wave)* (Tehran: Simãy-e Javãn, 1997).

69. Sayyed Mohammad Khatami (President of the Islamic Republic of Iran), Statement to the Eighth Session of the Islamic Summit Conference, (Tehran, 9 December 1997). *Bîm-é Mowj (Fear of the Wave)* (Tehran: Simãy-e Javãn, 1997), pp. 183–91.

70. Mehdi Bazargan was a French-educated engineer who became Professor at Tehran University and the leader of the Liberation Movement of Iran. After the Islamic Revolution in 1979, he became the first prime minister of the revolutionary regime, but resigned in November 1979 after the occupation of the US embassy in Tehran and the 'hostage affair'. He is the author of a number of books and articles through which he tried to reconcile Islam with modern science. He died in 1995.

71. Mohammed Arkoun was a Professor at the Sorbonne in Paris and is an author of books on Islam. One of his best works is perhaps *Pour une critique de la raison islamique* (Paris: Maisonneuve & Larose, 1984).

72. Hasan Hanafi is a Professor at Cairo University and is one of the leading figures of Islamic revivalism. One of his works is *Muqaddama fi 'ilm-il Istish-râq/Introduction to Occidentalism* (in Arabic) (Cairo: Dâr il-Fanniya, 1991) which is a reply to Orientalism. See also his article on 'An Islamic Approach to Multilateralism', in Robert Cox (ed.), *The New Realism* (Tokyo: Macmillan, 1997).

73. See Khatami, *Bîm-é*, pp. 183–91.

74. IRNA/Islamic Republic News Agency, 1 July 1998.

75. Francois Bourricauld, 'Modernity, Universal References and the Process of Modernization', in S. N. Eisenstadt (ed), *Patterns of Modernity*, Vol. I (New York: New York University Press, 1987), p. 21.

76. Jalãl Al-e Ahmad, an Iranian author whose writings had a decisive influence on the fall of the Shah's regime, described – not without exaggeration – the impact of Westernisation on Iranian society. See his book *Plagued by the West/ Gharbzadegi*, tr. Paul Sprachman (New York: Caravan Books, 1982).

77. See Toynbee, *Civilization on Trial*, p. 83.

78. Edgar Morin, *Penser l'Europe* (Paris: Gallimard, 1987).

79. See Hodgson, *The Venture of Islam*, Vol. III, p. 436.

80. See Shayegan, *Cultural Schizophrenia*, p. 34.

81. See Cox with sriclair, *Approaches to World Order*, p. 168.

82. See Shayegan, *Cultural Schizophrenia*, p. 23.

83. See Hodgson, *The Venture of Islam*, Vol. III, p. 441.

84. See Braudel, *A History of Civilizations*, p. 100.

8

An Islamic Perspective on Non-Alignment: Iranian Foreign Policy in Theory and Practice

Houman A. Sadri

Introduction

Contrary to the expectation of some Western observers,[1] the Non-Aligned Movement (NAM) is still strongly advocated by third world countries in general, and by Iran, in particular, in the post-Cold War period. Even during the Cold War, non-alignment was not just about rejecting the superpowers in a bipolar structure. It was really about providing policy options and a sense of independence for third world states soon after the decolonisation process. Since the demise of the Soviet Union, third world leaders, especially the Iranian political elite, still support a non-aligned policy and the Non-Aligned Movement in a world with only one superpower. This is evident by statements of former President Hashemi Rafsanjani[2] and the newly elected President Khatami.[3] Despite his accommodating statements regarding the general context of US – Iran relations in a January 1998 interview with CNN,[4] President Khatami stood strong in expressing the independent, anti-hegemonic, and non-aligned foreign policy of the Islamic Republic.[5] The fascination with non-alignment as a foreign policy strategy goes back to the early days of the Iranian Revolution, a turning point for Iranian foreign relations which shifted drastically from a close alliance with the United States to a non-aligned stance.

Understanding the nature, role and scope of non-alignment is salient to any analysis and estimation of Iranian foreign policy. Despite the significance of non-alignment, this concept has been ignored by most students of Iranian affairs. In one of the most authoritative books on Iranian relations with the superpowers, neither the contributors nor the well-known editors clearly or comprehensively explain what is described as Iranian 'neither East nor West' strategy, which is the Iranian version of non-alignment.[6] This article will address three basic questions about the non-aligned strategy of the Islamic Republic: Why did Tehran choose a non-aligned policy? What is the Islamic dimension of Iran's concept of non-alignment? How does this strategy apply to the conduct of the Iranian government, especially after the election in June of 1997? Before answering these questions, it is necessary to give a brief background about the context of Iranian non-aligned policy.

Background

Following the revolution, the Islamic Republic of Iran declared that it would conduct a non-aligned foreign policy – independent from the great powers. Shortly thereafter, Iran abandoned the Central Treaty Organisation (CENTO),[7] joined the Non-Aligned Movement and cancelled many weapons orders from the West. Iranian leaders believed that non-alignment would meet the foreign policy goals of Revolutionary Iran as a third world, Islamic state, whereas exclusive ties with any great power would not mesh with Iran's religion, culture or history. Moreover, an alliance or alignment would restrict policy options in establishing and maintaining mutually beneficial ties with states from any blocs and with certain third world states.

During the Cold War years, there was nothing unusual about the third world states' declaration to pursue a non-aligned strategy, even if a regime were clearly identified with either ideological bloc. For instance, Saudi Arabia became a member of NAM, even though it had no diplomatic relations with Moscow, and Cuba was a strong proponent of non-alignment, despite its membership in the Eastern camp and distaste for friendly ties with Washington. Moreover, Muslim states that joined the Non-Aligned Movement did not justify their policy based on Islam, but on the political options at the time. This applies to conservative Saudi Arabia as well as to, comparatively, more progressive Egypt. With the exception of Iran, the Muslim states make no direct connection between their non-alignment stance and Islamic heritage. This is especially significant as far as Pakistan and Mauritania are concerned because they are constitutionally and respectively the first and the second Islamic republics in the modern era. Neither one, however, has clearly and directly connected its policy to Islam in the way that has the third Islamic republic, Iran.

Iranian non-aligned strategy, enhanced by Tehran's independent stance, is a new chapter in the history of an ancient country that gained a different spirit and mission as a result of the 1979 Islamic Revolution. Some experts, though, have discounted the effects of Revolutionary Islam on the new Iranian leaders' political decisions by emphasising the element of continuity in geopolitical, historical and economic components of the policy; they conclude that Tehran's new strategy is not that original or radical.[8] Obviously, Iran was not a founding member of NAM, and Tehran's strategies in the pre- and post-revolutionary eras have some similarities, particularly due to geopolitics. Nevertheless, the Islamic Republic and Imperial Iran are philosophically and structurally different political units, and Tehran's declaration of non-alignment was a radical move, challenging the regional status quo at the time.

Why non-alignment?

Briefly, revolutionary Iranian leaders had four major policy objectives in declaring non-alignment: (1) to achieve autonomy in foreign policy-making, (2) to avoid a costly involvement in the American–Soviet rivalry, (3) to end Iran's dependence on one ideological camp, and (4) to improve ties with all states (except Israel and the former South African regime). Most of these goals were rooted in Iranian history, geopolitics and economy. In fact, the status and condition of Iran under the Shah was the main factor in shaping post-revolutionary foreign policy.

Regime stability dominated the Shah's domestic and foreign policies from 1953[9] and its pursuit created a vicious cycle: it required an alliance with the United States, which fostered a public image of military and economic vulnerability to non-Muslim foreigners. By emphasising such images, Ayatollah Khomeini characterised the Shah as an illegitimate, dependent and weak leader. This eventually weakened the regime both psychologically and politically. In sum, the revolutionary leaders claimed that their decision to follow a non-aligned strategy was taken mainly because dependency (that is, the trademark of the Shah's regime) was culturally an anti-Islamic and anti-Iranian notion.

What is significant about Iranian non-alignment?

Much is said about Iranian non-alignment, but ambiguities persist regarding Tehran's definition of this concept. For one ambassador of the Islamic Republic, non-alignment simply meant refusing to join an offensive pact.[10] Contrary to this rather passive interpretation of non-alignment, Ayatollah Mossavi Ardabili emphasised the active and con-flictual characteristics of non-alignment. He pointed out that Islam encompasses ideas that are at odds with both camps.[11] Former Foreign Minister Velayati defined non-alignment as maintaining independence from the two blocs and the consequent negation of foreign sovereignty in all aspects.[12] Ayatollah Khomeini, a strong advocate of a non-aligned strategy, did not offer a clear definition either, but referred to a slogan regarding the meaning of non-alignment, 'neither East nor West, [only] an Islamic Republic'.[13] Obviously, none of the above statements comprehensively defines the concept. Thus, it is necessary to have an analytical definition and discussion of the components of Iranian Islamic non-alignment, in order to examine its unique characteristics.

An analytical definition

Focusing on founder Ayatollah Khomeini's phrase, 'neither East nor West, [only] an Islamic Republic', one notes two parts. The first part negates external elements: the East and the West. It is a denial of formal or informal reliance (that is, alignment or alliance) on either the East or the West and refers to Iran's independent position. In this respect, Iranian non-alignment is similar to that of other NAM states. The second part refers to a specific type of regime: [only] an Islamic Republic. This is the unique aspect of Iranian non-alignment for two reasons. First, Tehran's definition is not secular like that of other third world states. Second, it implies a universalisation of one type of regime: a republic based on Shi'a Islamic values (not a monarchy like the Arab Gulf states although they are also NAM members). An examination of Iranian Islamic, legal and political values will help to better understand this unique approach to non-alignment.

The sources of Islamic non-alignment

An examination of the cultural, ideological and political context of Revolutionary Iran indicates that there are at least three major sources for this policy: religion, law and politics.

1. *Religious roots*

If one views non-alignment based on the idea of equilibrium or balanced relations (that is, the equidistance theory), then one might note that the Qur'an makes several references to the notion of equilibrium.[14] Iranian non-alignment, however, is not based on equilibrium, in which one seeks harmony with the environment.[15] On the contrary, Iranian Islamic non-alignment is, at least theoretically, not in harmony with its environment and is influenced by three Islamic, particularly

Shi'a, principles: *Tawhid* (Monotheism), *Hakemiyate Ellahi* (Divine Sovereignty) and *Jihad* (Holy War).

Monotheism (Tawhid). The Iranian non-alignment concept is rooted in monotheism, which is fundamental to understanding Islam.[16] Islamic monotheism is in contrast to the concepts of the Trinity[17] in Christianity and Dualism[18] in Zoroastrianism. In this context, Islam recognises no middle ground and historically challenged both Christianity and Zoroastrianism, the state religions of the Roman and Persian empires – the superpowers at the time Islam was a new religion. It is important to note that the first emerging Islamic state in Arabia did not align itself with either superpower at the time and neither did Revolutionary Iran centuries later.

Islamic monotheism refers to one God, one community of believers (*Umma*)[19] and one path of salvation – Islam.[20] Accordingly, other religions are unacceptable for a true believer in pursuit of salvation and solution to spiritual and worldly problems. Similarly, Iranian non-aligned strategy rejects the legitimacy of both Eastern and Western ideologies and models, considering them manmade (not divine), temporary (not permanent), and materialistic (not spiritual) in their nature and approach. Ayatollah Khomeini claimed that both ideological camps operated in an unjust international system based on might and not right. He added that no state is truly independent unless it confronts the hegemonic powers[21] and follows Islam. From this perspective, Revolutionary Iran joined NAM mainly because the non-aligned states reject hegemonic powers. Tehran, however, recognises that not all NAM states practise what they espouse. Thus, Iranian non-alignment is unlike that of other non-aligned states, and Revolutionary Iranian leaders have cast a great deal of doubt, from time to time, upon their strategy.[22]

Divine Sovereignty (Hakemiyat-e Illahi). The term Islam means submission to God, the only true sovereign. According to Shi'a theology, divine sovereignty passed from the Prophet to the Infallible Imams and by extension to the Most Learned *Faqih*. The latter is the basis of the concept *Vilayat-e Faqih*. In Revolutionary Iran, divine sovereignty is exercised by the *Vilayat-e Faqih* (rule of the leading jurisprudent) in the name of God and in the interest of *Umma*.[23] Thus, Iranian non-alignment takes a rather rigid and moralistic stand on sovereignty. One might ask why. In response, some leaders argue that Iranian political chaos and injustice during the Qajars and Pahlavi dynasties were created by the loss of true sovereignty to non-Muslim foreign powers. Therefore, they cautioned against unchecked ties with the great powers. This does not mean isolationism, but protecting one's sense of independence and identity while associating and cooperating with others.[24]

Holy War (Jihad).   Iranian non-alignment is also rooted in the concept of *Jihad*, the meaning of which is not limited to 'holy war'.[25] *Jihad* also means confrontation, struggle, or challenge, which refers to its diplomatic, as opposed to military, connotation. *Jihad* as a struggle of the powerless against the powerful is a significant aspect of Iranian foreign policy. *Jihad* glorifies a David versus Goliath type of confrontation, in which one finds both salvation and a deep connection to the mission of the Prophet Abraham. In fact, the Iranian Constitution requires the defence of the rights of Muslims anywhere, regardless of nationality, race, and severity of the crisis of the victims.[26] This justified Iranian efforts to help Afghans in their struggle against Soviets, Lebanese Shi'a verses Israelis, and Bosnians against Serbs. According to Ayatollah Khomeini, there is an inevitable struggle between the Islamic Republic and the hegemonic powers.[27] This struggle is not necessarily in the form of a full-fledged war, but rather as an ideological challenge. In this struggle, the revolutionary leaders insist that there is not much difference between the hegemonic powers (whether socialist or capitalist) as far as the policy goals or means are concerned, but there are fundamental differences between them and Iran. Unlike hegemonic powers, the latter does not initiate the usage of violence when challenging other states, although it preserves the right to resort to violence in self-defence.

2.   Legal roots

The Constitution of the Islamic Republic of Iran makes several references to the concept of non-alignment.[28] While four Constitutional articles address the general direction of foreign policy,[29] one focuses on non-alignment.[30] According to Article 152, Iranian foreign policy is based on:

(a) protecting the independence and territorial integrity of the Islamic Republic
(b) practising non-alignment toward hegemonic states and mutually peaceful ties with non-hegemonic ones
(c) rejecting any form of hegemony
(d) defending the rights of all Muslims

Therefore, the Iranian Constitution associates three notions with one another: the Islamic Republic, independence and non-alignment. Based on the notion of the Islamic Republic, Article 56 declares that absolute sovereignty belongs to God who has granted people the right to self-rule which no ruler should deny. Thus, the Constitution rejects the notion of dictatorship and foreign hegemony. Moreover, it relates foreign hegemony to dependence and attempts to end them both.

Citing a few examples regarding foreign advisers, treaties and military bases illustrates this point. First, although the need for industrialisation is recognised by the Constitution which allows the hiring of foreign consultants, Article 82 prohibits hiring foreign advisers unless it is absolutely necessary and then only with the approval of the Parliament (that is, Majlis). Second, any treaty that promotes foreign hegemony is void.[31] Finally, Article 146 explicitly prohibits the establishment of any foreign military bases in Iran, even for peaceful purposes.

3. *Political base*

Politically, the non-aligned strategies of Iran and others differ regarding the views of the existing world order, the nature of the policy and the notion of cultural independence. First, the founders of NAM were political realists who accepted the idea of an ideologically divided world order, based on a balance-of-power system. Thus, their non-aligned strategy was a mechanical solution and a foreign policy option to cope with the international status quo. On the contrary, the founder of the Islamic Republic was a revolutionary idealist who rejected the contemporary world order since he perceived it to be unjust and imposed upon the weaker nations.[32] On many occasions, Ayatollah Khomeini stated that there was no difference between the behaviour of the superpowers[33] since they were both materialistic, repressive in their own ways, and hegemonic toward the third world.

The second difference is that the founders of NAM did not intend to create a confrontational policy toward the superpowers. In fact, some NAM states, like India, had an instrumental value and acted as a means of communication between the superpowers during some international crises. Contrarily, Iranian non-alignment is, theoretically, an active and quarrelsome policy intended to challenge the great powers, although Tehran has not constantly and consistently confronted them in practice.

Finally, although all NAM states recognise the significance of cultural independence, the founder of the Islamic Republic went one step further in the defence of cultural independence by insisting that the great powers intended to destroy Islam – the core of Iranian cultural and religious identity. In terms of development, the clergy stated that the main problem of Iran had been *Gharbzadeqi* (or Western infatuation),[34] not industrialisation, and that these terms are not synonymous.[35]

Moreover, the problem was a mental dependence of many educated people on non-Islamic values. As early as the Constitutional Revolution, he argued, foreign-educated parliamentarians wrote the Constitution and established the educational and legal institutions based on non-Islamic foreign values.[36] For Ayatollah Khomeini, the most fundamental aspect of independence was its cultural dimension, represented by Islam,[37] despite some opinions that Revolutionary Iran had aimed equally for political, economic and cultural independence.[38] Even after the Ayatollah's death, Iranian revolutionary leaders still emphasise cultural independence and see themselves in a struggle against the influence of foreign, especially Western, values.[39]

Non-alignment: theory versus practice

The theoretical discussion of Iranian non-aligned strategy implies a moralistic, rigid and hostile policy, especially towards the great powers. In practice, however, the Iranian Islamic interpretation of non-alignment has been dynamic and has led to three distinct trends in foreign relations, each inspired by a different faction of revolutionary leaders. While all Iranian leadership factions have endorsed non-alignment, they each interpreted it differently according to the changing domestic and international circumstances. This led to three major trends in conducting Iranian non-alignment foreign relations in the first decade of the revolution: a two-track policy (1979 – July 1982), a conflictual policy (July 1982 – June 1985), and a conciliatory policy (June 1985–1989).[40] An examination of these trends will provide us with hints about the contemporary Iranian foreign policy posture, which will be discussed in the last section of this chapter.

A two-track policy

The two-track policy began when Bazargan's government took charge in February of 1979 and ended when Iranian forces moved the war into Iraqi territory in July of 1982. Shifting from a defensive to an offensive position in the Iran–Iraq war led some observers to argue that Tehran was exporting its revolution. Although many Iranian leaders insisted that exporting the revolution would be by word and not by sword,[41] there was evidence that the nature of the Iranian posture became less cooperative and more conflictual. Consequently, this action signified the start of a conflictual policy period, which will be discussed later.

The two-track non-aligned strategy consisted of one track oriented towards distancing Tehran from Washington and the other towards establishing more cooperative relations with Moscow. To distance itself from the United States, Iran took three major political measures including withdrawing from CENTO, abrogating the 1959 US–Iran Defense Agreement, and cancelling many Western military contracts. Although Tehran also revoked Articles 5 and 6 of the 1921 Iran–USSR treaty, some claimed that Moscow benefited from Tehran's decision to distance itself from the West while it established closer ties with some Russian allies like Syria and joined NAM. In general, non-alignment during this period was interpreted by many Iranian leaders as primarily a policy to reduce foreign, particularly Western, influence in Iranian affairs – a policy similar to Mossadegh's Negative Equilibrium.[42] Since the Russians did not have a significant presence in pre-Revolutionary Iran, they hoped to expand ties with the new regime. Tehran also began media campaigns against regional pro-Western states although pro-Eastern ones were not immune. Iran was soon blamed for a number of incidents which varied from demonstrations and acts of sabotage to hijacking and even an attempted coup. Considering the freedom that radical idealists enjoyed at the beginning of the revolution, such as operating centres like the Liberation Movement Office,[43] it is quite conceivable that some incidents received more than just a blessing from Tehran, despite the denial of top offcials.[44]

A more conflictual policy

In the second phase of its non-aligned strategy, Iranian policy toward the superpowers was more conflictual and uncompromising, particularly regarding the settlement of the war with Iraq.[45] Tehran's demand for the removal of President Saddam Hussein added to earlier suspicions about Iranian intervention in the domestic affairs of others and its attempts to export the revolution. This rigid position put Iran under a spotlight and isolated the country while it was already under domestic economic, political and military pressures.[46] To remedy the pressure, the leadership emphasised self-reliance and interpreted non-alignment as being similar to isolationism.[47]

Contrary to the earlier period when secular leaders like Bazargan and Bani-Sadr had an impact on the policy-making process, the clergy was in full control of all policy-making institutions after Khamene'i became president.[48] With the approval of Ayatollah Khomeini, the more radical clerics put a rigid tone on the Islamic non-alignment posture. The reason for this conflictual posture was that the tone of the policy was set by the more optimistic and idealistic revolutionary leaders who were confident that, despite some difficulties, they had run the country without foreign assistance. They could also see that time was on their side in bringing their new order not only to Iran, but also to the whole region. The radical leaders' growing sense of confidence was the result of a combination of some domestic and foreign successes which led them to become adamant in conducting their conflictual non-alignment policy towards the great powers and their allies.

A more conciliatory policy

The need for a more conciliatory approach in the non-alignment was partially rooted in the failure of the Iranian military to capture Basra. The latter is Iraq's second largest city and main port, populated mostly by Shi'a and located near the border with Iran. Despite inflicting heavy losses on the Iraqis, Tehran lacked the necessary hardware to break through the Iraqi defensive.[49] The Iranian leadership realised that the conflictual non-aligned position had limited the state's ability to end the war on its own terms.[50] The other root of the increasingly cooperative non-aligned posture was Iran's mounting economic and military hardships that led to increased domestic political pressure. The self-reliance policy had limited success, and Iran had major economic difficulties, such as astronomical inflation, food and medicine shortages, and stagnant salaries. Also, there were severe shortages of military spare parts for the weapon systems, and the infant domestic military industries had reached their qualitative and quantitative limits. Since Tehran could not match Baghdad's technological edge, it was forced to endure a much higher casualty rate in the war.

From late 1984, the more realistic revolutionary leaders, like Majlis Speaker Hashemi Rafsanjani, began to emphasize that non-alignment did not mean isolation from the rest of the world and aimed at changing the international image of the Islamic Republic. Iranian foreign policy began showing more conciliatory signs,[51] including Tehran's efforts to resolve the TWA hijacking and to end the radio propaganda war with the Russians.[52] Iranian diplomatic actions during this period showed that the emphasis was more on dialogue and less on defiance, although their rhetoric may have suggested otherwise. From 1985, Iran–Eastern bloc ties began to expand again. A year later, diplomatic relations with Western nations significantly improved despite the short-term downturn which occurred during the Salman Rushdie affair. The improvement of ties with the East and the West was an indicator of the realists' growing influence in policy-making following signs of moderation in

Ayatollah Khomeini. Furthermore, the Ayatollah's death in 1989 and the emergence of Rafsanjani as the main power broker smoothed some of the rough edges of the Islamic non-alignment policy.

Recent developments

Since 1989, Mr Hashemi Rafsanjani's bid for the leadership and ascendence to the presidency coincided with the rise of more realistic revolutionary leaders to the power centers. For the most part, this translated into a more accommodating non-aligned posture by the Islamic Republic towards both the great and regional powers. Nevertheless, this does not mean that the recent position of the Islamic Republic is the same as was that of Imperial Iran toward the West. Eighteen years after the revolution, the Islamic Republic neither maintains the same level or intensity of conflict towards the West (especially the United States), nor does it support the Western perspective on all regional issues, as did the Shah's regime. There are many examples. Contrary to the Western position, for instance, Tehran disapproves of the Arab–Israeli Peace Process since it forced many Palestinian problems into second priority negotiation issues, and it also meant that Palestinians could not negotiate on equal ground. Similarly, the Islamic Republic supports the rights of the southern Lebanese Shi'a more than does the West. The issue of human rights is another major point of contention between Iran and the West, especially the issue of the treatment of Iranian political opposition. There are instances in which Tehran's officials have been accused of involvement in the termination of political opposition in Europe. This behaviour of the Islamic Republic resembles that of Imperial Iran. These actions, however, are directed against Iranians, not Westerners.

Since the end of the Cold War, Tehran has further adjusted its non-aligned strategy. As a result, Iran conducted a more prudent and constructive policy during the Gulf War; in the Afghan civil war following the Russian withdrawal; in the Tajikistan conflict; and in the Armenia–Azerbaijan war, just to name a few. These examples, which will be discussed later, indicate that the Islamic leaders in charge of setting the policy agenda seem to have learned, or at least know, the limits of the Republic's capability to project its power and achieve its goals. Thus, the more realistic and pragmatic elements within the leadership are making and implementing policy.

One fundamental question here: Is a discussion of non-aligned strategy still appropriate with the end of the Cold War in the 1990s? The short answer is affirmative. Although the seeds of NAM were sowed during the hottest period of the Cold War, evidence shows that the Non-Aligned Movement and the strategy of non-alignment have a life of their own in the post-Cold War era. Their heads-of-state summits and the lower-level meetings are still held as usual and with the same fanfare style of NAM. The main difference is that there is understandably no attention paid to the ideological differences between the great powers, which divided the world across an East–West axis. However, there is much more emphasis on the North–South division of the world, and, in this fashion, NAM is playing the role of a union (of developing countries) versus the management (of the developed countries) at the global level.

The other major question regarding non-alignment is: Is there a possible role for non-aligned strategy in the post-Cold War period? The answer again is affirmative. We should recall that the essence of the non-aligned strategy was to provide a weaker state with more policy options. Using this strategy, many NAM states tried to avoid a costly involvement in the superpowers' conflicts, and their slogans suggested that they were neither in the Eastern nor the Western camps. This translated into the NAM states' obtaining some benefits from both camps. With the exception of states like Saudi Arabia and Cuba, most NAM members used this policy. Using non-aligned strategy, many NAM states took advantage of the opportunity provided by the natural conflict of interest among great powers. Today, there are no longer major ideological conflicts among these powers, but the end of the Cold War has not ended their natural clash of interests.

One can argue that there are now more clashing interests in the increasingly interdependent world than there were during the Cold War. Then, the superpowers focused mainly on security issues, and conflicts between the two camps were relatively few though intense. The quantity and quality of the conflicts were more or less managed by the superpowers in order to avoid the possibility of an accidental nuclear war. Conflicts within each ideological bloc, however, were either resolved in the interest of the community, in order to maintain unity against a global threat, or such disputes were discounted to avoid a fractured alliance.

Now, there is no more global threat, but the previously discounted or ignored disputes or conflicts have come to the surface, causing many regional problems on a variety of issues. The bulk of the conflicts are not limited to security issues any more, but include cultural, economic, legal and political problems. The nature of conflict in the global system has become so complex that it is not limited to two blocs challenging each other. Instead, members who used to be in the same bloc are now challenging one another on a number of fronts. Thus, the world has truly become an anarchical society.[53]

The examples of significant clashes among developed countries, especially the major powers, include: the growing division between the United States and European governments about the extraterritorial impacts of American laws on European companies that invest in Iran and Cuba; the American–Japanese controversy over the criminal behaviour of US servicemen in Okinawa and the closing of the base issue; the increasing objections of the French government to the Anglo (especially American) movie industry for projecting its culture and language in France; the Canadian, Australian and new Zealanders' complaints about the gradual loss of their national identity to the rapidly growing American symbolic presence in their respective countries; the intensified economic competition among multinational corporations of the United States, Japan and Germany for global and domestic market shares and resources; cases of cross-national industrial espionage among the American, European and Japanese companies; mutual security espionage between close allies like the United States and Israel; Sino-American disputes over the Chinese human rights record, unfair business practices and sales of missiles to Iran; and the growing gap between Washington and Moscow regarding the expansion of NATO, the oil of the Caspian Sea region, ethnic conflicts in the former Soviet republics, and Russian arms/technology sales to Iran and North Korea. Thus, the world is not a peaceful place yet, although the probability of nuclear annihilation has decreased to zero.

Considering that states have no permanent friends or foes (just interests), the above examples imply the obvious conclusion that where there is an interest, there is the possibility of conflict. It is the very existence of such conflicts that provide the non-aligned strategy with a window of opportunity. By balancing the interest of one power against another, a smaller state can not only survive but also thrive if the conditions are suitable.

In practice, the above strategy is the essence of the non-alignment policy of the Islamic Republic in this anarchical world. In Iran, the impact of revolutionary Islamic ideology (which gave a unique colour to Iranian non-alignment) on foreign policy is still visible, but there is also an appreciation for good old 'realpolitik'. Beyond the consensus among leadership factions regarding certain moral issues (for example, the support of Muslims around the world), Iranians are more willing to compromise now than during the early period of the revolution. For instance, Tehran supported the Islamic movement in Tajikistan (which shares the cultural heritage of Iran), but it also encouraged its client to negotiate instead of fighting hopelessly against the government. The final result was the July 1997 peace agreement which practically ended the civil war. In the Nagorno-Karabakh crisis in Azerbaijan, Iranians were concerned about the situation of the Azeri Muslims, many of whom are Shi'a, but Tehran maintained cooperative and working relations with Armenia to end the conflict in a reasonable fashion. Finally, Iran and the Gulf Arab states disagreed about the presence of US forces in the region, but they kept cordial relations, especially since the end of the Iran–Iraq war. These are only a few examples indicating pragmatic behaviour within the ideological context of the regime.

Beyond its borders, Iran will most probably maintain and expand its mutually beneficial ties with the great European powers, the Commonwealth member states and Japan. These countries are the major consumers of Iranian fossil fuel, and they are Tehran's main sources of industrial goods and hard currency. Since the 1979 revolution, however, Iran has tried to diversify its trade partners as well as its sources of technology in order to avoid overdependency on any foreign power. Of special significance are the growing Tehran–Moscow and Tehran–Beijing commercial and military relations that were historically restricted in terms of quality and quantity. Considering the earlier mentioned clashes of European, Chinese and Russian interests with those of the Americans, the Islamic Republic must be counterbalancing its troublesome US relations with its working ties with these powers. In other words, the non-aligned strategy is hard at work since Tehran does not have any exclusive ties with any major power, and the missing relations with the United States are compensated by those of the other great powers.

Mr Mohammed Khatami's successful bid for the presidency in June of 1997 was the most significant evidence of moderation among the Iranian masses and confirms that the more moderate elite within the leadership will continue to set the political agenda. The result of this election was unexpected, since a relatively unknown candidate was challenging the influential and charismatic Majlis Speaker, Mr Nateq Nori, known to represent the more radical factions and leaders. As mentioned earlier, President Khatami will most likely continue the pragmatic trend of conducting foreign relations as his diplomatic signals have indicated so far. The election results also indicate that the new leadership will work to prevent the Islamic Republic from being isolated again, as was the case during the conflictual period of non-alignment. It also means that leaders of the Islamic Republic will pursue a more accommodating non-aligned posture in order to maintain friendly, far-reaching, and fruitful ties with most countries, developed and developing (with the exception of Israel) and to neutralise the economic (and, indirectly, military) pressures of Washington on Tehran.

In sum, Iranian non-aligned strategy will continue in the post-Cold War period, although adjustments will be made to make it more applicable to the current global conditions. This policy will be the centrepiece of either the success or failure of Tehran's attempts to survive and nurture its revolutionary regime, despite all domestic, regional and international obstacles.

Notes

1. For a recent example of negative views toward the Non-Aligned Movement, please see the editorial piece, 'Review and Outlook: Flickering Flame', *The Wall Street Journal*, 8 April 1997, p. A22.
2. While visiting Nairobi, Kenya, former Iranian President Akbar Hashemi Rafsanjani urged support for the Non-Aligned Movement, in order to avoid exploitation by the West. See 'Iran Urges Support for Non-Aligned Movement', Africa News Service, 4 September 1996.
3. During a recent interview, newly elected Iranian President Seyyed Mohammad Khatami expressed his views about non-alignment by stating, 'We are nonaligned with an independent political system which, I hope, finds its proper place on the international scene.' Please see 'An Interview with Iranian President Khatami', *Middle East Insight*, vol. 13, no. 1, November/December, 1997: pp. 24–33, particularly p. 32.
4. President Khatami's interview by Christiane Amanpour on the Cable News Network, 7 January 1998, 6.00 p.m. ET.
5. See also 'Iran Paper Slams Khatami for Remarks to Americans', as reported by Reuters News Agency from Tehran, Iran, 8 January 1998. Available on Internet Infoseek News Channel, www.infoseek.com.
6. See Nikki R. Keddie and Mark J. Gasiorowski (eds), *Neither East Nor West: Iran, the Soviet Union, and the United States* (New Haven, Conn.: Yale University Press, 1990).
7. For information about CENTO see Zia H. Hashmi, *Iran, Pakistan, and Turkey: Regional Integration and Economic Development* (Lahore, Pakistan: Aziz Publishers, 1979), pp. 73–122.
8. For example, see Shireen T. Hunter, *Iran and the World: Continuity in a Revolutionary Decade* (Bloomington: Indiana University Press, 1990).
9. Robert Graham, *Iran: The Illusion of Power* (New York: St Martin's Press, 1980), pp. 245–54.
10. Muhammad Mokri, *Payam-e Emrooz*, 9 May 1979.
11. *Jomhori-e Islami*, 5 March 1983.
12. Statement by Dr Ali Akbar Velayati, *Kayhan Havai*, 2 May 1990.
13. Foreign Broadcasting Information Service, Daily Report: Near East & South Asia (henceforth FBIS/NE-SA), 10 December 1979.

14. The Qur'an speaks of a divine natural equilibrium and advises people to avoid excess in their conduct and to maintain a balance between earth and heaven, Sura Al-Rahman, Nos. 7–9.
15. The Qur'an states that God never leaves a path open for infidels to dominate the believers (Sura Al-Nesa, No. 141). This statement fuels the Muslim believers in their struggle against any form of foreign domination which would threaten their autonomy under divine sovereignty.
16. Monotheism to Islam is so significant that the Qur'an refers to it in several places (Sura Al-Baqara, No. 163; Sura Al-Nahl, No. 22; Sura Al-Moa' – menon, Nos. 91–2; Sura Al-Safat, No. 4; Sura Al-Ekhlas, No. 1). Ali Shariati states that *Tawhid* is not just one idea among others in Islam, but is the foundation of all Islamic principles. See Ali Shariati, *Islamshenasi* (*Understanding Islam*) (Mashhad, Iran: Chapkhaneh-i Tus, 1968), p. 73.
17. Sura Al-Maa da, Nos. 75–6.
18. Sura Al-Nahl, No. 51.
19. Sura Al-Hajarat, No. 13.
20. According to Shariati's analysis of monotheism in Islam, all other ideologies are only deviations from the true path. See Shariati, *Understanding Islam*, pp. 70–129.
21. R. K. Ramazani, *Revolutionary Iran: Challenge and Response in the Middle East* (Baltimore, Md: Johns Hopkins University Press, 1988), pp. 27–9.
22. For example, the Ayatollah considered Iran a truly non-aligned state which is a rare commodity (Ramazani, *Revolutionary Iran*, p. 22).
23. For more information, see A. Sachedina, *Islamic Messianism: The Idea of Mahdi in Twelver Shiaism* (Albany: State University of New York Press, 1981).
24. M. Mohammadi makes a similar argument based on Ayatollah Motahhari's views. M. Mohammadi, *Osol-e Siyasat-e Khareji-e Jomhori-e Islami-e Iran* (*The Principles of the Foreign Policy of the Islamic Republic of Iran*) (Tehran: Amir Kabir, 1987), pp. 47–9.
25. Focusing on *Jihad* only as a war has led some scholars to portray Islamic world order as rigid and prone to violent relations. See Majid Khadduri, *War and Peace in the Law of Islam* (Baltimore, Md: Johns Hopkins University Press, 1955). In fact, there are two types of *Jihad–Jihad Asqar* and *Jihad Akbar*. *Jihad Asqar* (the small holy war) is a defensive war that occurs between Muslims and their enemies without, while *Jihad Akbar* (the great holy war) occurs between an individual and the enemy within, that is, concupiscence. See A'skar Hoqoqi, *Falsafe-i Siyasi-i Islam* (*Political Philosophy of Islam*), Vol. 1 (*Tehran: Tehran University Press, 1975*), pp. 60–2.
26. Article 152.
27. R. K. Ramazani, *Revolutionary Iran*, p. 21.
28. For example, see Articles 3, 82, and 146.
29. Articles 152–5.
30. Article 152.
31. See Article 153.
32. For a discussion of types of revolutionary leaders, see Houman A. Sadri, *Revolutionary States, Leaders, and Foreign Relations* (New York: Praeger Press, 1997), especially p. 115.
33. In his speeches, Khomeini put both superpowers in the same category: *mustakberin* (oppressors) (see *Sahife-i Nur*, Vol. 11 (Tehran: Ministry of Islamic

Guidance), p. 17). He claimed that both superpowers would destroy the Iranian revolution from within (p. 108). The Ayatollah added that Iran should continue its struggle with the superpowers to eliminate all dependencies (p. 266).

34. This term literally means 'Westoxication' but it generally means adopting foreign values which include both the East or the West as the source of inspiration. However, the Ayatollah was not the first to refer to Iranian cultural dependence. See Jalal Al-Ahmad, *Gharbzadeqi* (*Westoxication*), reprinted in the USA (Solon, Ohio: Union of Societies of Islamic Students, 1979).

35. J. Mansori reached a similar conclusion, arguing that some developing countries mistakenly assume that the reason behind their national difficulties is their incompatibility with the West. J. Mansori, *Farhang-e Isteglal*: *The Culture of Independence*, (Tehran: Ministry of Foreign Affairs, 1987), pp. 1–4.

36. *Sahife-i Nur*, Vol. 11, pp. 183–4.

37. *Sahife-i Nur*, Vol. 12, pp. 122.

38. Mansori, *The Culture of Independence*, p. 251.

39. For example, Peter Waldman illustrates the clerics' fear of the promotion of Western values in Iran via satellite dishes. See 'Iran Fights New Foe: Western Television', *The Wall Street Journal*, 8 August 1994, p. A10. Also, the Associated Press reports that revolutionary Iranians introduced the Sara Doll (clothed in traditional Islamic dress) as an attempt to ward off Western cultural influences on Islamic children versus the barely dressed Barbie Doll. See 'Iranians Pit Doll Against "Evil Barbie" ', *Orlando Sentinel*, 25 October 1996, p. A6.

40. For a more detailed discussion of the three trends in Iranian foreign relations, see Sadri, *Revolutionary States*, pp. 93–109.

41. Ayatollah Khomeini's 9 August 1980 Speech in *Sahife-i Nur*, Vol. 12 (Tehran: Ministry of Islamic Guidance, January–February 1983), p. 283. Also see Hojatolislam Khamene'i's speech on 28 March 1980 in *Dar Maktab-e Jom'eh*, Vol. 2 (Tehran: Ministry of Islamic Guidance, January 1986), p. 87.

42. S. Zabih, *The Mossadegh Era* (Chicago, IU: Lakeview Press, 1982), pp. 88–96.

43. Helen Metz (ed.), *Iran: A Country Study*, 4th edn (Washington, DC: Government Printing Office, 1989), nn. 222–4.

44. Hojatolislam Rafsanjani has denied Iranian intervention in such affairs. For example, see his 18 December 1981 speech in *Dar Maktab-e Jome'h*, Vol. 4 (Tehran: Ministry of Islamic Guidance, Summer 1988), p. 152.

45. Iran's leaders referred to the war as the 'imposed war' and believed that the superpowers were in full support of the Iraqi goal of destroying the Iranian revolution (Sahife-i Nur, Vol. 14, pp. 107–8). Thus, Tehran's policy on the war serves as an indicator of its general non-aligned strategy although the latter usually refers to a state's relations with the superpowers.

46. Although Iran made some significant military achievements in the war (that is, liberating most of its territory in 1982 and capturing the Manjoon Islands in 1984 and the Fao Peninsula in 1986), the nation paid a high price in human and material losses (H. Metz, *Iran: A Country Study*, pp. 271–8).

47. *Sahife-i Nur*, Vol. 17, pp. 151–5.

48. The 1981 bombings, which killed many high-ranking revolutionary idealists (for example, Beheshti, Raja'i and Bahonar), had a major impact on Ayatollah Khomeini who 'withdrew his objection to the occupation of the highest offices of the state by clerics' and smoothed the way for the presidency of

Ayatollah Khamene'i on 2 October 1981. See Said Amir Arjomand, *The Tur-ban for the Crown: The Islamic Revolution of Iran* (New York: Oxford University Press, [Footnote] 1988), p. 154.

49. For details of this operation, see H. Metz, *Iran: A Country Study*, p. 276.
50. 'Iranian Minister Defends Policy', *Washington Post*, 27 November 1986.
51. On 28 October 1985, Khomeini confronted those idealists who had rejected relations with other governments. He decreed 'No man or wisdom accept [advocating isolationism] because its meaning is being defeated, annihilated, and buried' in *Sahife-i Nur*, Vol. 19, January–February 1983, p. 73.
52. James Bill dates the rapprochement to the recent Iranian attempts to get Western hostages freed. See J. Bill, 'The New Iran: Relations with Its Neigh-bors and the United States', *Asian Update*, August 1991, pp. 3–10.
53. See Hedley Bull, *The Anarchical Society: A Study of Order in World Politics* (New York: Columbia University Press, 1995).

Part IV

The Zen of International Relations

9
East–West Stories of War and Peace: Neorealist Claims in Light of Ancient Chinese Philosophy[1]

Roland Bleiker

Chuang-tzu and Hui Shih were strolling on the bridge above the Hao river.

'Out swim the minnows, so free and easy,' said Chuang-tzu. 'That's how fish are happy.'

'You are not a fish. Whence do you know that the fish are happy?'

'You aren't me, whence do you know that I don't know the fish are happy?'[2]

Neorealism has arguably been the single most influential contribution to the study of international relations (IR) since the 1980s. One of the paradigm's main purposes is to transcend time and space in order to recognise ahistoric and global patterns in the recurrence of interstate conflict. Yet, the key concepts of neorealist theory have been developed by Western scholars, largely based on analyses of interactions among Western states. How representative can such a grand Western vision be?

Neorealist thought – and, indeed, any form of intellectual endeavour – is inevitably influenced by time- and place-specific values. But such a proposition is not particularly new or insightful in itself. Hardly any approach to IR theory has come under harsher and more sustained criticism than neorealism. Ever since the late 1970s, when Kenneth Waltz introduced the tenets of a structural realist explanation of inter-state conflict,[3] scholars have found objection with just about every aspect of his parsimonious approach. We have heard of neorealism's state-centrism,[4] of its structuralist inability to account for agents and social change,[5] of its masculinism,[6] of its positivism and 'crude emperi-cism',[7] and of many other alleged shortcomings.

177

Despite this barrage of criticism – or, perhaps, precisely because of it – neorealism remains a highly influential approach to IR theory, particularly within North American academia. The publication patterns of the discipline's most influential journals testify to the continuous significance that neorealism holds in scholarly debates. The citation list would be endless,[8] but an illustrative example can be found in a recent discussion on the future of international relations, conducted in one of the discipline's new 'official' journals. Despite disagreements on a variety of fronts, the authors – all men, that is – return in the end to the inevitability of realist power politics. Or so at least argues the scholar who was given the task of summarising the contributions: 'most of the authors in this collection', he stresses, assume that 'the pursuit of power leads to the dynamics of realpolitik', and that 'such dynamics remain important in influencing the likelihood of international peace and order'.[9]

Equally prominent as the persistence of neorealist propositions is the belief, widely held among the paradigm's critics, that neorealism is a culturally specific *story* about war, rather than a detached and authentic representation of world political realities.[10] Such interpretations are particularly pronounced among scholars who are identified, in the broad sense of the term, with critical social theory and with the so-called English school, whose understanding of IR has always revolved around more historical and philosophical investigations, rather than the empirical generalisations that still characterise many approaches, particularly in the USA.[11]

This essay probes neorealist stories for their culturally specific traits, but does so in ways that differ from previous approaches. Rather than scrutinising the internal logic of neorealism or revisiting the criticisms that have been levelled against it, the essay seeks to identify the normative components of neorealism by examining the paradigm's main propositions in light of a tradition of thought that is concerned with the same issues, war and peace, but has emerged in an entirely different historical and cultural setting: ancient Chinese philosophy. The key task then revolves around the attempt to identify the elements of neorealist thought that are most likely shaped by specific spatio-temporal values. In order to compare realism with an entirely non-Indo-European stream of thought, I concentrate on Chinese philosophy during the Spring and Autumn (711–481 BC) and the Warring States (480–221 BC) periods, which roughly corresponds to what Karl Jaspers called the Axial Period. I focus primarily on specific thoughts within the two most influential schools, Confucianism and Taoism, refraining from examining competing contemporary thoughts and later influences on Chinese philosophy, such as neo-Confucian addenda to the *Analects*, the spread of Buddhism, or the more recent contact with Western ideas and ideologies.

The idea for such an unusual comparison across time and cultures has come to me via Nietzsche who, a good century ago, suggested that a person seeking to investigate 'our' European morality 'ought to proceed like a wanderer who seeks to know how tall the towers of a city are: s/he leaves the city'.[12] An adequate perspective on moral prejudices, Nietzsche stresses, can only be reached if one climbs up to some kind of position beyond good and evil or, since these lofty altitudes will always remain elusive to us earth-bound climbers, at least towards a position 'beyond *our* notions of good and evil'.[13] It is with this inherently impossible idea of an outside in mind that I am employing Chinese philosophical ideas, heterogeneous as they are, as means to leave the cultural hegemony of the realist city in order the examine the subjective but objectified foundations over which its towers of reality are built.

The essay begins by contrasting the broad conceptual and societal frameworks within which neorealism and ancient Chinese philosophy are operating. The subsequent sections deal with three sets of issues on which the two strains of thought diverge. First, I compare the methodologies of the relevant approaches. The focus rests on the use of levels of analysis, the academic and institutional organisation of the search for knowledge, and the key questions posed in the approach towards war and peace. Second, I examine the two intellectual traditions' attitudes towards reason with regard to ontology, epistemology and the search for solutions to the problem of war. Third, I concentrate on variations in the perceptions of the international system and the actors that comprise it. These domains of inquiry are, of course, not exhaustive. Countless other differences between neorealism and Chinese philosophy could be investigated too, such as their respective understanding of sovereignty, diplomacy and military strategy, or the gendered visions of society, conflict and peace. But given the limits imposed on an essay-length exposé, a more specifically targeted analysis must suffice, at least for now.

Needless, to say, a cross-cultural and cross-temporal comparison cannot claim to be an authentic series of representations. For one, I lay no claim to sustained disciplinary expertise in ancient Chinese philosophy. But even the most acclaimed expert would, I fear, never be able to climb up the hill of authentic knowledge and mount an epistemological platform from whence he or she could objectively gaze at the two systems of thought. No matter how high one claims, no matter how seriously and well-researched one approaches the issue, the structure of the English language forces the examiner to impose alien concepts on Chinese ideas because these ideas can only be expressed through references to values, experiences, terminologies and structures that possess meaning and identity within the Western cultural tradition. Thus, the present study does not claim to be more than a layperson's reading of ancient Chinese philosophy, a reading of thought in a distant time and place, conducted with the hope of rendering strange what has become frighteningly familiar and acceptable to us Westerners: a realist power politics that portrays violent conflict as inevitable, and perhaps even necessary for the sustenance of life in the global community.

Order, anarchy and change: contrasting stories about the international and the intercultural

In his *tour d'horizon* of IR theory, K. J. Holsti suggests that theories belong to one paradigm, the classical (realist) one, if they rely on the following three assumptions: (1) that the proper focus of study is the causes of war and the conditions of peace/security/order, (2) that the main units of analysis are the diplomatic–military behaviours of the only essential actors, nation states; and (3) that states operate in a system characterised by anarchy, the lack of central authority.[14] The latter assumption constitutes, from a neorealist perspective, the key structural variable around which explanations of interstate conflict must revolve.

Most of these assumptions about war are embedded in a deep-rooted intellectual tradition. Elements of realist thought can be recognised, or so at least it is claimed, in Thucydides' analysis of the Peloponnesian War, in the philosophical treatises of Niccolò Machiavelli, Thomas Hobbes and Jean-Jacques Rousseau, as well as in the (pre-structuralist) realism of E. H. Carr and Hans Morgenthau. These thinkers derived their hypotheses largely from the study of conflict within a particular, relatively homogeneous cultural environment: the European state system. Serious and culturally sensitive anthropological studies about warfare in other cultural spheres were not available until, at the beginning of the twentieth century, the (structural) functionalism of Malinowski and Radcliff-Brown introduced more systematic and culturally sensitive forms of ethnographies.

Even today, at the beginning of the twenty-first century, cultural homogeneity characterises most theories of international relations. Europeans and North Americans develop the major insights and paradigms. An empirical study suggests that in the 1980s scholars of anglophone countries, particularly the United States and Great Britain, dominated the field of IR theory.[15] It is unlikely that this pattern has changed fundamentally since then. As did their intellectual ancestors, most international relations scholars today derive their theories by and large from analyses of Western historical cases, particularly from the post-Westphalian European state system and its later global expansion. Only rarely do they consider patterns of warfare in premodern and non-Western contexts. Can realist assumptions thus retain any significance in cultural spheres other than the one from which they have emerged?

Western historians tend to agree that what could be called realist power politics characterised the political situation at the time when the classical Chinese texts were written. During the preceding period, the early Chou dynasty, there was no conflict among competing political entities because the patronage of a single emperor guaranteed unity. But from about 770 BC on, the order of this so-called golden age started to crumble, the empire disintegrated, and several independent states emerged. Louis Walker describes this epoch, the Spring and Autumn period, as one of disorder, central importance of state power and uncontrolled struggle for superiority.[16]

Rather than concluding, as structural realists would, that this system of competitive sovereign political entities inevitably breeds conflict, Chinese philosophers chose to envisage a world in which cultures interact without being dominated by the structural features of anarchy. I will discuss these alternative world views and their implications in more detail later in the essay. May it suffice, at least at this stage, to observe that none of the Chinese philosophers accepted the practices of warfare and the political structures at the time as naturally given. This tendency has been explained in various ways. The Confucian vision of orderly and hierarchical relations between individuals and aggregate of individuals is usually presented as an attempt to find the lost 'Tao', to reestablish the order and the harmony that existed during the preceding Chou, Shang and Hsia dynasties.[17] However, a full appreciation of the Chinese refusal to accept existing practices and structures as the sole reality can only be reached by touching upon the issue of dualism.

The way we perceive the interaction between dualistic entities has a crucial bearing on whether 'reality' is accepted as given or, rather, as subject to human influence. IR theory and Western conceptualising in general have traditionally been based on the juxtaposition of antagonistic bipolar opposites, such as rational/non-rational, good/evil, just/unjust, war/peace, or chaos/order. One side of the pairing is considered to be analytically and conceptually separate from the other one. The relationship between the bipolar opposites generally expresses the superiority, dominance, or normative desirability of one entity (such as peace) over the other (such as war). David Hall and Roger Ames argue that such dualist conceptualising leads to *ex nihilo* or 'transcendent philosophies'.[18] According to these doctrines, unconditioned elements determine the fundamental meaning and order of the world, such as, in neorealist thought, the transcendent source (the structure of the international system) defines the behaviour of the dependent variables (nation states).

Drawing upon the Taoist and Yin–Yang school, the dominant approaches in Chinese philosophy explicitly avoid dualistic conceptualising. Instead of thinking in the form of dichotomies, opposites are considered complementary because neither side can exist by itself. Since peace (or any other concept) can only prevail by virtue of its opposite – war – both form an inseparable and interdependent unit (yin and yang) in which one element is absolutely necessary for the articulation and existence of the other. Hall and Ames claim that operating along these forms of conceptual polarity leads to 'immanental philosophies'.[19] This is to say that events and actors are always interdependent, that there is no transcendent source which determines actions. Structures mediate thoughts and behaviour of agents, but the will of agents also influences structures. From this view, structures are not accepted as given and unchangeable, particularly the ones that may be responsible for a great deal of conflict.

Thus, rather than accepting the implications of the existing order, Chinese philosophers focused on human abilities to overcome the negative consequences of the existing 'realities'. The effects of this approach were not uniform. On a truly international level, the Chinese vision of world order had little or no impact because Confucian ideas never came even close to being hegemonic on a global scale. Yet, on the societal and to some extent also on the regional, intersocietal level, interactions among individuals and aggregates thereof were highly influenced by Confucian leitmotifs. A. C. Graham even argues that should ideas indeed have an impact on social forces, the Axial Period in China was an example of tremendous success.[20]

Ideas and their shaping of structures is a complex issue that cannot possibly be put to rest in this essay. Many critics of neorealism stress that the fundamental principles of international politics are subject to continuous change and that the direction of this change is at least partly a function of how we perceive and approach 'reality'. Not only is there no objective 'reality', but realities are always constructed. In short, discourse shapes practice. Hence, Robert Cox argues that there is no theory outside a specific spatio-temporal context, that 'theory is always for someone and for some purpose'.[21] There are, in Cox's view, two types of theories, problem-solving theories and critical theories. Problem-solving theories, of which neorealism is an example, consider the prevailing structures of the world as the given framework for action. They study the workings and impacts of the international system or address the problems that it creates. Such theories not only accept the existing order as given but also, intentionally or unintentionally, sustain it.[22] Critical theories, by contrast, attempt to transcend the prevailing world order with the objective of comprehending how it was created and how it could give way to less violent alternative orders.

While this is not the moment to scrutinise the relationship between structure and agency, one can reasonably assume that discourses on war and peace influence, at least to some extent, the formation of policy and, consequently, the occurrence and possible avoidance of conflict. For example, a Clausewitzian and a Confucian perspective are likely to lead towards different forms of state behaviour, even if the systems in which they operate were anarchic. Carl von Clausewitz considered war not as an aberration or a substitute for negotiations, but rather as a logical pursuit of diplomacy through other means.[23] Such a viewpoint influences decision-making because it not only delivers the explicit rationale for initiating and conducting violent encounters with other states, but also imbues these actions with philosophical and moral legitimacy. By contrast, a Confucian-oriented foreign policy is less likely to resort to violent means because it foresees the dissemination of influence not through wars, but via non-violent and persuasive methods such as education and indoctrination. Several studies have, indeed, suggested that the implicit and explicit theoretical concepts of policy-makers have a crucial impact on the occurrence of wars. For example, K. J. Holsti, based on an extensive survey of the issues over which armed conflicts were conducted between 1648 and 1989, argues that politicians' understanding of wars have influenced both the result of peace settlements as well as the emergence of subsequent conflicts.[24] Alexander Wendt goes a step further. He famously claims that anarchy does not necessarily have to create a security dilemma. The only 'logic' of anarchy is created by practices or, as he puts it, 'self-help and power politics are institutions, not essential features of anarchy. Anarchy is what states make of it.'[25]

Causes, circles and boundaries: methodological differences in the study of war and peace

In his influential analysis of international politics, Kenneth Waltz differentiates among three approaches to the study of interstate conflict.

Depending on whether the causes of war are seen in 'man' (individuals, if translated into less sexist language), the attributes of specific states, or the nature of the state system, he labels them first-, second-, or third-image analyses.[26] Most of the early and several contemporary theories, such as the ones of Hobbes, Rousseau, Grotius, Kant, Carr and Morgenthau belong to the first and second categories. While appreciating the general concept of power employed by these authors, neorealism has shifted the focus of inquiry from an ontological to a structural level. It is not human nature or the attributes of states but the systemic forces of the anarchical international system that are responsible for the recurrence of interstate conflict. In the absence of a global regulatory institution, the units of the system, sovereign states, must seek security through maximising their own defence capacities. This gives rise to a security dilemma, a vicious circle of continuous competition and conflict, according to which the very exercise of one state's security is a threat to the neighbouring states.

Such a structural explanation of conflict is alien to Chinese philosophy. The main subjects of study are individual ethics and societal order, that is, first-and second-image analyses. It is generally assumed that if harmony is reached at this level, global peace will follow automatically. Even Chinese philosophers who indirectly elaborate theories of international relations, such as Confucius or Han Fei Tzu would, in Waltz's definition, be 'reductionist' because they only study the behaviour of units, and not the impact of the system.[27] The very idea of separating among several levels of analyses is absent in Chinese philosophy. These differences in methodology are partly a reflection of how the search for knowledge is pursued.

The West has witnessed a long tradition of splitting up the organisation of intellectual endeavour. Assuming that the world cannot be explained by one single theory, that there is a need for demarcation, academia was separated into several fields. The social sciences alone are divided into various subfields. IR theory is only one of the subfields of political science, coexisting with others that range from political philosophy to comparative politics. Neorealist theory, in turn, is concerned with only one particular, and increasingly rare, type of armed conflict: interstate war.[28] Even within this already narrowly defined area of investigation, there has been a tendency towards increased specialisation on particular aspects or issues, such as regimes, alliances, or integration. The vision becomes even more narrow if we remember that the levels of analysis debate revolves around two different issues, as Barry Buzan stresses. On one side are ontological questions that have to do with determining the proper units of analysis (individuals, state, system and so on), and on the other side are epistemological questions that concern the proper research method, the manner in which one explains the units' behaviour.[29] By combining these two forms of delineating theoretical and analytical activities, the discipline of IR has turned into a rather narrowly sketched field of inquiry. A focus that is all too often confined to states and systemic factors is further restricted by limits imposed on the types of knowledge that are considered legitimate to understand global politics. The objectifying tendencies involved in this narrowing down of disciplinary debates become even more obvious if we recall Michel Foucault's suggestion that subdivisions of social knowledge do not represent an objectively existing 'reality' but, rather, constitute time- and place-specific rules and methods that control the production of discourses: systems of exclusion designed to define what is right and wrong, true and untrue, moral and immoral.[30]

Chinese philosophers do not share the belief that focusing on one precisely demarcated field of study will produce Pareto optimal conditions for the acquisition of knowledge. The rejection of dualist conceptualising is at the origin of this holistic approach. Since elements of bipolar opposition cannot exist by themselves and are defined always in relation to one another, events are seen as interdependent occurrences. Thus, Waltz's search for monocausality and his contention that one realm has to be separated from all the others in order to deal with it intellectually[31] are contrasted with the less parsimonious, but equally convincing, argument that the whole is greater than its parts, that the search for knowledge cannot, even for analytical reasons, be fragmented into different subfields. Consequently, Chinese philosophers reject intellectual endeavours that separate inquiries about conflict from philosophy, economics, religion and other fields of study.

One could, of course, go on and debate in great length the adequacy or intellectual usefulness of holism in comparison to academic specialisation. Such is not the task of this essay. For now we have to stay with the simple observation that the two approaches inevitably produce different outcomes. As a result of a holistic view, as prevalent in Chinese philosophy, the concern about war is only one theme among many. Armed conflict is inevitably linked not only to politics, but also to issues such as religion, economics, and even ethics and individual self-fulfilment. This direct link of conflict with ontology, history and culture implies that a (Chinese) theory about war and peace cannot exist outside of a time and place-specific context. By contrast, the separation of IR theory from other academic fields created a vacuum that has led to a search for atemporal structures that permanently mediate change. This view suggests that war is caused by, and peace can be found independently of, particular historical and cultural circumstances.[32]

Another methodological consequence of these diverging approaches to knowledge can be seen in perceptions of history. Operating along linear understandings of time, IR theory is mainly concerned with locating the causes of war. Among the crucial questions to be asked, Waltz points out, 'why does this occur?' and 'what causes what?'[33] It is only after finding out the answers to these questions that the conditions for peace can be searched for. Etiological (cause–effect) analysis plays a much smaller role among Chinese philosophers. In the same spirit as rejecting dualist thinking, they do not perceive history as a continuum of past, present and future but, rather, fuse these perceptions of time into a state of immediate awareness which takes the form of immanent or cyclical perceptions of history.[34] From this non-linear perspective of time, the search for solutions takes place independently from cause–effect analyses. Most experts agree that the main focus of Chinese philosophy is not searching for the truth, but locating the 'Way' (the *Tao*), not understanding the world, but making 'man' great, not determining the causes of war, but establishing the conditions for peace.[35]

The methodological and epistemological differences between neo-realism and ancient Chinese philosophy may be easier to recognise if we follow Nietzsche's advice once more and leave the city of IR in order to gaze at its crooked towers from a certain distance. Enter the domain of medicine which, if Foucault is right, should display similar culturally specific traits.[36] Ted Kaptchuk's detailed work on Chinese medicine does, indeed, support this suspicion.[37] Western medicine, he emphasises, is primarily concerned with either isolating disease categories or defining agents of disease. The rheumatologist, the neurologist, the gynaecologist, the optometrist, the cardiologist, the psychiatrist, the dermatologist, the urologist, the gastroscopist, the gastroenterologist, the otolaryngologist, the ophthalmologist, the endocrinologist, the oncologist and the haematologist, to name just a few examples, are all operating within well-demarcated spheres of inquiry. Few of them cross these demarcations and seek to understand the patterns of illness that may become visible if one were to gaze across disciplinary knowledges. But the prime objective of Western medicine, Kaptchuk stresses, is to detect a precise cause for a well-defined and self-contained illness. Chinese medicine, by contrast, is embedded in a holistic world view. It does not focus on specific disease entities. It does not trace symptoms back to causes. Instead, Chinese medical practices tend to focus on understanding the relationship of one organ to the whole, on patterns rather than causes of disharmony. Hence, restoring an overall balance between the body's yin and yang forces takes precedence over questions of cause and effect.[38] The field of medicine also reflects the difference between transcendental Western and immanental Eastern philosophies. Kaptchuk notes that Western medicine, in trying to discover pathological mechanisms behind apparent symptoms, attempts to discover the underlying causes of an illness independently from a specific patient or spatio-temporal circumstances. Chinese medicine, by contrast, only rarely relies on a transcendent body of theory. It considers the patterns of a patient's signs and symptoms as unique and therefore does not try to find solutions outside the idiosyncratic sphere of a patient's body.[39]

Logos, wisdom and experience: the role of reason in the explanation of conflict and the search for peace

Drawing on the (post-Sophist) Greek tradition, the belief in reason, logic and science guides Western thought. IR theory does not diverge from this pattern; reason and logic prevail in analyses and solutions of most theoreticians. It has been common in the West to argue, as Max Weber did, that the power of logos, of defining, and of reasoning was unknown to Chinese philosophers, that they were preoccupied with narratives while being ignorant of the 'empirical–etiological', 'rational–formalist' and 'speculative–systematic' approaches that were essential to Hellenic, occidental, Middle Eastern and Indian philosophies.[40] More recently researchers have claimed, however, that rational discourses were much more prevalent in ancient China than previously assumed.[41] Sophists like Hui Shih and Kung-sun Lung as well as the later Mohists, in an almost mirror-like image of the early Wittgenstein, rely heavily on reason and logical puzzles in their analyses. Hence, Graham concludes that Chinese philosophy was not unaware of the power of reason and logos, but that its most influential schools knowingly opposed or at least rejected an unlimited faith in it.[42] This scepticism towards reason is most pronounced in Confucianism, the Yin–Yang school and Taoism. It finds its most explicit representation in Chuang Tzu's anti-rationalism, contained in his second of seven 'Inner Chapters', called 'The sorting which evens things out'.[43]

Variations in the attitude towards reason influence the study of conflict in several ways. Drawing on Aristotles' concept of teleological action, the realist tradition generally assumes that under normal circumstances individuals and states act rationally, which is to say that policies result from a thought process that attempts to maximise utility through cost–benefit analyses. This assumption is the fundamental base, or even the *raison d'être*, of several approaches to the study of conflict, such as balance-of-power and game theories, or Robert Gilpin's application of economic (rational choice) theory to international politics.[44] Following from this assumed rational behaviour of states, the realist tradition concludes that the actions of states can also be understood in rational terms.[45] This belief appears so attractive that rational choice theory has, despite its limited relevance to political practice, become one of the most influential, if not the dominant, approach to the study of politics and international relations in North America.[46]

Confucians and particularly Taoists point out that the process of choosing between goals or options is often a spontaneous and intuitional rather than a rational process. They assume that before making an apparently conscious decision, subconscious and instinctive factors decide the outcome of the decision-making process. Hence, Chinese philosophers tend to consider a rational and logical analysis inappropriate for examining the dynamics of human thought and (inter)action. Rather, an assessment of a particular societal phenomenon should be based on such factors as detached awareness, instinct, wisdom and spontaneity. Confucians and Taoists thus favour a discursive, correlative or narrative approach which takes the form of poems, stories or aphorisms.

This contrasts with Hans Morgenthau's contention that 'a theory of politics must be subjected to the dual test of reason and experience'.[47] Chuang Tzu not only repudiates the utility of reason to a philosophical endeavour, but also questions the relevance of experiences for illuminating the issue of war and peace. Experiences, he would undoubtedly argue, cannot test (realist) theories because experiences are always judgements which are already mediated by a moral prejudice about what is right and wrong. Chuang Tzu's famous butterfly story exemplifies this scepticism about the existence of single reality:

> Once I, Chuang Chou, dreamed that I was a butterfly and was happy as a butterfly. I was conscious that I was quite pleased with myself, but I did not know that I was Chou. Suddenly I awoke, and there I was, visibly Chou. I do not know whether it was Chou dreaming that he was a butterfly or the butterfly dreaming that it was Chou.[48]

In its typical non-dualistic form, Chuang Tzu's story rejects the distinction between reality and unreality, object and subject, right and wrong.

The only way to liberate oneself entirely from these misleading structures is to undo and overcome the dualistic pairings, to break free from the prejudices and delusions built up by intellectually acquired and semantically conditioned thought-patterns. Thus, aesthetics and the search for emptiness through meditation become essential in the establishment of truth or, as Lao Tzu has expressed it, 'one who knows does not speak, one who speaks does not know'.[49]

Contrast this mystical approach, which one could call post-positivist in contemporary theory-speak, with the core principles of Western social science: realists generally presuppose the existence of a concrete and objective world, a reality that exists independently from human perceptions, a reality that can be understood as well as assessed, as long as our theoretical and analytical approaches are rational and systematic enough. Theories are only convincing if empirical examinations can validate them or, at the very least, if they successfully pass the scrutiny of Popperian falsification tests. Despite the prevalence of these positivist ideas within the realist tradition, Waltz is sceptical of purely empirical and heuristic methodologies. Basing his theory-building on C. S. Peirce's contention that experiences have no relevance as such, Waltz argues, in an almost Taoist way, that explanatory power is gained not by staying close to reality, but by moving away from it.[50] One key difference remains, however, between Waltz and Chuang Tzu. While both reject the possibility of gaining theoretical knowledge from examining (subjective) experiences, the former opts for a rational analysis while the latter employs an anti-rational and intuitive approach.[51]

These differences also left their mark on the respective searches for peace. The only way out of the security dilemma is, in Waltz's interpretation of Rousseau's stag hunt parable, a situation in which the individual acts rationally and is able to assume that everyone else does so too.[52] Most non-realist Western schools equally rely on reason for their solution. Martin Wight points out that theories which assert conceptions of global justice are based on the supposition that 'man' is a rational and social animal. As a result, 'his' rational nature leads 'him' to conform to a global order based on morality.[53] Immanuel Kant links reason to a didactic process. Human beings are, in his view, egoistic as well as rational. Paradoxically, it is the egoistic nature of individuals and the resulting occurrence of increasingly destructive wars which inevitably drive human beings towards greater respect for justice based on rationality.[54] Reason is also crucial to the solution advocated by the utilitarian tradition, which, according to Bentham, holds that beside public opinion, a rational body of international law is essential for the avoidance of war.[55]

These rational approaches to conflict resolution are much less prevalent in Chinese philosophy. Chuang Tzu would refute such solutions as misleading and, in a Western sense, as 'unreasonable'. An assessment of a particular problem and the solution to it does not, as already mentioned, require reason, but should be based on such factors as detached awareness, instinct and wisdom. Confucius equally rejects the establishment of peace through rational institutions such as laws, preferring instead an aesthetic approach that sustains a harmonious order through such elements as rituals and music.[56] Relying again on Chuang Tzu's ability to capture the essence of the matter in a few words, solutions cannot be based on reason because

> there is nothing that is not the 'that' and there is nothing that is not the 'this.' Things do not know that they are the 'that' of other things; they only know what they themselves know... Because of the right, there is the wrong, and because of the wrong, there is the right. Therefore the sage does not proceed along these lines (of right and wrong, and so forth) but illuminates the matter with Nature. This is reason.[57]

The differences between the logical realist approach and the embodiment of this anti-rational, Tao-oriented perspective on 'reason' find their clearest and perhaps most consequential manifestation in the perceptions the two streams of thought have of the nature of the international system.

Savage 'man', civil 'man' and the Tao: diverging stories of international utopia

Speculations about the state of nature play an important role in Western philosophies and indirectly in IR theory. This importance is partly derived from the belief that by knowing how individuals behaved in the state of nature, one could conclude which human characteristics are natural and which are artificially acquired by the influence of civil society. Descriptions of the state of nature vary from author to author, ranging from a peaceful, independent and egalitarian Rousseauian version to the Hobbsian state of war. Despite these differences, Western philosophers usually assume that anarchy, the absence of a central regulatory authority, was the most important feature of the state of nature.

Chinese philosophers are less explicit in their speculations about this subject. Among the few who explicitly elaborate on the state of nature are Mo Tzu, whose speculation bears many similarities with the anarchical, disharmonious and conflict-prone description provided by Thomas Hobbes and John Locke.[58] Taoist and even Confucian texts could also be interpreted as projecting a state of anarchy, or at least some form of initial equality among human beings. In a surprisingly Rousseauian way, the *Analects* (the most reliable source of Confucian doctrines) state that 'by nature men are alike. Through practice they have become far apart'.[59] However, this analysis of social dynamics differs from Confucius's normative viewpoint.

The important elements of the Confucian doctrine assume the existence of a preordained natural order. Central to Confucianism are the five cardinal relationships which characterise all human interactions in a very ordered and hierarchical way. They are sovereign–subject, father–son, old–young, husband–wife and friend–friend. It is likely that Rousseau would have criticised Confucius for not having reached the state of nature in his analysis, for speaking about civil 'man', and not savage 'man'. However, Rousseau himself argues that inquiries into this question cannot be based on scientific measurements and historic facts, for they are hypothetical and conditional reasoning.[60] Hence, the Confucian perception of a naturally hierarchical order cannot be regarded as right or wrong, it can only be acknowledged to exist.

Speculations about the state of nature are of direct relevance to the pursuit of conflict studies because IR theory has traditionally equated the interaction of individuals in the state of nature with the relationship among sovereign states in the international system. Among the authors who elaborate on this link, which Hedley Bull called the 'domestic analogy', are Spinoza, Hobbes, Locke, Rousseau and Kant, as well as the more recent realist theorists.[61] Thus, the state of nature and therefore the international system are characterised as decentralised and anarchic, which provides the *raison d'être* for most neorealist claims.

Chinese philosophy, in accordance with the emphasis on the 'Tao', is more critical in applying the 'domestic analogy'. The link between the state of nature and the international system is drawn only when this is compatible with the advocated conditions for peace. 'The ideal of an overarching Chinese polity remained strong', Yale Ferguson and Richard Mansbach stress, 'even during eras in which it was a fiction.'[62] Indeed, the very concept of an anarchical international system is virtually absent from the Chinese philosophical tradition. Benjamin Schwartz even argues that the entire Chinese world of thought shares one cultural assumption:

The idea of a universal, all-embracing sociopolitical order centering on the concept of a cosmically based universal kingship; the more general idea of the primacy of order in both the cosmic and human spheres; and the dominant tendency toward a holistic 'immanentist' view of order.[63]

The philosophy which provides the rationale for this vision is Confucianism. The five cardinal relationships, the norms of behaviour within the family, and the idea that all power should reside in one single ruler are applied to civil society and to the international system. Each 'unit' in this Sino-centric system has, according to its ability and function, a precisely defined place within a pyramidal international structure that ties the common citizen with the Chinese emperor and ultimately with heaven itself. The system is perceived to be a universal one, characterised by a set of tightly arranged hierarchical relationships.

Not only Confucianism but also most other Chinese philosophies assume the existence of order in the international system. Taoists, despite their commitment to laissezfaire principles and (anarchic) individual freedom, point out that the cultivation of inner virtues automatically leads to harmony among individuals and states. Mo Tzu, although presupposing conflict in the state of nature, advocates a cosmic order which is 'produced and maintained by the purposeful cooperation of Heaven, spirits, and men of good'.[64] This theory assumes that if the wisest man is chosen as the universal king of all civilisations, peace and global, indivisible love will automatically follow.[65] Even the Chinese legalist school, which can in many ways be compared to the realist tradition in IR theory, projects a certain image of universal order. In principle, legalists admit that the nature of the international system is conflictual because every state's objective is to maximise power. However, legalists stress that since every ruler is trying to become a hegemon by making his state paramount over all others, the end product is the establishment of a global order.[66]

It is not my intention to equate the Chinese vision of global order through hierarchy with a state of harmony or justice. Patriarchal and hierarchical Confucian principles have led to a great deal of oppression and discrimination. I only intend to use the Confucian vision of a global order to compare and contrast it to the neorealist concept of an anarchical international system that forces states to live in permanent competition with each other. Most realist hypotheses, such as the security dilemma or balance-of-power theories, depend on this assumed anarchy and would lose all meaning in the context of an orderly and hierarchical perception of the international system, no matter how oppressive and unjust its structure is. The only forms of hierarchy that penetrate realist thought are the ones that result from variations in prestige, the distribution of power, or unequal divisions of labour. This is the case because realists assume, as Raymond Aron summarises, that the oligopolistic character of the international system allows the main actors to influence the system more than the system can influence them.[67] However, realist perceptions of power hierarchies that operate within an anarchical system are different from the Confucian vision, because they do not rest on the assumption that the hegemon is legally established and formally recognised by the subordinate powers.

Confucianism also repudiates another essential assumption of neo-realism, the contention that sovereign nation states are the only consequential actors in the international system. From a Chinese viewpoint, interactions take place among cultures and not states. The very expression of 'Middle Kingdom' embodies the idea of cultural superiority, that is, China being the moral leader and the centre of humanity. As a result, it was perceived to be China's primary responsibility, as Adda Bozeman points out, 'to introduce civilisation into less privileged adjoining areas and thus prepare the barbarians for their ultimate inclusion in the world state'.[68] As opposed to armed conflicts being considered inevitable within a (realist) anarchical system, analysts tend to agree that given Confucius's rejection of power politics as an agent of diplomacy, the extension of the Chinese cultural realm to 'barbarian' areas is supposed to take place in a non-violent way, through education, virtuous example, persuasion, indoctrination, immigration and social intercourse.[69]

Conclusion

Conclusions are always temporary and tentative, especially if one compares two systems of thoughts that are as culturally and temporally removed from each other as neorealism and ancient Chinese philosophy are. Words of caution are all the more warranted since the present inquiry was able to focus only on a few representative domains. Within this limited sphere of inquiry, though, a number of clear differences have emerged. Presented in Western logical terms, they can be located in at least three different domains:

1. The methodologies of the two intellectual traditions differ in three ways:
    1.1 Neorealism separates among several levels of analysis and limits its approach to one principal level, the systemic one. The impact

of the structure of the international system on the formulation of state policies explains the reoccurrence of interstate conflict. This monocausal and parsimonious approach stands in contrast to the Chinese tradition, which focuses on the behaviour of individuals, and aggregates thereof, without limiting itself to precisely defined levels of analysis.

1.2 In order to maximise the search for knowledge, the West has divided academia into various fields and subfields. The relative separation of the study of international relations from other disciplines may be one of the factors that led to the neorealist search for a structural and ahistoric explanation of interstate conflict. The rejection of dualism and the resulting holistic framework of Chinese philosophy links the study of war with, among others, philosophy, religion and culture. It does not attempt to understand the ramifications of conflict outside specific spatio-temporal circumstances.

1.3 Dualistic conceptualising and linear perceptions of history partly explain the prevalence of cause–effect analysis in the neorealist approach to conflict. The key issue to be addressed is 'why do states go to war?' This question is only of minor relevance to Chinese philosophers. Cyclical and immanental perceptions of time as well as the belief in the social construction of reality led them to reject etiology in favour of searching for the conditions for peace independently from the causes of war.

2. The role of reason occupies a pivotal position in neorealist studies of conflict, but only a minor one in the Chinese approach to the issue. This difference manifests itself in at least three ways:

2.1 In the realm of ontology, neorealists generally assume that under normal conditions individuals and states act rationally; Chinese philosophers point out that the process through which actors choose among several options is dominated by intuition and spontaneity.

2.2 Following from 2.1, neorealists conclude that the behaviour and actions of states can be understood through rational means. They thus rely on rational and logical analyses to study war and assume that scientific–empirical research methods can test or at least falsify the established theories. Chinese philosophers, rejecting the prevalence of reason in epistemology, tend to approach the issue of conflict through narrative or correlative means that are based on detached awareness and wisdom. Scepticism about the existence of a single truth and reality makes testing of theories irrelevant to them.

2.3 The realist search for peace, to the extent that this is of concern to an etiological approach, is based on reason. An escape from, or containment of, the security dilemma can only be hoped for if a state acts rationally and can assume that the others do so too. Chinese philosophers tend to reject this solution as misleading and, instead, attempt to overcome conflict through the above-mentioned intuitive approach as well as through Confucian rituals, procedures and aesthetics.

3. The two traditions have radically different perceptions of the state of nature, the character of the international system, and the actors that comprise it:

3.1 The Western philosophies upon which neorealist concepts are built project the state of nature as one of anarchy, the absence of a central regulatory institution. The Confucian-influenced Chinese tradition assumes the existence of a preordained and hierarchical natural order among individuals.

3.2 Establishing an analogy with the state of nature, neorealists portray the international system as an anarchical one that inevitably breeds conflict among the system's only consequential actors, sovereign nation states. Confucianism displays a Sino-centric vision of a global community based on virtue, the supremacy of the Middle Kingdom, and a paternalistic–hierarchical interaction of cultures, rather than states.

While this essay has drawn attention to the differences between neorealism and ancient Chinese philosophy, one could – and should – also embark on a project that identifies similarities between them. The existence of 'realist' principles in Chinese philosophy has been mentioned briefly, particularly the elements of anarchy in Taoism and Mohism, the power politics of legalism, and the rational–logical character of Sophist and later Mohist thought.

Several key elements of ancient Chinese philosophy are also recognisable in IR theory and Western thought in general. Non-anarchical perceptions of the international system can be found in the premodern works of Dante and Thomas Aquinas, whose visions of a global harmony under either papal or imperial Christian authority bear many similarities with the hierarchical concept of the Middle Kingdom. The Chinese idea of peaceful interactions among societies, as opposed to antagonistic ones among states, can be seen in the ideas of early nineteenth-century liberals or in Karl Deutsch's concept of non-violent coexistence among regional pluralistic security communities.[70] Equally striking are the similarities between Taoism and various 'critical' approaches to IR theory. The immanental Chinese view that structure is both constituted and constitutive has more than just superficial resemblance with constructivist approaches to IR theory.[71] Chuang Tzu's mystical 'post-positivism' and Lao Tzu's reversal of priorities in chains of opposition find their Western counterpart in Derridean post-structuralists, who attempt reconceptualisation through the undoing of dualistic pairings and the reversal of hierarchies within existing dualistic concepts.[72]

The most striking similarity between neorealism and ancient Chinese philosophy is perhaps the patriarchal discursive framework that surrounds and drives both systems of thought. One could analyse at great length how and why two radically different cultural forms of masculinism have nevertheless led to similar gendered systems of exclusion. Crucial as this task is, to pursue it would have been beyond the scope of this essay. Its purpose was more modest and limited to identifying a few selective differences between the two respective traditions of thought.

What, then, is to be learned from such a specific cross-cultural and cross-temporal comparison of war and peace? For one, it is clear that neorealism is shaped and driven by values and political motives that are linked to a specific time and place. But if one compares this phenomenon with the striking similarities that exist between the two systems of thought, then one must also acknowledge that the differences between neorealism and Chinese philosophy are neither a result of cultural indoctrination nor a matter of mere coincidence. They are at least partly the expression of deliberate decisions taken by agents, individually or collectively. Of course, these decisions are never based on authentic insight into the realities of life. But they are nevertheless the produce of human will. Increased awareness of the theoretical choices we have made, and of the cultural context within which they are translated into practice, is the first and perhaps most important step towards creating an alternative and less violence-prone vision of world politics. This is why focusing our energies towards expanding or creating a new ahistoric and all-encompassing theory would not greatly improve our understanding of conflict or the prospects for peace. Instead, greater awareness of its inevitably subjective and culturally specific dimensions may help IR theory to become more effective in its search for the causes of war and its effort to overcome them.

Notes

1. This is a substantially revised version of an essay that was written in 1990 and appeared as 'Neorealist Claims in Light of Ancient Chinese Philosophy: The Cultural Dimension of International Theory', in *Millennium*, vol. 22, no. 3, Winter 1993, pp. 401–21; reprinted in D. Jacquin-Berdal, A. Oros and M. Verweij (eds), *Culture in World Politics* (London: Macmillan, 1998). I am grateful to Kal Holsti for encouraging me to pursue the topic, and to Stephen Chan for giving me the opportunity to revisit it. Such a revisit is an intricate affair, for one is inevitably torn back and forth between starting all over again and letting a text be what it is: an incomplete but nevertheless final arrangement of words which takes off in multiple directions and assumes a life of its own, independent of the author's initial intentions or subsequent efforts to retain control. The present revisit is located somewhere in-between these extremes. The essay's central arguments remain intact, but the framework within which they are presented has been substantially altered. Thanks to Doug Bond, Beth Kier and Kelly Wong for commenting on the essay at various stages of its conception.
2. Chuang-tzu, 'Stories about Chuang-tzu', in *Chuang-tzu: The Inner Chapters*, translated by A. C. Graham (London: Unwin Paperbacks, 1986), p. 123.
3. K. N. Waltz, *Theory of International Politics* (Reading, Mass.: Addison-Wesley, 1979). A selection of viewpoints presented by the paradigm's defenders, reformers and critics is contained in R. Keohane (ed.), *Neorealism and its Critics* (New York: Columbia University Press, 1986).
4. For instance David Campbell, 'Political Prosaics, Transversal Politics, and the Anarchical World', in Michael J. Shapiro and Hayward R. Alker (eds), *Challenging Boundaries: Global Flows, Territorial Identities* (Minneapolis: University of Minnesota Press, 1996); James N. Rosenau, *Along the Domestic–Foreign Frontier: Exploring Governance in a Turbulent World* (Cambridge: Cambridge University Press, 1997); and Gillian Youngs, *International Relations in a Global Age: A Conceptual Challenge* (Malden, Mass.: Polity Press, 1999).
5. For instance Alexander Wendt, 'The Agent–Structure Problem in International Relations Theory', *International Organization*, vol. 41, 1987; Andrew Linklater, 'Neo-realism in Theory and Practice', in K. Booth and S. Smith (eds), *International Relations Theory Today* (University Park: Pennsylvania State University Press, 1995), pp. 241–62.
6. For instance J. Ann Tickner, 'Hans Morgenthau's Principles of Political Realism: A Feminist Reformulation', in *Millennium*, vol. 17, no. 3, 1988, pp. 429–40; and 'Continuing the Conversation . . . ', in *International Studies Quarterly*, vol. 42, no. 1, March 1998; Christine Sylvester, *Feminist Theory and International Relations in a Postmodern Era* (Cambridge: Cambridge University Press, 1994).
7. Jim George, *Discourses of Global Politics: A Critical (Re)Introduction to International Relations* (Boulder, Colo: Lynne Rienner, 1994), p. 123. See also Richard Ashley, 'The Poverty of Neorealism', in *International Organization*, vol. 38, no. 2, 1984, pp. 225–86; and Steve Smith, 'Positivism and Beyond', in S. Smith, K. Booth and M. Zalewski (eds), *International Theory: Positivism and Beyond* (Cambridge: Cambridge University Press, 1996), pp. 11–44.
8. Indicative are the forum section on neorealism of the *American Political Science Review*, vol. 91, no. 4, Dec. 1997, especially Stephen M. Walt's 'The Progressive

198   *East–West Stories of War and Peace*

Power of Realism', pp. 931–5; and two significant monographs, D. A. Baldwin (ed.), *Neorealism and Neoliberalism: The Contemporary Debate* (New York: Columbia University Press, 1993); Charles W. Kegley (ed.), *Controversies in International Relations Theory: Realism and the Neoliberal Challenge* (New York: St Martin's 1995). Further examples include Stafano Guzini, *Realism in International Relations and International Political Economy: The Continuing Story of a Death Foretold* (London: Routledge, 1998); Mark Kramer, 'Neorealism, Nuclear Proliferation, and East–Central-European Strategies', in *International Politics*, vol. 35, no. 3, Sept. 1998; R. L. Schweller and D. Priess, 'A Tale of Two Realisms: Expanding the Institutions Debate', in *International Studies Quarterly*, vol. 41, no. 1, May 1997; Roger D. Spegele, *Political Realism in International Theory* (Cambridge: Cambridge University Press, 1996); J. Sterling Folker, 'Realist Environment, Liberal Process, and Domestic-Level Variables', *International Studies Quarterly*, vol. 41, no. 1, March 1997.

9. Stuart J. Kaufman, 'Approaches to Global Politics in the Twenty-first Century: A Review Essay', *International Studies Review*, vol. 1, no, 1, 1999, special issue on 'Prospects for International Relations: Conjectures about the Next Millennium', p. 195.

10. See, for instance, the work of Michael Shapiro: 'Sovereign Anxieties', in E. Lee and W. Kim eds, *Recasting International Relations Paradigms* (Seoul: Korean Association of International Studies, 1996); and *Violent Cartographies: Mapping Cultures of War* (Minneapolis: University of Minnesota Press, 1997).

11. For the authoritative statement on the latter see Tim Dunne, *Inventing International Society: A History of the English School* (London: Macmillan, 1998).

12. F. Nietzsche, *Die fröhliche Wissenschaft* (Frankfurt: Insel Taschenbuch, 1982/ 1882), pp. 276–7, Section 380.

13. Ibid., p. 277.

14. K. J. Holsti, *The Dividing Discipline: Hegemony and Diversity in International Theory* (Boston, Mass. Unwin Hyman, 1985), p. 10.

15. Ibid., pp. 102–8.

16. L. Walker, *The Multi-State System of Ancient China* (Hamden, Conn.: The Shoe String Press, 1953), pp. 73–9.

17. B. I. Schwartz, *The World of Thought in Ancient China* (Cambridge, Mass.: Harvard University Press, 1985), p. 63; R. Moritz, *Die Philosophie im alten China* (Berlin: Deutscher Verlag der Wissenschaften, 1990), p. 49.

18. D. L. Hall and R. T. Ames, *Thinking Through Confucius* (Albany: State University of New York Press, 1987), pp. 18–19.

19. Ibid., pp. 17–25. Lisa Raphals contrasts the two ways of thought in a similar way, but focuses on differences between theoretical and practical knowledge as well as on questions related to (metic) intelligence and Language: L. Raphals, *Knowing Words: Wisdom and Cunning in the Classical Traditions of China and Greece* (Ithaca, NY: Cornell University Press, 1992).

20. A. C. Graham, *Disputers of the Tao: Philosophical Argument in Ancient China* (La Salle, ILL.: Open Court, 1989), p. 5.

21. Cox, 'Social Forces, States and World Orders', in R. Keshane (ed.), *Neorealism and its Critics* (New York: Columbia University Press, 1986) p. 128. See also R. W. Cox, 'Gramsci, Hegemony and International Relations: An Essay in Method', *Millennium* vol. 12, no. 2, 1983.

22. Cox, 'Social Forces, States and World Orders', p. 130.

23. C. von Clausewitz, *Vom Krieg* (Stuttgart: Reclam, 1980), pp. 329–38.

24. K. J. Holsti, *Peace and War: Armed Conflicts and International Order 1648–1989* (Cambridge: Cambridge University Press, 1991).

25. A. Wendt, 'Anarchy is What states Make of It: The Social Construction of Power Politics', *International Organization*, vol. 46, no. 2, 1992, p. 395.

26. K. N. Waltz, *Man, the State and War* (New York: Columbia University Press, 1959).

27. Waltz, *Theory of International Politics*, pp. 18–37.

28. On the decreasing occurrence of interstate war see K. J. Holsti, *The State, War, and the State of War* (Cambridge: Cambridge: Cambridge University Press, 1996).

29. Barry Buzan, 'The Level of Analysis Problem in International Relations Reconsidered', in Booth and Smith, *International Relations Theory Today*, pp. 203–5. See also Hollis and Smith, Beware of Gurus: Structure and Action in International Relations', *Review of International Studies*, vol. 17, no. 4, 1991, pp. 394–5;and *Explaining and Understanding International Relations* (Oxford: Claredon Press 1990), pp. 92–118.

30. M. Foucault, *L'Ordre du discours* (Paris: Editions Gallimard, 1971), pp. 31–8.

31. Waltz, *Theory of International Politics*, p. 8.

32. For a more sustained discussion on the relationship between universalism and culture in IR theory see R. B. J. Walker, 'East Wind, West Wind: Civilizations, Hegemonies, and World Orders', in R. B. J. Walker (ed.), *Culture, Ideology and World Order* (Boulder, Colo: Westview Press, 1984), pp. 2–22.

33. Waltz, *Theory of International Politics*, p. 8.

34. See, for example, Chuang Tzu, 'The Chuang Tzu', translated by W. T. Chan, in *A Source Book in Chinese Philosophy* (Princeton, NJ: Princeton University Press, 1963), pp. 165–6.

35. A. B. Bozeman, *Politics and Culture in International History* (Princeton, NJ: Princeton University Press, 1969), p. 140; Graham, *Disputers of the Tao*, p. 4; J. M. Koller, *Oriental Philosophies* (New York: Charles Scribner's Sons, 1970), p. 197; Schwartz, *The World of Thought in Ancient China*, p. 414; H. Schleichert, *Klassische Chinesische Philosophie: Eine Einführung* (Frankfurt a.M.: Vittorio Klostermann, 1990), pp. 18–19.

36. M. Foucault, *Naissance de la Clinique* (Paris: Presses Universitaires de France, 1963).

37. T. J. Kaptchuk, *The Web That Has No Weaver: Understanding Chinese Medicine (New York: Congdon & Weed, 1983).*

38. Ibid., pp. 1–33, 256–66.

39. Ibid. pp. 34–5.

40. M. Weber, *Die Wirtschaftsethik der Weltreligionen: Konfuzianismus und Taoismus: Schriften 1915–1920*, Gesammelte Schriften, Vol. 19, edited by H. Schmidt-Glintzer (Tübingen: J. C. B. Mohr, 1989), pp. 309–13.

41. A. C. Graham, *Later Mohist Logic, Ethics and Science* (Hong Kong: The Chinese University Press, 1978); and J. Needham, *Science and Civilization in China* (Cambridge: Cambridge University Press, 1954).

42. Graham, *Disputers of the Tao*, pp. 7–8, 75–94, 137–212.

43. Chuang Tzu, *Chuang-tzu: The Inner Chapters*, pp. 48–61.

44. R. Gilpin, *War and Change in World Politics* (Cambridge: Cambridge University Press, 1981).

45. R. O. Keohane, 'Realism, Neorealism and the Study of World Politics', in R. O. Keohane (ed.), *Neorealism and its Critics*, in note 2, p. 7. It should nevertheless be noted that a number of realist theorists, particularly the ones with a (neo) liberal outlook, are critical about certain aspects of reason. For example, the traditional liberal view emphasises that rationality only applies to endeavour, and not to outcome, or that various external and internal factors are responsible for decision-makers acting 'only' under bounded rationality. See R. Gilpin, *The Political Economy of International Relations* (Princeton, NJ: Princeton University Press, 1987), p. 28; and R. O. Keohane, *After Hegemony: Cooperation and Discord in the World Political Economy* (Princeton, NJ: Princeton University Press, 1984), pp. 111–14.

46. See Jonathan Cohn, 'Theory vs Politics: When did Political Science Forget About Politics?', in *The Australian*, 27 October 1999, pp. 30–2, reprinted from *The Republic*.

47. H. J. Morgenthau, *Politics Among Nations: The Struggle for Power and Peace* (New York: Alfred A. Knopf, 1978), p. 4.

48. Chuang Tzu, 'The Chuang Tzu', p. 190.

49. Lao Tzu, *Tao Te Ching*, translated by D. C. Lau (Harmoundsworth: Penguin Books, 1986), p. 117.

50. Waltz, *Theory of International Politics*, p. 4.

51. For an elaboration on how Waltz's rejection of experience-based knowledge is nevertheless articulated form within a positivist framework see George, *Discourses of Global Politics*, pp. 123–4.

52. Waltz, *Theory of International Politics*, p. 169. See also Gilpin, *War and Change*, p. 226.

53. M. Wight, *Power Politics*, edited by H. Bull and C. Holbraad (Leicester: Leicester University Press, 1978), p. 290.

54. W. B. Gallie, *Philosophers of Peace and War* (Cambridge: Cambridge University Press, 1978), pp. 28–9.

55. F. H. Hinsley, *Power and the Pursuit of Peace* (Cambridge: Cambridge University Press, 1963), p. 88.

56. Graham, *Disputers of the Tao*, p. 30.

57. Chuang Tzu, 'The Chuang-Tzu', pp. 182–3.

58. Mo Tzu in Schwartz, *The World of Thought in Ancient China*, p. 142; T. Hobbes, *Leviathan*, edited by C. B. Macpherson (London: Penguin Books, 1968), p. 185; J. Locke, *Second Treatise of Government*, edited by R. H. Cox (North Arlington, Ill.: Harlan Davidson, 1982), pp. 3–10.

59. Confucius, *The Analects*, translated by W. T. Chan, *A Source Book in Chinese Philosophy*, p. 45. The Rousseauian passage is, of course, 'Man is born free, but everywhere he is in chains.' *Du Contract Social* (Paris: Flammarion, 1966), p. 41.

60. J. J. Rousseau, *Discours sur l'origine et les fondements de l'inégalité parmi les hommes* (Paris: Gallimard, 1965), p. 49.

61. H. Bull, *The Anarchical Society* (New York: Columbia University Press: 1977), p. 46; Waltz, *op. cit*, in note 2, pp. 163, 172; M. Wight, 'Western Values in International Relations', in H. Butterfield and M. Wight (eds), *Diplomatic Investigations: Essays in the Theory of International Politics* (London: George Allen & Unwin, 1969), pp. 102–3. See also Hidemi Suganami, *The Domestic Analogy and World Order Proposals* (Cambridge: Cambridge University Press, 1989).

62. Yale H. Ferguson and Richard W. Mansbach, 'The Past as Prelude to the Future: Identities and Loyalties in Global Politics', in Y. Lapid and F. Kratochwil (eds), *The Return of Culture and Identity in IR Theory* (Boulder, Colo.: Lynne Rienner Publishers, 1996), p. 26.

63. Schwartz, *The World of Thought in Ancient China*, p. 413.

64. Ibid., p. 141.

65. Ibid., p. 148. This concept, masculine as it is in its terminology and substance, evokes certain parallels with Plato's idea of a philosopher king.

66. A. Waley, *Three Ways of Thought in Ancient China* (New York: Doubleday Anchor Books, 1956), p. 177.

67. R. Aron, *Paix et guerre entre les nations* (Paris: Calmann-Lévy, 1962), p. 103.

68. Bozeman, *Politics and Culture in International History*, p. 144.

69. Ibid., pp. 134–5. See also M. Haas, 'Asian Culture and International Relations', in J. Chay (ed.), *Culture and International Relations* (New York: Praeger, 1990), p. 173; and J. K. Fairbank and S. Y. Teng, 'The Chinese Tradition of Diplomacy', in J. Larus (ed.) *Comparative World Politics: Readings in Western and Premodern Non-Western International Relations* (Belmont, Calif. Wadsworth Publishing, 1964), p. 192.

70. See K. J. Holsti, 'The Necrologists of International Relations', *Canadian Journal of Political Science*, vol. XVIII, no. 4, 1985, p. 678; A. Lijphart, 'Karl W. Deutsch and the New Paradigm in International Relations', in R. L. Merritt and B. M. Russett (eds), *From National Development to Global Community* (London: George Allen & Unwin, 1981), p. 239; and D. J. Puchala and S. I. Fagen, 'International Politics in the 1970s: The Search for a Perspective', in R. Maghroori and B. Ramberg (eds), *Globalism versus Realism: International Relations' Third Debate* (Boulden colo: Westview Press, 1982), p. 48.

71. See, most notably, Anthony Giddens, *The Constitution of Society: Outline of the Theory of Structuration* (Berkeley: University of California Press, 1984) and, for more IR specific debates; Wendt, 'The Agent–Structure Problem', pp. 335–70; David Dessler, 'What's at Stake in the Agent–Structure Debate?', *International Organization*, vol. 43, no. 3, Summer 1989, pp. 441–73; Martin Hollis and Steve Smith, 'Beware of Gurus: Structure and Action in International Relations', *Review of International Studies*, vol. 17, no. 4, 1991, pp. 393–410; Walter Carlsnaes, 'The Agency–Structure Problem in Foreign Policy Analysis', *International Studies Quarterly*, vol. 36, Sept. 1992, pp. 245–70; Vivienne Jabri, *Discourses on Violence: Conflict Analysis Reconsidered* (Manchester: Manchester University Press, 1996).

72. See, for instance, R. K. Ashley, 'Living on Border Lines: Man, Poststructuralism, and War', in J. Der Derian and M. J. Shapiro (eds), *International/Intertextual Relations*: Postmodern Readings of World Politics (Lexington, Md: Lexington Books, 1989). J. Derrida, *A Derrida Reader: Between the Blinds*, edited by P. Kamuf (New York: Columbia University Press, 1991), pp. 259–76.

10
Selling Culture: Ancient Chinese Conceptions of 'the Other' in Legends

Qing Cao

Introduction[1]

For over two millennia,[2] the Chinese considered their country to be the Middle Kingdom (*Zhongguo*), the terrestrial focal point of 'all under heaven' (*tianxia*) and the source of all civilisation. They had never faced a rival strong enough to challenge their cultural supremacy until the mid-nineteenth century when British gunboats broke through their 'isolation'. China's conception of the Other was deeply imbedded in this tradition. However, apart from this 'isolation', there are other factors that determine the Chinese sense of their position in the world and their relations with the Other. The following two are important. First, unlike Europe, Africa and other parts of Asia where kingdoms and empires rose and fell to form different nations, China has sustained what Wang Guangwu terms a 'historical oneness'.[3] This 'oneness' is a unity of the largest ethnic group on earth, the Han Chinese,[4] with their sinicised peripheries, an extensive settled land, and a consistent and continuing culture. The unit of this 'oneness' is the so-called civilisation-state. Second, China as an empire was not established by conquest of other nations[5] like other great empires, such as the Greek, Roman, Persian, or, in modern times, British and French. Recent imperial conquests stretched over long distances, even across oceans. They survived as long as their military power could sustain them. No armies ever marched out of the confines of the traditional 'Middle Kingdom'[6] in China's two thousand years of 'imperial' history. Given these traditions and characteristics, China's conceptions of the Other operate in a very different framework from that of the West where a Westphalian system was established in 1648.

China is rich in legends, folktales and myths. They form a vast repertoire of cultural resources in which perceptions of the Other were preserved, transmitted and reproduced throughout history. Folklore
operates within the framework of culturally approved schematic knowledge. In China, this schematic knowledge with reference to images of
'self' and Other bears distinct features. To begin with, major strands of
conceptions of the Other were developed two thousand years ago, and
recorded in a relatively small number of classics during the Spring and
Autumn (770–256 BC) and Warring States (475–221 BC) periods. These
ideas, like other basic Chinese worldviews, survived the millennia primarily through two institutions: *sishu* (traditional form of school) and
keju (state examination for the selection of bureaucrats). The former
used Confucian classics as textbooks, through which orthodox ideas
were widely diffused and penetrated every single cell of the society.
The latter tested the knowledge of these classics, giving them the status
of undisputed 'truth'. Next, the presentational style of these classics,
unlike that of earlier Western thinkers such as Aristotle, is characterised
by an extensive use of 'stories' to illustrate theoretical points.[7] Later,
many of these stories became household *chengyu* or *diangu* (idioms,
aphorisms, or epigrams, allegories) typically expressed in a four-
character idiom.[8] This narrative style of presentation, shared by wider
early writings, contributes to the blurring of borders between literature,
history, and even philosophy in early China a phenomenon that raises
debates about Chinese image/intuitive thinking and Western logic/
scientific thinking.[9] This narrative tradition, combined with holistic
thinking, forms an important context in which folklore functions as
an essential part of cultural process in Chinese society.

Moreover, the 3000-year-old Chinese writing system has been an
enduring force stronger than power-greedy emperors in keeping Chinese culture intact.[10] It is more saturated with ideological function and
content than any other major writing system, and therefore termed as a
'Chinese ideological machine' by Hodge and Louie.[11] The unified script
can be read by people across the country speaking hundreds of different
dialects. Popular stories recorded in written form such as the case study
story in this article could temporally and spatially reach a vast audience
and therefore have a sustained life. These features ensure that 'stories' in
Chinese society carry more cultural messages and are therefore important in tracing the Chinese sense of 'us' and the Other.

This chapter aims to explore traditional Chinese conceptions of and
strategies for the Other through an analysis of legend. A combination of
methods will be utilised, including structuralist and discourse analysis,

to deconstruct the narrative of the selected case study story, 'Seventh Capture of Meng Huo'. This legend offers a typical example of how conceptions of the Other are represented in a popular cultural form based on underlying assumptions rooted in dominant Confucian tradition. It demonstrates that while sharing some similarities with the West, the Chinese conceptions of the Other are significantly different in a number of ways. The differences could be understood as manifestations of fundamental features of the Chinese culture itself.

Theoretical framework

Structuralism is a way of thinking about the world which is primarily concerned with the perception and description of structures. It carries with it the assumption that the full significance of any experience cannot be perceived unless it is integrated into the structure of which it forms a part.[12] In summarising the structuralist study of folklore, Alan Dundes distinguishes two types of analysis – syntagmatic and paradigmatic.[13] The former is represented by Propp's seminal study on the morphology of Russian fairy tales,[14] focusing on the structure of formal organisation of a folkloristic text following the chronological order of the linear sequence of elements. The latter is represented by Claude Lévi-Strauss[15] who emphasises the pattern underlying the folkloristic text, focusing on an *a priori* binary principle of opposition. Lévi-Strauss believes linear sequential structure is apparent or manifest content, whereas the paradigmatic structure is the more important latent content. Therefore, the task of structural analysis is to reveal the true underlying paradigmatic pattern of organisation beneath the superficial linear structure. Paradigmatic analysis recognises the culture-specific nature of the meanings of folklore. This study will draw largely on the second type of structuralist method in the analysis of binary oppositions in the Chinese conceptions of the Other through cultural categories constructed in the legend.

However, this study aims to locate the Chinese conceptions of the Other in a historical dimension. Discourse analysis, therefore, provides a convenient supplementary method. Taking a theoretical and methodological approach to language and language use as its main concern, discourse analysis relates text to a wider social process as a historical context. This study adopts Norman Fairclough's framework that defines a discourse as a particular way of constructing a particular (domain of) social practice.[16] Fairclough emphasises text production and interpretation as an integral part of text analysis and develops different levels and dimensions of analysis.[17] In differentiating textual, intertextual and contextual analysis, Fairclough gives centrality to intertextuality, in contrast to conventional focus on textual domain, as linking the text as a product and discourse as a process. Intertextual context is defined as 'histories' within which discourses and texts occur. To analyse these 'histories' one needs to reveal which series a text belongs to, and therefore what can be taken as common ground for participants, or presupposed. These presuppositions, evident in the text, are a trace of the text producers' interpretations of intertextual context.[18]

Closely related to intertextuality is reproduction of socio-cultural identity through discourse practice, a stage of analysis termed 'explanation' by Fairclough.[19] The task at this stage is to uncover how discourse is determined by social structures, and what reproductive effects discourses can cumulatively have on those structures, sustaining them or changing them. Reproduction is generally an unintended and unconscious effect of production and interpretation through drawing on schematic knowledge as interpretative procedures of texts. Thus, social structures shape schematic knowledge, which in turn shapes discourse; and discourse sustains or changes schematic knowledge, which in turn sustains or changes social structures. Thus conceptualised, this study will focus on the dominant influence of traditional culture upon the discourse of folklore with reference to the notion of the Other which is an important vehicle in sustaining the existing social structures of Confucian China.

Seymour Chatman[20] distinguishes 'story' in the content plane and 'discourse' in the expression plane in the study of narrative. The present study focuses on the latter to examine the set of narrative statements, where 'statement' is the basic component of the form of the expression, independent of any particular manifestation – that is, the expression's substance such as folklore. This difference could also be understood as a 'story' that is a specific and local transformation of a deep structure of binary oppositions essential to a culture within which they circulate as 'myth'.[21] The case study legend 'Seventh Capture' is used in this sense as a particular 'story' that expresses and realises underlying cultural 'myths' of the Other.

Case study story: analysis and discussion

The story and its formal features

The story 'Seventh Capture of Meng Huo' is an episode from *Romance of the Three Kingdoms*, one of the four classic Chinese novels, reputedly written by Luo Guanzhong, a Confucian scholar of the Ming dynasty

(1368–1644), based on folktales and scattered historical records.[22] The novel is about wars between the three kingdoms during the Three Kingdoms period (220–280). The four-chapter episode I will examine depicts how Zhu Geliang, the prime minister of the kingdom Shu, successfully subdues a major rebellion led by an arch-villain Meng Huo in Southern China, a peripheral region at that time. It reveals how the people on China's periphery were perceived, treated and subsequently brought within China's cultural orbit.

Vladimir Propp defines the smallest narrative units – motif in terms of functions[23] – and demonstrates that all the folktales which he examines conform to a limited number of functions (31 in all) performed by 'dramatis personae'.[24] Based largely on Propp and Northrop Fry, Silverstone[25] develops a concept of 'mythic narrative' which combines syntagmatic and paradigmatic structuralist analysis to deconstruct wider narrative structures. According to this view, there are two dimensions of a 'mythic narrative': a chronology of events, principally as heroism and adventure, and a logical structure of concrete categories. The first provides the narrative with its momentum; the second with a base in experience and ontology. Heroic narrative follows the pattern of heroes, quests and tests, a pattern explored in the work of Propp. Logical narrative provides explanation and description deemed appropriate to discursive reasoning. Therefore one is the narrative of action and battle, the other of classification, justification and demonstration; though both are unnatural as representations of reality. Following the model provided by Propp, Lévi-Strauss and Silverstone, I will draw a sketch of the *mythic* structure of *Seventh Capture* to outline the story and its basic functional elements.

1. *The initial situation*   A powerful barbarian king, Meng Huo, rebelled against the Middle Kingdom (China). This poses a serious challenge to the authority of the emperor Liu Chan. The equilibrium was broken.
2. *Dispatch*   The prime minister Zhu Geliang was dispatched by the emperor to wipe out the threat.
3. *Departure*   Zhu Geliang departed with a dozen generals and 500,000 soldiers.
4. *First donor*   A detailed map of the barbarian land was obtained from a wise man who offered to become a guide.
5. *First victory*   Meng Huo was captured in direct combat, but subsequently set free because he claimed to have been caught through treachery.
6. *Receipt of a magical agent*   Guided by a mountain god, Zhu Geliang obtained the use of magic water in 'An Le Spring' (Spring of peace and

happiness), and a magic herb, 'Xieyie Yunxiang'. Zhu also possessed the magical power of commanding the wind to overcome the wild animals controlled and used by a cave leader, an ally of Meng.

7. *Subsequent victories* Meng was caught another five times in a series of fierce battles, but Meng still refused to accept his defeat. In order to win his whole-hearted subjugation, Zhu treated him well and released him each time to allow him to fight 'a fair battle'.

8. *Final victory* Upon his seventh capture, Meng was overwhelmed by Zhu's wisdom, military might, and his humanity and generosity. Zhu Geliang finally won the heart and mind of Meng, pardoned his sin, and returned all the occupied land. Meng became a 'good' king of China's southern periphery and promised never to rebel again.

9. *Return and transfiguration* Zhu Geliang triumphantly returned to the Middle Kingdom and was received as a hero by the emperor. The troubled southern barbarian land became a peaceful, tribute-bearing region. The equilibrium was restored.

The actorial structure, following Propp, can be presented as shown in Figure 10.1.

A number of transformations are accomplished in this narrative. First, temporally a history of interactions with a tributary region is rendered highly intelligible within the short space of an episode. Second, a remote peripheral culture has been rendered not only 'familiar' but reassuring. Third, unconscious but powerful parameters have been offered to the reader in viewing the peripheral regions. All of these could not happen without the second aspect of the mythic narrative – logic, or an organising structure of concrete categories that provide both the building blocks of the narrative and a way in which that narrative grounds its material in the fundamental experience of a culture. These

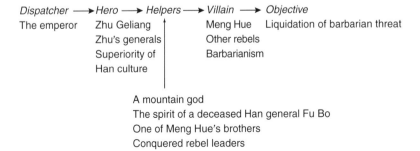

Figure 10.1

categories focus on the organisation of a textual expression of the basic ordering capacity of humankind. This logic provides the frame for a presentation of the Other grounded in an articulation of a series of simple oppositions: civilisation and barbarism, culture and nature. These binary oppositions, or 'grand dichotomy' as Jack Goody[26] puts it, forms the basis of the logical structure shown in Figure 10.2.

The model of the mythic logic of a narrative must work with categories that are readily understood and acceptable by the culture that receives it. The narrative in its movement through this structure tells a cultural story with two sets of basic but interrelated codes: civilised versus savage and cultural versus natural. Both categories and their oppositional relationships are textually established. I will use these categories to analyse the story in the following sections.

Textual domain: value systems

Culture and ethnicity

A central concept of 'us' as Han Chinese and 'them' as '*man*' (see below) is defined through two sets of codes in Figure 10.1. The Han people are described as possessing the attributes on the left and top whereas *man* people bear those on the right and bottom. This Sinocentric view is realised through a series of classifications that impose an order of 'us' and 'them'.[27] Similar to a zoning system in early Zhou,[28] an abstract notion of '*wanghua*' is used to present a concentric sphere system of Confucian influence. '*Wanghua*' means 'civilisation' (literal meaning 'emperorisation'[29]). Meng and his followers were described as being 'outside *wanghua*', whereas Zhu's mission was to bring '*wanghua*' to the rebellious natives. The word '*man*' is used to refer to Meng and his people and means 'rough, unreasonable.'[30] *Man* and *wanghua* are often used together: 'to subject *man* people to *wanghua*', '*Man* people are far from Central China so they are not used to *wanghua*'.

Through these classificatory terms, relations with the Other are conceptualised in terms of culture used as a predominant factor determining territory measured by distance from the centre and the level of Confucian influence, and even ethnicity seen mainly in terms of customs, for example, diet, mating, dress, cooking. There was no clear sense of 'border' in the Chinese conception of *tianxia* (all under heaven). It extends as far as Confucian cultural norms were practised. Nor was ethnicity clearly defined and so did not play an important role in differentiating 'us' from the Other. The tension between 'us' and 'them', therefore, was not Chinese against non-Chinese. It was those

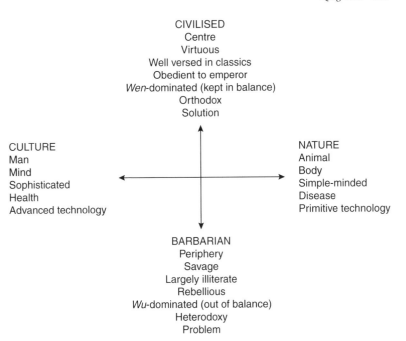

CIVILISED
Centre
Virtuous
Well versed in classics
Obedient to emperor
Wen-dominated (kept in balance)
Orthodox
Solution

CULTURE
Man
Mind
Sophisticated
Health
Advanced technology

NATURE
Animal
Body
Simple-minded
Disease
Primitive technology

BARBARIAN
Periphery
Savage
Largely illiterate
Rebellious
Wu-dominated (out of balance)
Heterodoxy
Problem

Figure 10.2   The mythic logic in the legend, 'Seven Captures of Meng Huo'

Chinese who had civilisation as opposed to all those who did not have it. Those who did have it included non-Chinese as well as other Chinese.[31] This was in line with the traditional view that there were three types of being in the world: humans, barbarians and animals. *Huaxia* (Central China) is most civilised; barbarians are less so; animals are not at all civilised.[32] This conception of the Other is reflected in terms used to refer to China's peripheral tribal peoples: *yi* (eastern), *man* (southern), *rong* (western) and *di* (northern). All these terms carry the connotation that they are less civilised. Collectively they are called *yi*.

Cultural power versus military power

A central strategy adopted by Zhu to subdue the rebellion is 'It is better to win hearts and minds than to attack towns and cities' (*gongxin weishang, gongcheng weixia*), and 'A battle for winning hearts is wiser than a battle of arms' (*xinzhan weishang, bingzhan weixia*).[33] This pacifist strategy seems to have the advantage of securing a long-lasting peace with the '*man*' in Southern China, so that Zhu could focus on reuniting

China by defeating the other two 'illegitimate' kingdoms on the northern and eastern fronts. However, it carries with it some underlying cultural assumptions. First, as '*yi*' were seen as 'uncivilised', an important goal, therefore, is to bring them to the Confucian cultural orbit. This aim is different from internal conflicts where main issues were legitimacy of the throne (by royal blood) and/or the level of benevolence in the reign (when changing dynasty). In these conflicts, military conquest is invariably the solution. Second, cultural tradition dictates that cultural power is sufficient to bring the rebellious Other to 'our' cultural sphere (to be discussed later).

Military power, on the other hand, was presented as being used as a deterrent. Zhu claimed to be able to catch Meng any time like 'taking a thing from my bag' (*nangzhong quwu*), but was patient enough to wait for Meng's final remorse and total subjugation, so that Meng would never pose a threat. Military power was thus used to serve the projection of cultural power. Moreover, in dealing with the *yi* at the periphery, establishing and maintaining a tributary state had always been preferred to an occupation. Tribute-paying is more a ritualised affirmation of China's claimed cultural superiority than an activity of economic significance. China seemed to be content to maintain such a loose relationship. Upon withdrawal of his troops, Zhu was pleased to have 'established peace without having to leave any men to rule and provide any additional resources'.[34] Around two hundred tributary tribal regions were established as a result of this expedition. This was the best result the emperor had hoped for.

Moralism

In a dichotomous account of Meng and his followers, a moral order was established based on a Confucian vision of a moralised universe. In this hierarchical world, the emperor as the 'son of heaven' (*tianzi*) is the supreme moral symbol of all under heaven. To defy the wishes of the emperor implies lack of morality.[35] Thus, Zhu's expedition was seen as primarily a moral mission. The legitimating power derives from resolving *an act of immorality* (a rebellion) in the name of *tianzi*. Zhu accused Meng of moral perversion: 'the emperor has treated you kindly, how dare you rebel?' The accusation assumes an indisputable imperial authority over the *man* population who were morally bound to obey the imperial court. The unity of civil and moral power is a unique feature of Chinese culture.[36] This nature of relationship is defined in a chapter title[37] 'Prime Minister mobilised forces to combat Southern aggressors [*nankou*]; *Man* King was caught when resisting the heaven's army [*tianbing*]'. The word *tian* (heaven) represents both a cosmic order and the emperor, conveying the meaning of both a moral and imperial power. The morality-oriented legitimating power is further confirmed when Zhu, trapped in an ominous valley, was assisted by a temple god because he was carrying out a civilising mission to restore a Han moral order entrusted to him by the late emperor Liu Bei.

Confucian moral superiority was described as recognised by *man* natives as well. Prisoners of war sang praises of Zhu's Confucian civility. Even Meng acknowledged his own inferior culture upon his seventh release: 'Though I am from outside civilisation, I know correct conduct and righteousness [*liyi*]. How can I be so shameless?' In the end, Meng was made a moral loser, which was precisely what Zhu designed to achieve. Meng's moral 'inferiority' was also exposed by those close to him, often in dramatic ways. In Propp's classification of 'dramatis personae', Meng's essential 'lack'[38] is morality – the real cause of his villainy. One of Meng's brothers denounced Meng as 'unreasonable and evil, not following *wanghua*'. Meng's followers deserted him in the heat of battle, believing 'Zhu is a benevolent man [*renren*], it is ominous to do evil things and oppose him'. Tired of conspiring with Meng, fellow chieftains even caught Meng as a gift to deliver to Zhu. To rebel against Meng seemed the best way of a moral redemption. Throughout the story, maintaining a high moral ground is more important than diplomatic manoeuvres and the use of naked force. Morality became the real magical agent in Propp's sense of the term.[39]

Universalised morality, as an important philosophical tradition, is best expressed in the concept of *tianren heyi* (unity of heaven and man)[40]. In this moral regime, man follows the cosmic order that has its moral will. The emperor, as the supreme moral symbol, is responsible to heaven for his own conduct and for maintaining a good moral order. Cross-cutting natural and human worlds, the moral regime knows no boundaries. Seen through this lens, the act of rectifying the perversity of *man*'s rebellion elevated Zhu to the status of a hero of the Han and a saviour of the *man*. Upon his victory, Zhu was even revered as 'a benevolent father', enjoying ceremonial sacrifice in a dedicated temple established by *man* natives. Interestingly, even today, Zhu's accomplishments are recognised in standard history books: 'to secure the interior land, he [Zhu] improved relations with ethnic minorities in what is now Guizhou and Yunnan provinces, and strengthened political, economic and cultural ties between the Han nation and ethnic minorities in Southwest China'.[41]

Intertextual domain: discursive background

The values expressed in 'Seventh Capture' are deeply embedded in Chinese culture. As outlined earlier, major schools of thought in China find their roots in the classical time of the 'one hundred schools'.[42] During the Warring States era when interstate wars were rampant, most schools favoured a non-violent solution to 'interstate relations'. Despite eventual unification under Qin Shihuang who adopted the legalist thinking[43] of using brute force as a political instrument, the non-violent tradition represented by Confucianism emerged as dominant thinking from the Han dynasty[44] on. 'Seventh capture' reflects this mainstream political ideology. Not only the frame of thinking but some of the very expressions are drawn from pre-Qin classical works.

Zhu's strategy of projecting a cultural power resembles closely Confucius's view of cultivating a 'soft' relationship (*huairou*) with remote areas: 'If remote people are rebellious, our civil culture is to be cultivated to attract them to our virtues; and when they have been attracted, they must be made contented and tranquil.'[45] Confucius likened cultural virtues with the north polar star: 'He who exercises government by means of virtues may be compared to the north polar star, which keeps its place and all the stars turn towards it.'[46] This *yide laizhi* (attract by virtues) line of thinking resonates with Mencius'[47] famous theorising of the virtue of moral power:

> To govern the people not with a fortified boundary; to defend a country not with the natural barrier of deep valleys; to reign all under heaven not with armed forces. Those who possess justice get abundant assistance; those who abandon justice get scanty assistance. Relatives will desert those scarcely assisted; all under heaven will rally with those who are abundantly assisted. To use all under heaven to combat those abandoned by relatives, a victory is assured if gentlemen choose to fight a war.[48]

This idealistic doctrine of cultural power[49] clearly guided the story's line of reasoning. However, pacifist tradition is not limited to Confucianism. The Mohist School[50] is famous for its strong stance against any form of using force,[51] a theory known as *jianai* (universal love) and *feigong* (non-invasion). A well-known story, 'Gongshu', tells of how Mozi, the founding father of Mohism, successfully persuaded State Chu to abandon an invasion through his eloquence, bravery and clever defence strategies.[52]

Taoism developed a political philosophy of *wuwei erzhi* (reign by non-activity) in which wars are to be totally avoided. Lao Zi abhorred the use of violence: 'the more sharp weapons people have, the more benighted the state'.[53]

Early traditions of pacifism could be found in other writings as well, for example, *Zhan Guo Ce*, one of the earliest historical chronicles about Warring States. A household idiom, '*nanyuan beizhe*', originating in this chronicle, compares going to war to someone travelling towards the north when his destination is in the south. The faster one travels, the further away is his destination.[54] Drawing on this rich cultural repertoire, 'Seventh Capture' makes a particular point about the expedition: a benign war fought with the power of virtue, a dominant Confucian[55] interpretation of war, in particular in relation to tribal 'barbarians'.

In portraying a triumph of Confucian virtues over peripheral villainy, the author inherited a Sinocentric view as well from the early thinkers. Confucius took Chinese cultural superiority for granted: 'The tribal land of the east and north ruled by princes are not as good as China even when there is an absence of sovereign.'[56] Mencius is more influential in this respect: 'I only know to transform *yi* with *xia* [China], and have never heard of transforming *xia* with *yi*.'[57] Adopting Chinese culture was likened by Mencius to a bird coming out of a dark valley to the sunny arbor tree, but adopting *yi* culture is exactly the opposite. Mencius' conception of *xia* is, again, predominantly cultural rather than ethnic. He eulogises *yi* scholar Chen Liang for unparalleled accomplishments in Confucianism, but despises Chen's Chinese disciple for learning *yi* doctrines[58]. By learning *xia* culture, Chen became 'us' and, correspondingly, his disciple became 'them'.

Mencius' culture-dominated definition of binary *xia*–*yi* relations leaves a deep imprint in Chinese history. Tang scholar Chen Yan's view reflects this influence: 'Some people are born in barbarian lands but their actions are in harmony with rites and righteousness. In that case, they are barbarian in appearance only but they have a Chinese heart and mind.'[59] Fung Youlan stresses an emphasis on culture over ethnicity as explaining China's acceptance of foreign rulers during the Yuan and Qing dynasties, which adopted Confucianism as the dominant ideology: 'They, the Mongols and Manchus, ruled China politically, but China ruled them culturally. China's main concern is whether Chinese culture or civilisation remains intact.'[60] Foreign rulers of Yuan and Qing are therefore recognised as orthodox by the Chinese.

Identifying 'us' and 'them' by cultural practice is abundantly evident in 'Seventh Capture'. Meng's brother, Jie, was immediately recognised as 'us' by his conduct. Jie has a typical Confucianist image – sophisticated, modest, well-versed in the classics, dressed in a white robe and living in a simple cottage surrounded by carefully selected plants. It explains why Jie, with his barbarian origin, was a legitimate source to provide the magic to save Zhu's army. The power was clearly endowed by Confucian culture, regardless of its holder's ethnicity. Even the image of Meng changed from being a 'villain' to a 'hero' when he was finally subjected to Confucian culture and followed Zhu's admonition of governance by virtue. *Man* people eventually became converted to become 'us', rather than remaining a conquered but uncivilised people. The practice-based view of the Other may account for the slow absorption of peripheral ethnic minorities into Chinese culture over the centuries. Anthropologist James Watson calls this feature of Chinese culture 'performative', therefore Han Chinese were 'not racial or biological in any overt sense'.[61] Hahm argues that this is different from the Western notion of culture which 'tries to combine the "genetic" and the "social"'.[62]

Cultural reproduction: the symbol of *wen* and *wu*

Operating within a socio-culturally conditioned framework, 'Seventh Capture' draws on existing cultural categories and, through this discursive practice, reproduces them. This is chiefly realised through the success of the image of Zhu, who represents a classic balance of two principal ways of dealing with the Other – *wen* and *wu*. This pair of words, like *yin* and *yang* familiar in the West, are philosophical terms to describe fundamental categories of two different but supplementary forces, which are widely applicable in life in various forms. The binary concept can roughly be translated as 'cultural–military', 'cultivation–force', or 'mental–physical', 'literati–warrior', according to the specific context.[63] In the foreign policy domain, *wen* and *wu* principally mean 'to use military force' or 'to use pacifist means'. However, like *yin* and *yang*, *wen* and *wu* should be combined in a fine balance to optimise the force because both are sources of power. Nevertheless, as *wen* tradition had been stronger in a Confucian state,[64] a pacifist policy had been preferred to a *wu* militarist approach. As cultural categories, *wen* and *wu* are endlessly versatile and can be applied to many concrete instances. 'Seventh Capture' applies them both as strategic approaches and cultural symbols.

Zhu Geliang, as one of the most enduring artistic creations in China, represents an ideal *wen* symbol. First, he uses primarily his wisdom and 'virtues' to subdue a peripheral rebellion – a pacifist *wen* strategy. Second, he was moderate in using his military might which could easily smash the *man* forces – an essential *wu* force but under *wen* control. Traditionally, *wu* force was often viewed with suspicion. *Wu* is believed to be a natural force that must be seasoned with *wen* cultivation in order to be productive. A naked *wu* power would either be destructive (like Meng) or fail to achieve its aim. An ideal combined use of *wen* and *wu* is *yin er bu fa*, meaning reserving military force, but not to make use of it. The constraint is *wen*, the deterrent is *wu*. On his triumphant return, Zhu made a moving prayer at a river bank, weeping to the ghosts of those dead from both sides in battle. This *wen* ritual serves to redress *wu*'s destructive, though necessary, force.

Third, Zhu's appearance represents a typical *wen* symbol – wise, sober, benevolent and refined, often seen holding a delicate feather fan in a hand, while examining the topography of the battlefield. The visual image marks him as different from other generals with a typical *wu* image – awesome face, broad shoulders, and a suit of armour – such as Guan Yu and Zhang Fei, the two most powerful of Zhu's generals. This symbolises not only an emphasis of *wen* over *wu*, but a Confucian bureaucrat's control over the military. Fourth, in contrast to Zhu, Meng demonstrates primarily *wu* qualities: mightly, fierce, glamorous, arrogant, though unsophisticated. Unlike Guan Yu and Zhang Fei whose *wu* image is positive (kept in balance), Meng's *wu* image is negative (out of balance). Therefore, Zhu's *wen* image represents a Confucian superior culture and Meng's *wu* image represents a barbarian culture.

'Seventh Capture' represents a glorious victory based on an alleged successful expedition. The reality however is far from glamorous. China was constantly harassed throughout history by tribal peoples on the borders, in particular Central Asia's nomads. The *wen* and *wu* approaches were frequently debated in the imperial court. But pacifist *wen* policy often got the upper hand due to a *wen*-oriented tradition. The military as a profession was not even listed in the four occupational classes – *shi* (scholar), *nong* (farmer), *gong* (artisan) and *shang* (merchant). However, it does not follow that there was no realpolitik in traditional thinking on foreign relations. Many of the concepts of modern international relations, such as the balance of power, collective security, diplomatic manipulation, and interstate treaties and alliance, developed in China as early as the Spring and Autumn period.[65] Numerous stories illustrating these strategies were recorded in early historical books such as *Zuo Zhuan*, *Zhan Guo Ce*, *Sun Zi Bing Fa*, and *Shi Ji*.[66] However, the historical record suggests that for most of the Chinese dynasties, the Confucian *wen* paradigm was preferred to the *wu* realpolitik paradigm.[67]

The Confucian world view sees the world as harmonious, orderly and hierarchically structured with a moral 'son of heaven' both at the top and centre. 'Conflicts are regarded as largely deviant phenomena rather than the nature of things and should/can be managed through means other than the use of brute force.'[68] In this *wen*-dominated strategic thinking and practice, an invasion by the northern nomads remained a serious threat. Fairbank even concludes that 'a reasoned pacifism' is one of China's 'deepest weaknesses, an inability to avoid alien conquest from the grasslands'.[69] Situated in this historical context, the Mongol conquest of Yuan China seems almost inevitable. However, Confucianist *wen* culture, in turn, claims to have sinicised *wu*-dominated Mongols, and through this absorbed the Mongols into the Chinese orbit.

Zhu's *wen* conquest of Meng falls into the category of *zhaoan* tradition – a practice of offering a bureaucratic position to a worthy convert-rebel (preferably before the conquest). The objects of *zhaoan* were usually powerful charismatic rebel leaders such as Meng. *Zhaoan* could save bloodshed and avoid social disruption. Nevertheless, conditions for such an offer are total repentance and subjugation to the imperial court. However, *zhaoan*, more often applied to internal rebellions, was not as typically used as *heqin*, a standard *wen* strategy in foreign relations. It is a practice of pacifying northern nomads by marrying imperial daughters to their chieftains. Stories about *heqin* are numerous in history. In contrast to glorious *zhaoan*, *heqin* legends are typically sad laments of imperial daughters in a foreign land, such as Wang Zhaojun,[70] one of the four celebrated beauties in Chinese history, who was married to a Mongol prince and died from grievous nostalgia for her homeland. Both peace by offering office and peace by matrimonial ties are culturally approved *wen* strategies.

Cultural symbolism embodying these underlying assumptions has been disseminating in Chinese society for centuries, reinforcing Confucian values. The image of Zhu Geliang is so successful that he has become a household name in China for his wisdom and virtues. This story has also circulated in various other popular forms, such as comics, local operas, *shuoshu* (a form of story-telling in tea houses) and, in modern times, film and television drama. The unfailing popularity of Zhu as a cultural symbol indicates that some Confucian assumptions are still alive.

Conclusion

Samuel Kim, in his authoritative summary of Chinese foreign relations past and present, distinguishes two schools – the *exotica sinica* 'continuity' and revolutionary 'discontinuity'.[71] Both 'schools' study the past with the assumption that it will contribute to an understanding of China's present international behaviour, and therefore contribute to how to *deal with* it. This is entirely understandable. However, this problem-solving approach does conceal a seldom-asked question. Does China's traditional 'foreign' behaviour merit study in its own right? Or does China's traditional thinking have any ontological value? In reality the answer is negative. So it seems perfectly normal to find philosophical or political theories of international relations having only European names.[72] Therefore when Samuel Huntington predicts a clash of civilisations,[73] the West is disturbed, and 'the rest' disagree.[74] Disturbed because it may come true; disagree because it is not true. The difference is first of all that we do not even share the same definition and *experience* of what is *civilisation*, *culture* and *clash*.

I have demonstrated, through the analysis of a legend, how the Other is conceptualised in ancient China and the strategies for dealing with it. These dominant conceptions and strategies are a reflection of how the world as a whole is perceived by the ancient Chinese, and therefore are products of the collective consciousness of a nation. However, when a militarily powerful and 'morally unjust' West emerged on the Chinese horizon, they were drastically changed. In a new 'Warring States' of the modern world, China is yet to establish a new system of thought to survive in a world it is still striving to come to terms with.[75]

Notes

1. Unless otherwise noted, the translations from classical and modern Chinese are my own.
2. From 221 BC when China was first unified under the Qin dynasty to the Opium War in 1840. However China as a civilisation existed long before its first unification.
3. G. Wang, *The Chinese Way: China's Position in International Relations* (Norway: Scandinavian University Press, 1995), p. 52.
4. The Han Chinese constitute 93 per cent of China's population.
5. The first Qin dynasty unified China by conquering other Han principalities rather than other 'nations'.
6. The Chinese tributary states are different from European colonies in that the Chinese had not conquered or governed any of the states outside imperial borders.
7. Y. Fung, *A History of Chinese Philosophy* (Peiping: Henry Vetch, 1937), p. 4.
8. Q. Cao, 'Yuanyu lunyu de chengyu yu chuantong wenhua' (Idioms from Confucius's *Analects* and traditional culture), *Journal of Inner Mongolia Teachers College*, vol. 53, 1993, pp. 66–9.
9. There is a vast literature on this topic. For a general discussion, see F. S. Northrop, 'The Complementary Emphasis of Eastern Intuitive Philosophy

and Western Scientific Philosophy', in C. A. Moore (ed.), *Philosophy, East and West* (Princeton, NJ: Princeton University Press, 1946); Y. Fung, *Zhongguo zhexue jianshi* (*A Concise History of Chinese Philosophy*) (Beijing: Beijing University Press, 1985), ch. 1, pp. 3–20; and S. Liang, 'Dongxifang wenhua jiqi zhexue' (Culture and Philosophy of East and West) and 'Zhongguo wenhua yaoyi' (The Essence of Chinese Culture), in J. Cao, (ed.), *Ruxue fuxing zhilu: Liang Shouming wenxuan* (*Road to Rejuvenation of Confucianism: Selected Works of Liang Shouming*) (Shanghai: Shanghai Yuandong chubanshe, 1994), pp. 3–130, 133–369.

10. See K. Dong, 'Hanzi: shiji de zaoyu, pingjia he qianzhan' (The Chinese Character: Centuries of History, Assessment and Prospect), in L. Xi, (ed.), *Ershiyi shiji zhongguo zhanlue da cehua: zhuming xuezhe fangtanlu* (*China's Strategic Planning in the 21st Century: Interviews with Prominent Scholars*) (Beijing: Hong Qi Chubanshe, 1996), pp. 385–405; and J. Ren, ' "Cong shutong-wen" dao "yutongyin" ' (From 'common written language' to 'common spoken language'), ibid., pp. 380–4.

11. B. Hodge, and K. Louie, *The Politics of Chinese Language and Culture: The Art of Reading Dragons* (London: Routledge, 1998), p. 49.

12. T. Hawkes, *Structuralism and Semiotics* (London: Methuen, 1977), ch. 1.

13. A. Dundes, in V. Propp, *Morphology of the Folktale* (Austin and London: University of Texas Press, 1968), pp. xi–xvi.

14. V. Propp, *Morphology of the Folktale.*

15. See C. Levi-Strauss, *The Raw and the Cooked* (London: Cape, 1969); and 'The Structural Study of Myth', *Journal of American Folklore*, vol. 68, 1955, pp. 428–44.

16. N. Fairclough, *Media Discourse* (London and New York: Edward Arnold, 1995), p. 76.

17. N. Fairclough, *Language and Power* (London and New York: Longman, 1989), chs 2, 5 and 6; 'Discourse and Text: Linguistic and Intertextual Analysis Within Discourse Analysis', *Discourse and Society*, vol. 3, no. 2, 1992, pp. 193–217; *Discourse and Social Change* (Cambridge: Polity Press, 1992).

18. Fairclough, *Language and Power*, pp. 152–5.

19. Ibid., p. 26.

20. S. Chatman, *Story and Discourse: Narrative Structure in Fiction and Film* (Ithaca, NY, and London: Cornell University Press, 1978), ch. 1.

21. See J. Fiske, *Introduction to Communication Studies* (London: Routledge, 1990), pp. 122–3.

22. Historical evidence about Zhu's southern expedition in 225 is mainly recorded in *San Guo Zhi* (*Record of the Three Kingdoms*) written by Chen Shou in the Jin dynasty (265–420). See Chen Shou, *San Guo Zhi* (Beijing: Zhonghua Shuju, reprinted 1959).

23. *Morphology of the Folktale.* V. Propp

24. Ibid., p. 25.

25. R. Silverstone, *The Message of Television: Myth and Narrative in Contemporary Culture* (London: Heinemann Educational Books, 1981); and 'Narrative Strategies in Television Science – a Case Study', *Media, Culture and Society*, vol. 6, 1984 pp. 377–410.

26. J. Goody, *The Domestication of the Savage Mind* (Cambridge: Cambridge University Press, 1977), p. 146.

27. For functions of classification of the world with language, see R. Hodge, and G. Kress, *Language as Ideology*, 2nd edn (London: Routledge, 1993), ch. 4, pp. 62–84.
28. In ancient China *tianxia* (the world) is conceptualised in a vague zoning system institutionalised in the Zhou period. At the centre is the central plain in the Yellow River middle valley, surrounded by vassal states, and then subordinate tributaries scattered along peripheries, beyond which were 'barbarians'. This zoning system represents a basic pattern of China's configuration of the world. See C. Hsu, and K. M. Linduff, *Western Chou Civilisation* (New Haven, Conn.: Yale University Press, 1988); and C. Hsu, 'Applying Confucian Ethics to International Relations', *Ethics and International Affairs*, vol. 5, 1991, pp. 15–31.
29. Given the tradition of adaptation of Confucianism as official ideology, there is little difference between 'civilisation', 'Confucianisation' and 'emperorisation'. The first character *wan* in *wanhua* can be used as a verb, meaning 'to rule benevolently'.
30. In the standard Chinese language dictionary *Xinhua Zidian* (*New China Dictionary*), there are three definitions of the word '*man*': (1) rough, unreasonable, (2) a term used in ancient China to refer to ethnic groups in the south, (3) very'. See Shangwu yinshuguan, *Xinhua Zidian* (Beijing: Shangwu Yinshuguan, 1993).
31. See G. Wang, *The Chineseness of China: Selected Essays* (Hong Kong: Oxford University Press, 1991), p. 147.
32. See Y. Fung, *Zhongguo zhexue jianshi* (*A Concise History of Chinese Philosophy*), p. 221.
33. G. Luo, *Sanguo yanyi* (*Romance of the Three Kingdoms*) (Jinan: Shandong renmin chubanshe, 1980), p. 748.
34. Ibid., p. 780.
35. For more discussion of morality in Chinese culture and foreign relations, see C. Shih, *China's Just World: The Morality of Chinese Foreign Policy* (Boulder, colo and London: Lynne Rienner, 1993).
36. The emperor as a moral being means not only that he represents the highest level of morality but that he has the legitimate authority to launch a moral crusade.
37. Chapter 87. This 'Seventh Capture' episode covers four chapters from 87 to 90.
38. For Propp's description of 'lack' as a dramatis persona, see Propp, *Morphology of the Folktale*, pp. 35–6.
39. For Propp's description of the 'magical agent', see Propp, *Morphology of the Folktale*, pp. 43–50.
40. For more discussions, see Y. Fung, *A History of Chinese Philosophy*, 2nd edn, Vol. 1 (Princeton, NJ: Princeton University Press, 1952).
41. Bai Shouyi (ed.), *Zhongguo tongshi gangyao* (*An Outline of a Complete History of China*) (Shanghai: Shanghai renmin chubanshe, 1980), p. 159.
42. Late Spring and Autumn (770–476 BC) and Warring States (475–221 BC) periods.
43. The most important thinker of legalism, Han Feizi (?–233 BC), believes that neither power (*shi*), nor methods of government (*shu*) nor law (*fa*) can be neglected. They must be used together to gain a supreme authority, a view similar to Machiavelli. He says:

Shi [power] is the means for gaining supremacy over the masses... Therefore, the intelligent ruler carries out his regulations as would Heaven, and employs men as if he were a spirit. Being like Heaven, he commits no wrong, and being like a spirit, he falls into no difficulties. His *shi* enforces his strict teachings, and nothing that he encounters resists him... Only when this is so can his laws be carried out in concert. (In Fung, *A History of Chinese Philosophy*, p. 320)

44. The rule of the first unified dynasty of Qin was extremely brutal and lasted only sixteen years (221–206 BC). It was followed by the Han dynasty (206 BC–AD 220) which adopted Confucianism as its official ideology.
45. Confucius, *Analects*. In J. Legge, trans., *The Four Books* (Hong Kong: Wei Tung Book Co., 1971), p. 143.
46. Ibid., p. 7.
47. Mencius (372–289 BC) is a founding father of Confucianism, famous for his emphasising 'people are more important than rulers' and anti-war thinking.
48. Mencius, *Mengzi zhengyi* (*Works of Mencius*) (Beijing: Zhonghua shuju, 1957).
49. This quotation of Mencius is often summarised in one phrase, *Dedao duozhu, shidao guazhu* (Those who posses justice get abundant assistance; those who lose justice get scanty assistance), and has exerted strong influence on Chinese society until modern times. In his criticism of American and Soviet imperialism during the Cold War, Mao Zedong quoted this famous phrase which became a popular slogan in the Chinese foreign policy discourse.
50. The Mohist School was founded by Mozi (about 479–381 BC). See Fung, *Zhongguo zhexue jianshi* (*A Concise History of Chinese Philosophy*), ch. 5, pp. 61–73.
51. There is a difference between Mencius and Mozi in their condemnation of war. The former thought it was not righteous; the latter thought it was not profitable.
52. See Guoxue Zhenglishe, *Zhuzi jicheng* (*A Complete Collection of pre-Qin Thinkers*), vol. 4 (Beijing: Zhonghua shuju, 1954), pp. 292–6.
53. Lao Tzu, *Tao Te Ching* (Harmondsworth: Penguin Books, 1963), p. 118.
54. See Liuxiang (Han dynasty) (ed.), *Zhanguoche*, vol. 2 (Shanghai: Shanghai guji chubanshe, reprinted 1978), p. 907.
55. A distinction needs to be made between classical Confucianism (pre-Qin period) and imperial Confucianism (from the Han dynasty when it became official ideology). The latter is primarily used to support the imperial reign. Confucianism used in this article takes its general meaning comprising both periods of Confucianism.
56. Confucius, *Analects*. In J. Legge, trans., *The Four Books* (Hong Kong: Wei Tung Book Co., 1971), p. 15.
57. Mencius, *Meng Zi*, in Jiao Xun (ed.), *Men Zi Zheng Yi*, vol. 2 (Beijing: Zhonghua shuju, reprinted 1957), p. 214.
58. Ibid., p. 217.
59. R. J. Smith, *Chinese Maps: Images of 'All Under Heaven'* (Hong Kong: Oxford University Press, 1996), p. 8.
60. Fung, *Zhongguo zhexue jianshi* (*A Concise History of Chinese Philosophy*), p. 221.
61. J. L. Watson, 'Rites or beliefs? The Construction of a United Culture in Late Imperial China', in L. Dittmer and S. S. Kim (eds), *China's Quest for National Identity* (Ithaca, NY: Cornell University Press, 1993), pp. 80–103, p. 83.

62. C. Hahm, 'The Clash of Civilisation Revisited: A Confucian Perspective', in S. Rashid (ed.), *'The Clash of Civilizations?' Asian Responses* (Karachi: Oxford University Press, 1997), pp. 109–26. p. 125.
63. For discussion of cultural categories of *wen* and *wu*, see K. Louie, and L. Edwards, 'Chinese Masculinity: Theorising *"Wen"* and *"Wu"'*, East Asian History, vol. 8, 1994, pp. 135–48; B. Hodge, and K. Louie, *The Politics of Chinese Language and Culture: The Art of Reading Dragons* (London: Routledge, 1998), pp. 121–37; and J. K. Fairbank, *China: A New History* (Cambridge, Mass: Harvard University Press, 1992), pp. 108–12.
64. See Z. Huang, *Nan Song junzheng yu wenxian tansui (An Investigation into the Military Administration and Texts of the Southern Song)* (Taipei: Xinwen feng chubanshe, 1980), p. 398.
65. See R. Walker, *The Multi-state System of Ancient China* (Hamden, Conn: The Shoe String, 1953), pp. 20–40.
66. These three historical books were written respectively in the Spring and Autumn, Warring States and Western Han dynasty periods.
67. See M. Mancall, *China at the Center: 300 Years of Foreign Policy* (New York: Free Press, 1984).
68. J. Yuan, cited in G. Chan, *Chinese Perspectives on International Relations: A Framework of Analysis* (London: Macmillan, 1999), p. 59.
69. Fairbank, *China: a New History*, p. 109.
70. The story of Wang Zhaojun is a well-known legend. She was actually not an imperial daughter. The story goes that the emperor promised a Chinese wife to a Mongol chieftain, but did not want to marry the imperial princess away on this occasion. Wang was selected among his unseen concubines based on her picture. Upon seeing Wang, the emperor was struck by her beauty. He faced a difficult decision of losing trust with the Mongols and losing his favourite concubine. He finally chose trust with the nomads and killed the artist who painted the picture because he cheated the emperor.
71. See S. Kim, 'China and the World in Theory and Practice' in S. Kim (ed.), *China and the World: Chinese Foreign Relations in the Post-Cold War Era*, 3th edn (Boulder, Colo, San Francisco, Oxford: Westview Press, 1994), pp. 3–41.
72. For example, in the most recent book by David Boucher, *Political Theories of International Relations: From Thucydides to the Present* (Oxford: Oxford University Press, 1998).
73. See S. P. Huntington, 'Clash of Civilizations', *Foreign Affairs*, vol. 72 no. 3, 1993, pp. 22–49; and 'If not Civilization, What? Paradigms of the Post-Cold War World', *Foreign Affairs*, vol. 72, no. 5, 1993, pp. 186–94.
74. See, for example, J. Wang, (ed.), *Wenming yu Guoji Zhengzhi: Zhongguo xuezhe ping hengtingdun de wenming chongtulun (Civilization and International Politics: Chinese Scholars' Critique of Huntington's Theory of the Clash of Civilizations)* (Shanghai: Shanghai renmin chubanshe, 1995). For a summary of this book, see C. Hughes, 'Globalization and Nationalism: Squaring the Circle in Chinese International Relations Theory', *Millennium*, vol. 26, no. 1, 1997, pp. 103–24. Also see S. Rashid, (ed.), *'The Clash of Civilisations?' Asian Response* (Karachi: Oxford University Press, 1997).
75. The most obvious evidence is that there are more changes in foreign policy in the last one and half centuries than in the previous two millennia.

11
The Zen Master's Story and an Anatomy of International Relations Theory

Xiaoming Huang

It may well be an over-ambitious undertaking to argue that Zen is more than just a convenient escape for those who have genuine distrust in positivist attempts to portray the world in general, and international relations in particular, and found it difficult and often painful to reconcile the consequent disciplinary effects of these attempts with their own learning and insights. But it is the underlying argument of this chapter that, beyond what people usually tend to associate with it, Zen envisions a world larger than the one that positivists would allow themselves and others to recognise and has a clearer vision of the steps and their logical connection in the evolution of one's experience with that world.

It is larger because Zen includes in its vision not only the world we normally see, but also the one we would eventually identify with and attach ourselves to, and one that may not necessarily manifest itself only in the form of what Popper calls World 1 (Popper, 1991). For Zen, knowing the world is not sufficient. The real challenge is how knowledge acquirers relate themselves to it through the process of knowledge acquisition. This process of relating is primarily an experience of the individual knowledge acquirer, no matter how powerful the collective effects of their actions and interactions might be.

For Zen, such a meaningful and positive relating requires not only a constant search of the world, but also that of oneself. Since whether the knowledge acquirer should be an active part of the knowing process has been a defining issue among IR debaters, the problem of how the knowledge acquirer should relate to the subject matter raises the issue to a higher level.

There seems to be a view that a possible solution to the paradigmatic conflicts in international relations theory may be found only at the level of ontology and epistemology.[1] It is not so much the complexity of international relations that prevents us from reaching and sharing its meaningful understanding; rather it is the circumstances in which we are led to pursue such an understanding that have forced us into different camps. The circumstances could be linguistic, cultural, as well as those of real world interests. For Zen, such a view, while recognising the fundamental problem in our attempts to understand international relations, does not provide a formula that would deal with the problem of our natural desire for knowledge and progress, even only at the 'intersubjective' level.

Against this backdrop, this chapter first introduces the world as Zen envisions it. In fact, there are three worlds of intellectual activity in Zen's world vision: the Real World in which one objectifies what one intends to understand; the Political World in which one resists objectification by others and therefore politicises what is intended for explanation; and the Cultural World in which one is emancipated not only from the obsession with mastering the reality and overcoming differences as in the Real World, but also from the need, as in the Political World, to correct the 'structural violence' of the Real World by simply denying the legitimacy or even existence of such a world, and effectively excluding the possibility of common interests and desirability of common good.

The second part relates the discussion to the three major debates in international relations theory: realism versus idealism in the 1920s and 1930s; traditionalism versus scientism in the 1960s; and the latest one, the challenging side of which has been in the constant making for the past decade, from post-structuralism in the late 1980s and early 1990s to constructivism in the late 1990s. The chapter argues that the three debates are important turning points in the field's fast and often painful growth up and search for its scientific form and substance for the past century. But there is something fundamentally missing or wrongly promoted in these debates, which, in the view of Zen, has not only created constant tensions among those debaters, but also prevented international relations theory from moving further and beyond, and becoming a positive and humane knowledge.

The central argument advanced here is that international relations theory, like any other field of intellectual activity, operates in all three worlds of Zen's vision: Real, Political and Cultural. Unlike others, however, the lines in international relations theory between the three different worlds are not as clear as we tend to think, and human crucial (rather than accidental) involvement is much deeper than we want to recognise and are willing, or even able, to deal with. This substantially complicates its mapping of international relations.

Realists and neorealists alike believe that what they 'theorise' in the Real World is simply what exists in the real world. To them, the Political World of postmodern visions is no more than a politicisation of the Real World by those who fail to come to terms with the hard reality in international relations. On the other hand, post-structuralists and constructivists alike see things the other way around. For them, it is the Political World that correctly relates IR theory with international reality, thus not only better depicts the true nature of international relations but also more accurately reflects the relationship of IR theory to its subject matter. There is no more truth beyond this.

What is missing in their debates is a realisation that international relations theory also operates, and if not yet, should be nurtured or 'civilised' to operate, in the Cultural World in which, according to Zen, there is common good (the big Self; Abe, 1985) accepted to which each individual small self (the knowledge acquirer) surrenders. International relations theory operates in this world on the expectation that all individual selves, rather than trying to overcome each other as in the Real World or deny one another, as in the Political World, submit themselves to the common good of the IR community. This, at the personal level, is a progressive process of what Zen calls self-cultivation or 'awakening' from a low level of existence to a higher one, and eventually to the highest state of humanity. As for the matters called international relations theory, the notion of the Cultural World opens new space[2] for antagonised IR debaters to think international relations creatively and humanely. It also points to a direction in which the efforts of knowledge acquirers in international relations theory to seek a realistic balance between science and humanity can be morally promoted.

The Zen master's story and the three worlds

The illustrative Zen story to lead the discussion in this chapter happened in the Tang dynasty of ancient China. One day, there was a conversation between a Zen master and his pupil. The Chinese Zen master, Qing-yuan Wei-xin, described how he understood the world differently in three distinct stages of his Zen cultivation:

> Thirty years ago, before I began to study Zen, I said, 'Mountains are mountains, waters are waters.'

After I got an insight into the truth of Zen through the instruction of a good master, I said, 'Mountains are not mountains, waters are not waters.'

But now, having attained the abode of final rest [that is, Awakening], I say, 'mountains are really mountains, waters are really waters.' (Abe, 1985; p. 4)

This story, like many other Zen stories, is capable of becoming unintelligible to many ordinary readers. What is the point in mentioning the plain fact that mountains are mountains? How can mountains no longer be mountains? And how do mountains become mountains again? For those with some measure of advanced training, the story may remind them of some basic lines in those intellectual battles they are familiar with: a fact as simple as this could be either the effect of a judgement or a truthful reflection (traditionalism versus scientism); mountains can no longer be mountains because of the power of interpretations (positivism versus constructivism); and mountains could become mountains again – have you ever heard of Hegel? But this Zen master's story seems to go beyond that. The three stages of the master's Zen cultivation can be seen as 'symbolising' three epistemological worlds of which the debates in international relations, and for that matter in social sciences in general, have so far limited themselves mainly to the first two.

In the first world, or the Real World, the knowledge acquirers take themselves out of what they intend to understand and explain, and build a relationship between them as the observing subject and the mountains, or waters, as the observed object. Here the international structure is an international structure because there is a central system, or 'the sovereign interpretive center', in Richard Ashley's words (Ashley, 1989a, p. 261), in international relations theory. The central system defines 'international structure' through established procedures and processes. The knowledge acquirer acts as the defender and refiner of such a system and which together form what might be called the central or collective subject in relation to the observed object. In this world, knowledge is gained primarily through the function of the knowledge acquirers' senses, their cognitive capacity, and their ability to extend logical reasoning beyond empirical evidence, following the disciplinary guidelines of the central system.

As one can see, this Real World is one where the detached knowledge acquirer sees or perceives the real world of international relations. The knowledge acquirers supposedly have nothing to do with this world, or should follow strict procedures to make sure their depiction leaves no room for human contamination or distortion. There are two small problems though. First, the real world is not fixed, waiting for the knowledge acquirer to depict it, world affairs are dynamic. Therefore, the problem of change becomes a daunting task in international relations theory.[3] If one wants to accurately account for changes, however, one's model needs to be able to account for non-linear variables and, better yet, the human factor. Then the problem of quantification of the unquantifiables follows.

On the other hand, the knowledge acquirer is also responsible for the formation of the central system and its defining criteria and paradigmatic procedures. These not only need to make sure that their empirical depiction is accurate, but also that the criteria and procedures with which they reach the depiction are valid. The validity issue will eventually lead to the fundamental problem of scientific unity (Kuhn, 1970).

The Real World is very much the one in which modern social sciences operate, on the basic positivist principles. In this world, objectification is first and foremost important in developing a credible knowledge. Consequently, the debates about the location of the original substance of human activities and the valid methodology for its accurate description and explanation have been the cornerstone for modern social sciences.[4]

In the second world, the Political World, objectification is rejected. There is no such thing as a pure knowledge acquirer. Everyone (or his or her group) can be a knowledge acquirer and disseminator one way or another. Each has individual motivations and interests in acquiring and promoting certain knowledge. There is no respected central system defining what is a valid knowledge about, say, world affairs. Mountains may not be mountains for a particular person (group) because viewed from their vantage point, they are not, should not, or just cannot, be mountains. They could be just land, trees, rocks, or bushes. The reasons for the world definable by a central system of knowledge to become a world in which truth is contestable can be looked at in many different ways. It may have to do with how one *interprets* an event or phenomenon. Even with exactly the same event or phenomenon, one's cognitive condition does affect its interpretation. The US bombing of the Chinese embassy in Belgrade, for example, may say something to the Chinese, but quite another thing to the Americans.

It may also have something to do with how one *approaches* an event or phenomenon, thus there is an issue of perspective. One looks at an event or phenomenon from one's particular physical or institutional position, which limits what he can capture and how he captures it. Concerning the causes for the Asian crisis, for example, the IMF, the World Bank and various Asian countries offered very different explanations of their own, from the over-expansion of the public sector, to the inefficiency and low productivity of the private sector, to the lack of regulation of the emergent global capital market.

Finally it may also have to do with the 'political' agenda knowledge acquirers may have, for example, the IMF agenda in the case of the Asian crisis and the 'American conspiracy' in the case of the NATO bombing. The United States and New Zealand perhaps would have a difficult time defining what is 'free trade' when it comes to the export of New Zealand lamb products. The possibility that Beijing and Washington might agree on what constitutes human rights is extremely remote. These are just examples of how the political agenda can dominate the knowing process. When a political agenda is involved, neutral, independent and objective truth can hardly emerge. A central system to define an event or phenomenon can barely function. Knowing the world, or disseminating one's knowledge about the world, becomes a political exercise.

A world where self becomes problematic

We cannot go directly to the definition of Zen's third world, the Cultural World, without first putting the Real World and Political World in perspective. In the Zen master's view, the contention between world visions in the Real and Political worlds is just another round of the century-long battle over the ontological nature of the human world. Fukuyama (1989) is not new in what he tried to suggest as he never shies away from his Hegelian inspirations.

But until the arrival of those envisioning the Political World in the second half of the twentieth century, the ontological wars were confined mainly to a bifurcated framework in which Reality and Ideas fought each other for the status of the primary signifier and generator of human activity. Scientific realism believes the former; historical idealism the latter. At issue is the location of the original substance and the generative power associated with it. Historical idealism argues that 'the contradictions that drive history exist first of all in the realm of human consciousness, i.e., on the level of ideas', and human behaviours are the effect of the interplay of ideas (Fukuyama, 1989, p. 5). It is argued that reality could be meaningful only within a local context of significance (Geertz, 1973), and that a better world starts from a better ideal (Frost, 1986).

On the other hand, scientific realism insists that the forces behind human history exist first in reality. Human knowledge, judgment, theories and belief systems are generated from and by the reality. The reality is conceptualised and generalised through accurate measurement (Singer's *Correlates of War* project, for instance; Singer, 1980), logical reasoning (Waltz's international structure; Waltz, 1979), or both (for instance, Axelrod's decision structure; Axelrod, 1976).

This is what came to be understood as *modern* intellectual traditions, or what might be called *modern visions*. For both Zen and postmodernism,[5] these visions are all stories of the Real World. Looking beyond the bifurcated framework and the fine differences among these visions, however, one can see clearly that they share something fundamentally. It is the notion of the original substance that motivates and limits all these modern visions. Consequently, it is the anxiety, expectation and almost religion-like faith driven by these visions in searching for and proving the original substance that, according to post-structuralism, have been constantly moving us away from the very simple fact that there is nothing 'deep there' waiting for us to discover, whether a generative structure or influential ideas. The notion of the existence of such a structure or ideal is simply an illusion, one that has severe consequences for a field's further growth. It is the attachment of the ultimate truth to the ever elusive original substance, agrees Zen, that creates tensions as well as progress, and ultimately, through their 'relentless pursuit' of modern forms and substance, sacrifices human individuality and marginalises divergent interests.

For both Zen and postmodernism, the problem lies in the notion of original substance and the consequent central system of knowledge, ideas and values built upon it. For those with postmodern visions, the solution is to be found in the negation of the idea of original substance and the power of the central system. For the Zen master, however, that creates more problems than it solves and this is where Zen's Cultural World fits in.

When Qing-yuan Wei-xin said 'mountains are mountains and waters are waters', he actually touches upon three things: an observed object, an observing subject, and the 'Ego' behind the subject.[6] The mountains and waters are objectified, defined and interpreted. The activities of objectification, definition and interpretation are those of the subject. When a person makes a judgement such as 'mountains are mountains', and then asks himself who made the judgement, the answer would be 'I'. If he goes on to ask who the 'I' is, the answer again would be 'I'. The question–answer process could go on indefinitely. In the process of answering the question, he makes a distinction between the 'I' who makes the judgement and the 'I' who asks himself the question, a distinction between the intellectual self (subject) and the True Self (Ego). Each time he asks who the 'I' is, the True Self goes one step back behind the intellectual self. As the process continues indefinitely, the True Self would retreat indefinitely and always stay behind the intellectual self. While the True Self is *the original substance* or *constructive sovereign* of what makes 'I', it is ever elusive and probably never attainable.

For the Zen master, the notion of the ever-elusive True Self lies at the heart of the problems of the modern world, material and intellectual. What makes scientific realism and historical idealism share the same Real World is that both of them constantly search for the original substance: Waltz for international structure; Morgenthau the nation state; Wallerstein the capitalist world system; Cox global productional forces; Fukuyama liberal ideas, and so on. These in themselves are not a problem. But as suggested earlier, the search for original substance is an indefinite process, and, in fact, the constructive sovereign could well be unattainable, because the process involves an endless separation of the original substance from the acting agent, that is, the international structure from the nation state; the nation state from the individual; human ideas from human interests, and so on. In the pursuit of the original substance, both scientific realists and historical idealists aim at an unreachable goal: to define the objectified from a never-definable original substance. For the Zen master, the tension can never be resolved because the original substance, or the constructive sovereign, is always in the process of defining itself.

Post-structuralism is an attempt to go beyond the modern obsession with original substance. Ashley (1989b, p. 272) argues that post-structuralism neither endorses the proposition that 'practice depends on structure', nor embraces the argument that 'structure depends on practice'. For postmodernism, the two propositions 'describe a paradox'. The opposition is undecidable (Ashley, 1989b, pp. 272–3). It is a paradox because modern visions try to define concepts and their relationships on a foundation yet to 'become itself' (or always in the process of becoming itself). The desire to impose an order or structure upon human phenomena comes from the modern expectation (or faith) that such an order or structure is ontologically justifiable. Since such an ontological basis is never attainable, the efforts to establish such an order or structure can be no more than a history of constant paradigm- and revolution-making (both in Kuhn's sense; Kuhn, 1970).

What postmodernism tries to do, however, is to problematise the notion of original substance and, in doing so, challenges the legitimacy of any central system of knowledge, ideas and values. With the refutation of the notion of original substance, such a system is deprived of the basis for its paradigmatic authority. Postmodernism breaks the 'legitimising link' between the original substance and the central system, and releases involuntary participants – at least psychologically – from the pressures to comply with modern forms and procedures, dictated by such a central system and in fact by the imagined original substance.

For the Zen master, the opposite views on the notion of original substance separate postmodern visions from modern ones at one level, but unite them at another, perhaps deeper, level. While a sense of intellectual confidence for those of modern visions has to be constantly secured and resecured, with each step supposedly making them closer to the original substance, the postmodern challenge intends to destroy the confidence – without necessarily providing an alternative. For the Zen master, both modern and postmodern visions seem to have failed to recognise the living nature of the human world. As the Zen master himself experienced, in the Real World where mountains are mountains and waters are waters, it is the central system that dictates their definition and description on the basis of an imagined original substance. The interests, observations and inspirations of the observer (IR specialist, for example) are not allowed as they function only to distort the faithful observation. Individual particulars of the observed (the nation states, for example) are irrelevant, as they prevent the observer's moving up the ladder of generalisation and reaching the original substance. Mountains are mountains, full stop, just like when Waltz says international politics is international structure, regardless of how Clifford Geertz (1973) sees it or whether the 'inter' 'national' is between the United States and China, or between the United States and the Bahamas. Obviously the Real World is an uncomfortable and frustrating place to live in, with all its disciplinary and centralising regimes.

Leaving, or pretending not to operate in, the Real World may not necessarily lead to genuine freedom as postmodernists may wish. One still has to face 'mountains' and use 'water' every day, make judgements, and develop useful knowledge. But this certainly could not normally take place in a world where mountains refuse to be mountains and the qualities of water are constantly subject to interpretations or political manipulation. This is where the Zen master sees what is messed up by postmodernists, very much the same way as many young Zen converters do when they leave the real world initially, not so much because of their love for the Zen style of living, but rather because of their frustration and perhaps even hatred of the 'real' world.

For the Zen master, postmodern visions misplace the blame in their refutation of the original substance and therefore the central system of knowledge, ideas and values. The world should be the same to everyone who sees it. In that sense, modern visions have legitimate reasons to believe mountains are mountains. On the other hand, the world cannot be the same in its reception by individuals. Postmodernists are certainly right in exposing the political, cognitive and linguistic dynamics that define mountains in a particular way in inter-subject interaction.

What puts modern and postmodern visions in the same basket is not so much whether there is an original substance *out there*, but the fact that they are all driven by one *in themselves*. It is the ever-elusive, never-satisfiable and never-attainable True Self in both modernists and postmodernists that drives their anxiety, obsession and faith, and consequently their relentless pursuit of their respective visions. The problem with postmodernism is that while they are right in calling our attention to the suppressive and hegemonic nature of modern visions, they seem to fail to realise that it is not the pursuit of original substance in the Real World that causes much of their sufferings. After all, the notion of original substance and the consequent central system are themselves the products of our intellectual activities. Underlying these activities, like any other human activities, is one's (modernists', postmodernists', or anyone else's) unfailing desires to be secure, free and achieving. It is a unique combination of one's desires, surrounding environment and personal conditions that moves him into the drive to become a modernist, or forces him to declare his deep suspicion in modern visions.

So for the Zen master, the postmodernist's move to the Political World is not insufficient, much in the way that Karl Popper argues that indeterminism is not enough 'to make room for human freedom' (Popper, 1991, p. 114). The real turning point in one's 'Zen' cultivation, and in fact in one's efforts to relate to the world, is the realisation that the real problem is not out there in the world, but right here in one's *self*.

It is likely that mountains themselves are ambiguous or problematic, which inhibits their instant and genuine depiction, so there is a need for scientific realism. It may also be true that what is constructed in our mind complicates our job of understanding and interpretation, thus there needs to be praise for postmodernists. But it is the elusive and unsatisfied self behind every knowledge acquirer that shapes what happens in both the Real and Political worlds. For the Zen master, the ultimate release of the tensions in both worlds could only come from a realistic defining of one's self. Postmodernism cannot serve as a mean-ingful alternative to modern visions because its politicisation of the field further intensifies rather than reduces the tensions. While postmodern-ists claim postmodernism is about whether there is the ultimate truth, it appears that it is really about who has the truth.

The realistic definition of the self is difficult. Not everyone can become a Zen convert, nor can every Zen convert become a Zen master. But the idea does have its value: unless we human beings learn how to discipline *ourselves* and relate ourselves to others in a positive way, we probably will never see knowledge and process in international relations theory.

What does it all have to do with IR?

Good question. In fact, it may indeed not have that much to do with IR, as it involves no vocabulary, subject matter or paradigmatic debates often found in international relations theory. The Zen master's story is not an alternative IR theory. It does not explain international relations. It does not engage in IR debates. One perhaps need not expect anything intelligent about international relations from a century-old story of a hermit. But this is precisely the point. It is not what one does, but how one does it that matters most. The problems in international relations theory are not really those of IR debaters. The fundamental flaws one side accuses the others of in the debates may not be flaws at all but themselves the manifestation of the dynamics of a broad social process, and shared by all sides.

It is at this level that one can find the fundamentally intelligent point in the Zen master's story. Viewed from the Zen master's perspective, international relations theory, like the subject matter it tries to make sense of, is still at an early stage of evolution where curiosity about truth precedes concern about values and common good; where the central system is in constant self-making; and where the biggest challenge of realistic self-definition can never seriously take place.

Along this line of argument, the recent history of international relations theory can be seen as a good example of how political a science-bounded young enterprise can get if the value of human quality is overwhelmed by concern for the imagined truth. And the key to the strengthening of such human quality is a realistic definition of one's self. International relations theory has been, since early in the twentieth century, marked by several major debates about the fundamental nature of international relations and therefore effective methods for its management and manipulation.

From the early debate between realism and idealism in the 1920s and 1930, followed by the second between traditionalism and scientism in the 1960s, to the recent one between neorealism to postmodernism, one can see clearly the strong desire and tremendous efforts among IR theorists to turn the 'art of diplomacy' into a real science. And yet international relations theory has never been less 'scientific'.

It seems that IR theory, unlike any other field of knowledge, can hardly become a real science because of the very nature of international relations. On the other hand, politicisation of the field does not go beyond the recognition of the 'indeterminism' embedded in international relations, and therefore no real 'thinking space' is created by such politicisation. However, both the making of the Real World and the challenges of the Political World are a normal part of the field's growing up. The problems associated with them cannot be properly overcome by themselves. The field will eventually surpass them once it grows into a new Cultural World where the selves are properly defined, their boundaries with others are responsibly established and respected, and the common good is articulated and widely accepted. Mountains are mountains again, because there can be an inter-subject agreement that is built upon such a sense of common good.

Shaping of the Real World

Seeds of the illusion of a science of international relations were planted in the first major debate between E. H. Carr and his idealist contemporaries, notably among whom is President Wilson. The starting point for Carr's challenge to idealism was the need to get our knowledge of international relations to its necessary scientific foundation.[7]

For Carr, the prospects of international relations theory becoming a real science of world affairs lie firmly in the fact that international relations is an objective reality that is shaped by an internal logic of its own. What concerns Carr most is as much the 'scientific integrity of international relations theory' as the flaws of idealism. While conventional interpretations tend to focus on Carr's criticism of Wilsonian idealism, his more significant contributions seem to lie in his 'modernisation' of the long tradition that started with classical realism, incarnated in the works of Thucydides, Machiavelli and Hobbes in their attempts to search for the essence of world affairs and therefore the foundation for a scientific knowledge of world affairs.

Carr's cause is faithfully carried on by Hans Morgenthau. Modern realism seeks to expand the search for and further define the internal logic. In Morgenthau's vision, world affairs are shaped by the persistent pursuit by the nation state of power, status and prestige. This logic not only determines the confrontational nature of international relations, but also the only effect of its manipulation, that is, balance of power (Morgenthau, 1948). Various studies, on the basis of Morgenthau's framework, have tried to look further at the factors at various levels that shape the international behaviour of the nation state: cognitive and psychological factors (Steinbruner, 1974), human nature (Niebuhr, 1960), group dynamics, political system (Waltz, 1979), decision-making process (Allison, 1971), national attributes (ideology, culture, national resources, and so on) and international systems. (Kaplan, 1957).

   Classical and modern realism, in their fellow critics' view, lack the rigidity and systemic quality that a science should have. As neorealism (Waltz, 1979 and Gilpin, 1981) tries to expand the realist paradigm on the theoretical front, scientism (or behaviourism: Singer, 1980; Axelrod, 1984, for example) enhances it on the methodological front. Both intend to put realism on a firmer scientific ground. Taking issue with classical and modern realism, scientificism of the 1960s forcefully promoted the idea that international relations should be built following universally applicable scientific procedures and methods. It must be systematic rather than selective; objective rather than judgemental; and statistically accurate rather than reliant mainly on case studies (Singer, 1968, 1969).

   On the theoretical front, neorealism, through the pioneering works of Waltz (1979) and Gilpin (1981), hoped to fine-tune the realist visions so more rigour and explanatory power could be built into them. Like Carr and Morgenthau before them, Waltz's and Gilpin's main concern is again a science of international politics, built upon concepts and methodology that are universally applicable: Waltz makes his landmark case on the concept of international structure and methodological reductionism; Gilpin makes his on the principles of micro-economics and rational choice.

   Problems of both scientism and neorealism are well documented (Keohane, 1984 and Vasquez, 1983). These problems, however, are not the defects of these two visions. Rather, they are the inevitable consequences of the efforts these two visions carry on from classical and modern realism to move international relations theory further towards a science. The extensive scientific qualities that scientism and neorealism have intended for international relations theory intensify the tensions among those of different visions, and at the same time move the discipline further away from the living and rich reality.

Along with realism of various versions, there are equally enthusiastic efforts in search of the internal logic, but in an opposite direction. If realism believes that the generative power of such an internal logic is embedded in reality, idealism tries to relocate it in human ideas. There are two aspects to the idealist challenge. The first one is what E. H. Carr took issue with in the 1920s and 1930s: the school of thought that world affairs should be disciplined and regulated according to human values and ideals. This aspect of idealism turned out to be an insignificant challenge and has been very much marginalised through the history of IR theory.

A more serious challenge comes from the other aspect of idealism, a tradition that goes even further back than the Wilsonian idealism of early in the twentieth century, but is still echoed in contemporary debates: a tradition that originated in German idealism and is carried on by contemporaries such as Francis Fukuyama. Rather than simply arguing that human values and ideals are desirable and imperative, this vision believes that world affairs, like any other human activities, are just the effects of the interplay of human ideas. It is the human ideas that are the original substance of world affairs. Struggle for power, war and conflicts, peace and security, development and human rights are all phenomena driven by various human ideas and ideals.

With all the idealist noises, classical and modern realism could still reign in the field. But when neorealism and scientism had their way, the tensions created by the illusion of a science of international relations could no longer be contained. The advent of postmodernism in IR theory in the 1980s suggested a need for hard soul-searching for IR thinkers. For those outside the field, this is perhaps necessary in forcing them to seriously reflect on the fundamental nature of international relations theory and how it could help them better relate to world affairs.

Three turns make an all-new world

The challenge to modern visions has not come in one clear form. There is tremendous confusion about the form and substance of the postmodern challenge. International theorists, having fought the first battle between realism and idealism and the second one between traditionalism and scientism long ago, have not wasted their time in calling the latest exchanges between postmodern challengers and realist defenders a third debate.[8] Yet, after the initial wave of attacks on neorealism led by Richard Ashley, the challenge has appeared to be larger than we thought, joined by interpretationism and lately constructivism. This has turned the whole IR debate into a completely different game.

The confusion about the nature of postmodernism in IR theory is reflected in the fact that various and sometimes confusing terms are used to represent the new challenge. These include postmodernism, post-structuralism, post-positivism, critical thinking, and so on. James Der Derian, for instance, preferred post-structuralism to postmodernism, arguing that postmodernism as a theoretical response 'has begun to take on more meaning than it can sensibly carry' (Der Derian, 1992, p. 34). While also recognising it as a reaction to the excessive claims and aspiration of the 'behaviour revolution', Holsti (1989, p. 255) labelled the challenge as postmodernism instead.

For some, there is not much difference between postmodernism and post-structuralism (Rosenau, 1992, p. 3); while for others, post-positivism was hailed as a new intellectual movement against the strict empiricism and tight paradigmatic discipline associated with modern visions (Lapid, 1989, p. 235). There are still others who treated the new wave as critical thinking or an 'agenda of dissent' (George and Campbell, 1990; and Ashley and Walker, 1990). Finally, there were also people who used different terms for different purposes. The most notable among them is Richard Ashley. He used post-positivism (Ashley, 1987), post-structuralism (Ashley, 1989b), and dissident agenda (with Walker, 1990) to address different aspects of modern discourses that were laid out in his earlier work on neorealism (Ashley, 1984).

Various labels aside, the postmodern challenge is led by three major schools of thought, each of which represents a 'turn' away from modern visions, from the Real World, and towards the new Political World, where the key issue is not about the location of the original substance, but whether such a substance ever exists: the post-structuralist turn in the late 1980s led by Richard Ashley, the interpretative turn in the early 1990s led by R. B. Walker, and the constructivist turn led by Nicholas Onuf in the 1990s.

Post-structuralism is the closest among the three to Zen's second world. For post-structuralism, the key problem in the Real World is the increasing alienation of the realists from real international relations in the name of scientific knowledge and the suppressive nature of realist visions, their theories and methods. Ashley's sophisticated treatment of classical realism and neorealism (Ashley, 1984 and 1987) suggests that it is neorealism which overplays the scientific side of realism, consequently tightens the thinking space for IR specialists, and turns the field into a political battleground. As such, IR theory is no longer (perhaps never was) a pure 'academic' turf for the faithful reflection of international relations. Mountains are no longer moutnains. In fact, the political nature of international relations theory is so substantive that the line between IR theory as the collective observing subject and international relations as the observed object is blurred, and one can hardly argue that international relations theory is only a reflection of international relations.

The attention of the interpretivists however is not so much on the political nature of IR theory, but more on the interpretive nature of our knowing process itself (Kratochwil, 1988 and 1989) and how cognitive diversity would prevent the formation of a scientific knowledge of international relations. Sharing the same view as Zen regarding the Political World, the interpretivists believe that the knowing experience is primarily the individual's experience and the most important is the human cognitive process where knowledge is actually formed. Moreover, the individual's particular cognitive architecture – effects of the person's linguistic build-up, cultural habits and real-world interests, among other things – is an effective filter that gives their knowledge an individualist shape. When this cognitive filter functions in international relations theory, it becomes much more complicated because of the collective effect of cognitive processes. In effect, interpretivism rejects the possibility of universal truth, not because of the political intentions of knowledge acquirers, but because of the limits in their knowing capacity itself.

Finally, constructivism (Adler, 1997; Hopf, 1998; Ruggie, 1998; and Ckeckel, 1998) starts with the same premise as in interpretivism: that it is the knowledge acquirer who gives meaning to an event or phenomenon. But its intellectual individualism differs in two important ways. First, the knowing exercise could be intentional, rather than just an unfortunate consequence of human cognitive bias. Second, the knowing exercise is part of the reality formation, rather than just a manipulation of its interpretation. In fact, the knowing process and its product (as Popper's World 3) becomes the primary source of international relations theory.

Constructivism also shares post-structuralism's belief in the political dynamism of knowledge acquisition. But for constructivism, political intentions in knowledge acquisition and dissemination are not necessarily something that needs to be deplored or eliminated. They are the driving force behind the grand process of social formation. What constructivism is interested in is a recognition of the generative power of IR theory, not a judgement of such power.

The three turns, while offering different explanations/justifications for a decentralised field of international relations theory, all see the root of the problems in IR theory in the conformist dynamism of the Real World. Post-structuralism is the most radical among the three. It challenges the Real World by denying the central system, but without, perhaps being incapable of, offering an alternative which would bring back confidence in intersubjective communications. On the other hand, conscious of the dead end post-structuralism has brought about, the constructivists instead subject the Real World to one of their own making. Between them, there is interpretationism which neither challenges the Real World nor provides one of its own, but only survives on the contextualising of the Real World.

This is, in the Zen master's view, where the problem is for the challenges to modern visions and also where Zen fundamentally differs from the postmodern visions. Postmodernism correctly points out that modern visions ignore the complexity in subject configuration and the dynamic nature of reality formation in international relations, and therefore seriously underestimate the problem of political, cognitive and social distortion and construction in the building of a knowledge of world affairs. The farther the field is pushed towards a science based on a central defining system, the more tense the relationship would become between competing visions.

On the other hand, dignifying distortions (mountains are not mountains), or reversing the direction in the causal relationship between international relations and their theory (mountains of 'our own making'), does not deal with the problem of how we can make a better world. Postmodernism may help us become psychologically relieved from the repressive structure framed in modern visions but leaves us in the state of excessive indeterminacy where some key human values such as knowledge and progress become problematic.

The greatest challenge is ourselves

The excessive indeterminacy promoted by postmodernism in the Political World turns concepts and relationships in IR theory into unnecessary contestation. Concepts like national interests, world order and international structure become no more than the disguise of local political interests, intentions and agendas.

To the extent postmodernism goes, the political nature of IR theory can be seen as reflecting the unsettledness in the constant process of self-making of the central system of knowledge, values and meaning in

IR theory (the successive debates are the core part of the self-making). It is the indeterminacy of such a hard-sought interpretative centre that keeps international relations theory as a political game. But if one looks further at the deeper source of the indeterminacy and thus the real problem of modern as well as postmodern visions, the indeterminacy of international relations theory is indeed the consequence of the indeterminacy of the modernist and postmodernist self.

Without a realistic definition of the self, one is constantly in a state of insecurity and barely has a sense of the line between oneself and others. Naturally one would continuously seek the expansion of one's living and thinking space and greater control over it. Consequently, the common good is at the mercy of those who have greater space and greater control. Any service this process of security-making might do to the common good can only be accidental. In the end, whether one's security can be protected and promoted is also very much contingent.

To make IR theory 'humanely determinant', one needs first to make oneself humanely determinant. What makes a good IR theory? It is the fact that the theory promotes good human qualities in international relations. What makes us a good knowledge acquirer in IR theory? It is also the fact that knowledge acquirers commit themselves to such humane qualities. Accordingly, such a knowledge needs not necessarily to be scientific but, certainly to be political. As the knowledge acquirer, we do face difficult ethical decisions in satisfying demands from different directions. Humane principles are as important as scientific values and political wisdom. When they are in conflict, humane principles should prevail in directing our building the knowledge of international relations.

Most importantly, humane principles do not start with others. They should work primarily in oneself. In that sense, postmodern visions of world affairs are arguably as problematic as modern ones as they also see the problem on the *other* side. This is indeed a giant claim, but not necessarily an unfriendly one. The problems with both modern and postmodern visions are not something that have to be corrected or overcome. They are simply an unavoidable part of the field's growing pains. In the formative years, there is a natural curiosity about the ultimate truth of things around. As one grows up, one will come to realise that things are much more complicated than straight truth. At the same time, the question about oneself becomes dominant.

For the Zen master, one needs to go further beyond these two stages in the process of our knowing and also relating to the world. What makes that final transition possible is not the overcoming of the Others, but rather that of oneself. It is this self that drives the initial curiosity that results in many unnecessary tensions in the Real World. It is also this self that feels the need to be protected in the Political World. The overcoming of the self is not simply its denial as we might think in terms of Zen teachings. It is to positively relate ourselves to the world. It is a search for a reasonable boundary between oneself and others, rather than a pursuit of the limitless expansion of one's space.

A science of international relations is 'a mission impossible' for the modern visions. In the process of pursuing such a mission, modern visions are responsible not only for mis- or under-representations of reality, but also for the confrontational and mutually destructive nature of the community of international relations theory. Postmodern visions are correct in pointing out the political nature of the Real World, but still pursue a world where the other side is problematic. Further development in IR theory thus should start with the courage to see one self as part of the problem and with the idea that a humane definition and positive relating of one's self is not just a crucial concern for the world of international relations, but more importantly for that of international relations theory.

Notes

1. The view is shared among those of post-structuralism and lately constructivism. See for example, Ashley (1984 and 1987), Walker (1984 and 1990), Walker and Mendlovitz (1990); onuf (1989). Also for general discussions of the issue from a more neutral perspective, see Ferguson and Mansbach (1991) and Adler (1997).
2. More thinking space not only for postmodernists (George, 1989, p. 235; and Lapid, 1989), but also for realists and in fact anyone else.
3. In fact, studies on change and continuity have become a major focus in IR across the 'party' line. See Gilpin (1981), Czempiel and Rosenau (1989), Kennedy (1987), Keohane (1980), Ruggie (1982), Vasquez and Mansbach (1983), Walker (1987).
4. For an overview of the issue, see Bernstein (1983).
5. Postmodernism here is used in its broad sense that includes the three latest movements in international relations theory that challenge modern visions: post-structuralism, interpretationism and constructivism.
6. The interpretation of Qing-yuan Wei-xin's discourse is heavily drawn from Abe (1985), ch. 1, 'Zen is not a philosophy, but...'
7. Carr starts his critique of the idealism of the intra-war period with a discussion of the 'science of international politics' (Carr, 1964, pp. 1–21).
8. *International Studies Quarterly*, vol. 33, no. 3, 1989 and vol. 34, no. 3, 1990.

References

Abe, Masao (1985) *Zen and Western Thought* (Honolulu: University of Hawaii Press).

Xiaoming Huang   241

Adler, Emanuel (1997) 'Seizing the Middle ground: Constructivism in World Politics'. *European Journal of International Relations Theory*, vol. 3, no. 3, pp. 319–63.

Allison, Graham T. (1971) *Essence of Decision: Explaining the Cuban Missile Crisis* (Boston, Mass: Little, Brown).

Ashley, Richard K. (1984) 'The Poverty of Neorealism', *International Organization*, vol. 38, no. 2, pp. 225–86.

—— (1987) 'The Geopolitics of Space: Toward a Critical Social Theory of International Politics', *Alternative*, vol. 12, pp. 403–34.

—— (1989a) 'Imposing International Purpose: Notes on a Problematic of Governance', in Ernst-Otto Czempiel and James Rosenau (eds), *Global Changes and Theoretical Challenges: Approaches to World Politics for the 1990s* (Lexington, Md: Lexington Books), pp. 251–90.

—— (1989b) 'Living on Border Lines: Man, Poststructuralism, and War', in James Der Derian and Michael Shapiro (eds), *International/Intertextual Relations: Postmodern Readings of World Politics* (Lexington, Md: Lexington Books), pp. 259–321.

—— and R. B. J. Walker (1990) 'Speaking the Language of Exile: Dissident Thought in International Studies', *International Studies Quarterly*, vol. 34, no. 3, pp. 259–68.

Axelrod, Robert (1984) *The Evolution of Cooperation* (New York: Basic Books).

Axelrod, Robert (ed.) (1976) *Structure of Decision* (Princeton, NJ: Princeton University Press).

Bernstein, Richard J. (1983) *Beyond Objectivism and Relativism: Science, Hermeneutics, and Praxis* (Philadelphia: University of Pennsylvania Press).

Carr, Edward H. (1964) *The Twenty Year Crisis: 1919–1939* (New York: Harper & Row).

Checkel, Jeffrey T. (1998) 'The Constructivist Turn in International Relations Theory', *World Politics*, vol. 50, no. 1, pp. 324–48.

Czempiel, Ernst-Otto and James N. Rosenau (1989) *Global Changes and Theoretical Challenges* (Lexington, MD: Lexington Books).

Der Derian, James (1992) 'The Gulf War/Game: A Case for a Poststructuralist Approach', The Center for International Studies Seminar, University of Southern California, Los Angeles.

—— and M. J. Shapiro (1989) *International/Intertextual Relations: Postmodern Readings of World Politics* (Lexington, Md: Lexington Books).

Ferguson, Yale H. and Richard W. Mansbach (1991) 'Between Celebration and Despair: Constructive Suggestion for Future International Theory', *International Studies Quarterly*, vol. 35, no. 4, pp. 363–86.

Frost, Mervyn (1986) *Toward A Normative Theory of International Relations Theory* (Cambridge: Cambridge University Press).

Fukuyama, Francis (1989) 'The End of History?', *The National Interest*, vol. 16 (Summer), pp. 3–18.

Geertz, Clifford (1973) *The Interpretation of Cultures* (New York: Basic Books).

George, Jim (1989) 'International Relations Theory and the Search for Thinking Space: Another View of the Third Debate', *International Studies Quarterly*, vol. 33, pp. 269–79.

—— and David Campbell (1990) 'Patterns of Dissent and the Celebration of Difference: Critical Social Theory and International Relations', *International Studies Quarterly*, vol. 34, no. 3, pp. 269–93.

Gilpin, Robert (1981) *War and Change in World Politics* (Cambridge: Cambridge University Press).

Holsti, K. J. (1989) 'Mirror, Mirror on the Wall, Which are the Fairest Theories of All?', *International Studies Quarterly*, vol. 33.

Hopf, Ted (1998) 'The promise of Constructivism in International Relations Theory', *International Security*, vol. 23, no. 1, pp. 171–200.

Kaplan, Morton A. (1966) 'The New Great Debate: Traditionalism vs. Science in International Relations', *World Politics*, vol. 19, no. 1.

Kennedy, Paul (1987) *The Rise and Fall of the Great Power: Economic Change and Military Conflict from 1500 to 2000* (New York: Random House).

Keohane, Robert O. (1980) 'The Theory of Hegemonic Stability and Changes in International Economic Regimes, 1967–1977', in Ole R. Holsti, Randolph Siverson and Alexander George (eds), *Change in the International System* (Boulder, Co 10: Westview Press), pp. 131–62.

——(1984) *After Hegemony* (Princeton, NJ: Princeton University Press).

Kratochwil, Friderach (1988) 'Regimes, Interpretation and the "Science" of Politics: A Reappraisal', *Millennium: Journal of International Studies*, vol. 17, pp. 263–84.

——(1989) *Rules, Norms and Decision* (Cambridge: Cambridge University Press).

Kuhn, Thomas S. (1970) *The Structure of Scientific Revolutions* (Chicago, Ill.: Chicago University Press).

Lapid, Yosef (1989) 'The Third Debate: on the Prospects of International Relations Theory in a Post-postivist Era', *International Studies Quarterly*, vol. 33, pp. 235–54.

Morgenthau, Hans (1948) *Politics among Nations: The Struggle for Power and Peace* (New York: Knopf).

Niebuhr, Reinhold (1960) *Nations and Empires: Recurring Patterns in the Political Order* (London: Faber & Faber).

Onuf, Nicholas (1989) *World of Our Making: Rules and Rule in Social Theory and International Relations* (Columbia: University of South Carolina Press).

Popper, Karl R. (1991) *The Open Universe: An Argument for Indeterminism* (London: Routledge).

Rosenau, Pauline M. (1992) *Post-modernism and the Social Sciences: Insights, Inroads, and Intrusions* (Princeton, NJ: Princeton University Press).

Ruggie, John (1982) 'International Regimes, Transactions, and Change: Embedded Liberalism in the Postwar Economic Order', *International Organization*, vol. 36, no. 2, pp. 379–415.

——(1998) 'What Makes the World Hang Together? Neo-utilitarianism and the Social Constructivist Challenge', *International Organization*, vol. 52, no. 4, pp. 855–85.

Singer, J. David (1969) 'The Incomplete Theorist: Insight Without Evidence', in K. Knorr and James Rosenau (eds), *Contending Approaches to International Politics* (Princeton, NJ: Princeton University Press), pp. 62–86.

——(1980) *The Correlates of War* (New York: Free Press).

——(1968) *Quantitative International Politics* (New York: Free Press).

Steinbruner, John (1974) *The Cybernetic Theory of Decision* (Princeton, NJ: Princeton University Press).

Vasquez, John A. (1983) *The Power of Power Politics: A Critique* (London: Pinter; New Brunswick, NJ: Rugers University Press).

—— and Richard W. Mansbach (1983) 'The Issue Cycle: Conceptualizing Long-term Global Political Change', *International Organization*, vol. 37, no. 1, pp. 257–80.

Walker, R. B. J. (1984) 'World Politics and Western Reason: Universalism, Pluralism, Hegemony', in R. B. J. Walker, *Culture, Ideology, and World Order* (Boulder, colo: Westview Press), pp. 182–216.

—— (1987) 'Realism, Change and International Political Theory', *International Studies Quarterly*, vol. 31, pp. 65–86.

—— (1990) 'The Concept of Culture and International Relations', in Jongsuk Chay (ed.), *Culture and International Relations* (New York: Praeger), pp. 3–20.

—— and Saul H. Mendlovitz (1990) *Contending Sovereignties: Redefining Political Community* (Boulder colo: Lynne Rienner).

Waltz, Kenneth (1979) *Theory of International Politics* (Reading, Mass: Addison-Wesley).

Bibliographical Note:
Has Chinese IR Progressed?

Wang Yi

In Stephen Chan's survey article of non-Western IR literature (Stephen Chan, 1994), the section on China took up barely two pages, which in a way reflected the paucity of Chinese writings on IR theory at the time. Now seven years later, has there been any progress? The simple answer is yes. The publication at the end of the 1990s of Gerald Chan's book-length survey of Chinese IR writings points to a proliferation of the literature during the intervening period.

While only a handful of theoretical works were cited in Stephen Chan's article, seven years on the bibliography, as well as the list of interviewees, is much longer in Gerald Chan's book. As Gerald Chan himself admits, a book like this would have been almost impossible 'a decade or so ago because of a dearth of source materials and a lack of openness in the Chinese system' (Gerald Chan, 1999, Preface, p. xi). Chan's book has identified four main themes of Chinese IR works: power, Marxism, culture and modernisation. He notes that power is the cornerstone and driving force of China's international relations and foreign policy and that power politics in interstate relations as a feature of Chinese history since the days of the Spring and Autumn Period starting in the eighth century BC has exerted a marked influence on contemporary IR thinking in China.

In discussing the impact of Marxism, Chan finds that although Marxism remains a potent force in shaping the international behaviour of the Communist-led country, recent IR literature in China reveals a gradual shift away from the traditional method of class analysis. In terms of culture, Chan believes that it is easy to fall into the trap of cultural determinism in analysing Chinese foreign policy and argues that although culture has a more profound influence on Chinese IR thinking than most scholars would admit, culture itself is not an actor in world politics and is best treated as an intervening variable rather than as an independent variable. Chan's treatment of modernisation is the briefest of the four themes identified, pointing out that modernisation as a national goal has played an influential role in the state-building efforts in China's recent history, a feature well-reflected in the literature.

Chan concludes his survey by stating that the development of Chinese IR studies in recent years adds an interesting dimension to the existing body of knowledge in the wider IR community. But he also points out that IR theory is a relatively new subject in China and a lot of work needs to be done before a distinctively Chinese school of thinking emerges. He cites the state ideology of Marxism, the lack of resources and the limited knowledge in China of the inter-paradigm debates in the West as some of the main problems hindering the further development of Chinese IR.

As the first comprehensive and systematic review of contemporary Chinese IR literature, Chan's book provides a fair, though very brief, summary of the major works produced by Chinese IR scholars in the past dozen years. Nonetheless,

Gerald Chan, in spite of his Chinese origin, has approached Chinese IR as an outsider rather than adopting a more empathic reading of Chinese works and has therefore overlooked some publications that are regarded as important by those working in the field within China.[1] A case in point is the systematic study of China's national interest by Yan Xuetong published in 1996, well before Chan's survey was completed.

If Chan's book testifies to the growth of Chinese IR literature in quantitative terms, Yan's work demonstrates that such growth has been punctuated, if only occasionally, by originality and quality. After completing his political science PhD at Berkeley in 1992, Yan has been working as a research fellow in the Chinese Institute of Contemporary International Relations in Beijing. He regards himself as a realist, but unlike many realist authors who tend to take national interest for granted, Yan tackles the concept head-on in order to develop a more effective method for analysing the often intangible notion.

Yan takes issue with many of his contemporaries who equate national interest with the interests of the ruling class. For him, national interest is different from state interest and should be defined as the totality of material and spiritual concerns of the entire population of a given country. This definition allows Yan to challenge many of the existing notions about national interest. Proceeding from such a definition, Yan argues, for instance, that the realisation of the national interest need not be at the expense of individual interests and that national sovereignty is just one of the many interests of a nation that may be traded off for the fulfilment of a more compelling interest of that nation. Coming from someone working within China, this line of thinking is unusual because it implies, in practical terms, a departure from the Chinese government's argument, often made in defence of its human rights record, that state sovereignty is paramount and that collective interests take precedence over individual rights.

But Yan does not stop at the conceptual level. His main aim is to develop a framework for quantifying or measuring the national interests of China, or any other country for that matter. For this purpose, he classifies national interest into four main categories: security, political, economic and cultural, and then uses the concept of 'utility' measured in terms of importance and urgency to build an analytical framework. For Yan, the relative importance of a given category of national interest depends on its position on a scale of priorities ranging, in descending order of significance, from national survival, political recognition and economic benefit, to international status and contributions to the world. The urgency of a given interest depends on the time-scale involved in the realisation of such an interest. The resulting matrix allows Yan to assign a relative utility value to each of China's security, political, economic and cultural interests at any given time. For instance, he concludes that China's top national interest in the mid-1990s was economic construction because the end of the Cold War rendered the erstwhile vital interest of national security less urgent. As a result, he ranks the four main categories of China's national interests at the time of writing in the following order: economic, security, political and cultural. On the basis of such a ranking, Yan goes on to apply his analytical framework to the details of China's foreign policy scenarios in actual circumstances and puts forward policy recommendations.

It is impossible to do justice in such a short summary to the sophistication of Yan's book, but the reader comes away convinced that he has basically achieved his aim of devising a more effective way of theorising and analysing China's national interests for the benefit of the country's policy-makers.

Because of its policy relevance, the second part of the book, with details of policy analysis including copious quotes from China's late leader Deng Xiaoping, represents an anti-climax to a work of rare theoretical insights, but in a country where pure theorising is still regarded as a luxury and where the state maintains a grip on the media, this is hardly surprising and is in fact understandable. It is a pity that Yan's book, written in Chinese, is not yet widely available, but I was happy to learn from the author himself that it is now being translated into English.

If Yan's book has not been given due attention in Gerald Chan's survey because of oversight, then *The Rise of China* (1998) and *The Tide of Democratisation* (1999) are not included because they were both published after Chan's book had gone to press. This in itself is a reflection of how rapidly IR literature in China grows these days.

The Rise of China is worth mentioning because it is a co-authored book on China's international position written at a time when nationalism was running high in China as a result of the country's phenomenal economic growth and its frustration at not being treated as an equal by the USA-led West. The four authors made a cool-headed analysis of China's international environment and counselled caution to their readers when such polemics as 'China Can Say No' were dominating the market.

Proceeding from a theoretical and historical perspective, the authors argue that only those countries with comprehensive national resources, not just in economic strength but also in political and military terms, have the potential to rise to the status of a great power and that in the post-Cold War world, only Japan, Germany, Russia and China have such potential. The realisation of such potential, they argue, depends as much on the international environment as on the internal strength of the countries concerned.

According to the authors, to make a sound judgement on whether the international environment is favourable to the rise of China (or the other countries in question), at least three factors need to be considered: the level of security risks to the country under discussion, the state of its political relations with other major countries in the world and the speed of expansion of its overseas economic interests. If a country of great power potential can expect a long lead time before getting drawn into a military conflict, finds its own strategic interests more or less in harmony with those of other major countries and is able to increase its share of the international market rapidly, then the international environment for that country's rise to great power status can be judged as favourable; otherwise it should be judged as unfavourable.

As the above three variables can be measured, comparisons may be made across different countries as to how each of them relates to the international environment at a given time. For this purpose, the authors assign numerical values to various combinations of the three variables on a scale of 1 to 4, with 4 representing 'very favourable', 3 representing 'relatively favourable', 2 representing 'relatively unfavourable' and 1 representing 'very unfavourable'. In 1995, for example, China's expected lead time before involvement in a conflict was longer than that of Russia, but shorter than that of Japan and Germany due to possible conflict over the Taiwan issue. China's international acceptability seen by the other major countries, especially the United States, was similar to that of Russia, but much lower than that of Germany and Japan. The share of China's exports on the world market in that year grew moderately, similar to Russia, but still faster than Japan and Germany. In aggregate, China scored 2.33 points on the 1–4 scale, compared with 3 for Japan and Germany respectively and only 1.67 for Russia. In other words, China's international environment in 1995 was found to be less favourable than that of Japan and Germany, but more favourable than that of Russia. By extending this line of assessment over a number of years, the authors are able to plot the movement of China's international position on a chart and reflect on the longer trend of the international environment for China's development. They conclude that China's path to great power status is a twisty one, but is unlikely to deteriorate to 'very unfavourable' in the near future.

Apparently believing that this line of reasoning alone is not adequate, the authors also devote much space to a historical examination of the successive rise of Britain, France, Germany, Russia, Japan and the United States at various times in history. They find that the path to international greatness is a long and arduous one, taking decades or even centuries to materialise, and that the process tends to undergo two or three stages: the preparatory stage, the take-off and the consummation. They believe that contemporary China has only just entered the threshold of the second stage and is a long way from achieving great power status. The talk of 'the China threat' is therefore exaggerated and the declaration of 'China can say no' is premature.

If the works mentioned earlier are primarily concerned with China's international relations, Cong's book on democratisation is more international in its coverage. As the first systematic response by a Chinese author to Samuel Huntington's book *The Third Wave: Democratisation in the Late Twentieth Century*, Cong's work examines the theory and practice of democracy as affecting the political, economic, cultural and diplomatic aspects of modern societies in various parts of the world. The book surveys the democratisation process in Asia, Africa, Latin America, the Middle East, the former Soviet Union and Eastern Europe, covering more than eighty countries in its purview. Cong believes that democracy is the best way so far of organising our societies, although it is by no means 'the end of history'. Historically, according to Cong, the worst mistake ever made by a democracy has been to terminate its own existence by handing over power to a few individuals. Although democracy as we know it today originated in the West, it has spread rapidly to the rest of the world, especially during the last quarter century, referred to as the 'third wave' by Huntington. This not only testifies to the appeal and vitality of democracy itself, but also stems from the fact that different cultures across the world share common traits as human societies and that there is much compatibility among them. It is therefore inappropriate, as Huntington does, to exaggerate the differences between cultures or to predict clashes between civilisations as the major problem of the post-Cold War world.

After surveying the different regions of the world, Cong concludes that there is no one correct model of democracy that may be applied across the world and that the trend has been towards localisation of democracy in line with the indigenous conditions of a given country rather than towards universalisation of political cultures in the Western democratic mould. In other words, the 'Western wind' of democracy has swept across the seas, causing giant waves in its wake, but leaving the deep ocean currents of local cultures relatively undisturbed. The author thus raises the possibility that this trend of localisation rather than universalisation probably means that the third wave of democratisation has pushed the outward expansion of Western political culture to its limits and that the tide is perhaps beginning to turn from a largely one-directional projection of Western influence upon the rest of the world into a two-way interchange between various civilisations.

The books reviewed above represent only a small, though select, sample of the works produced by Chinese IR scholars in the past decade, but they do give a sense of the mileage covered by such scholars up to now. If Chinese IR specialists were still busy translating and introducing Western works ten years ago, the few recent books highlighted above at least demonstrate that a small but significant number of theory-conscious scholars have emerged in China who have started to build upon the earlier introductory works of their peers in order to develop a more systematic way of observing, understanding and explaining the world and China's place therein. Such a development shows not only that Chinese IR has grown in volume in the past decade, but that we are beginning to witness a qualitative difference in the more recent pursuits of the small IR community in the country. The trend is still rather tentative of course, but it is making a start.

Note

1   Gerald Chan's outsider approach is also reflected in his repeated reference to the current open policy of China as the 'open-door policy'. The latter is a mistranslation of the Chinese term *'dui wai kai fang zheng ce'*, which simply means 'the policy of opening to the outside world' and contains no reference to the metaphor of the door. This is important because the fallacy often appears in the Western media, which confuses the current Chinese policy with the imperialist practice of 'the open door and equality of opportunity' promoted by the United States at the turn of the century in its rivalry against other Western powers for an equal share of the profit and concessions in China. Due to the politically sensitive nature of the translation, the official English press in China, along with some knowledgeable and sensitive Sinologists in the West, has been careful to avoid the usage of the door analogy in referring to the current Chinese policy.

Books reviewed

Chan, Gerald, *Chinese Perspectives on International Relations: A Framework for Analysis* (Basingstoke: Macmillan, 1999).
Cong, Riyun, *Dangdai Shijie de Minzhuhua Langchao (The Tide of Democratisation in the Contemporary World)* (Tianjin: Tianjin People's Press, 1999).
Yan, Xuetong, *Zhongguo Guojia Liyi Fenxi (Analysis of China's National Interest)* (Tianjin: Tianjin People's Press, 1996).
Yan, Xuetong, Wang Zaibang, Li Zhongcheng and Hou Ruoshi, *Zhongguo Jueqi: Guoji Huanjing Pinggu (The Rise of China: Assessing the International Environment)* (Tianjin: Tianjin People's Press, 1998).
See also:
Stephen Chan, 'Beyond the North-west: Africa and the East', in A. J. R. Groom and Margot Light (eds), *Contemporary International Relations: A Guide to Theory* (London: Pinter, 1994).

Index